teach
yourself®

world cultures:
italy

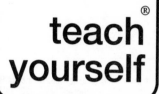

world cultures:
italy
derek aust
with mike zollo

For over 60 years, more than
40 million people have learnt over
750 subjects the **teach yourself**
way, with impressive results.

be where you want to be
with **teach yourself**

The publisher has used its best endeavours to ensure that the URLs for external websites referred to in this book are correct and active at the time of going to press. However, the publisher has no responsibility for the websites and can make no guarantee that a site will remain live or that the content is or will remain appropriate.

For UK order enquiries: please contact Bookpoint Ltd, 130 Milton Park, Abingdon, Oxon OX14 4SB. Telephone: +44 (0) 1235 827720. Fax: +44 (0) 1235 400454. Lines are open from 09.00–18.00, Monday to Saturday, with a 24-hour message answering service. Details about our titles and how to order are available at: www.teachyourself.co.uk

For USA order enquiries: please contact McGraw-Hill Customer Services, PO Box 545, Blacklick, OH 43004-0545, USA. Telephone: 1-800-722-4726. Fax: 1-614-755-5645.

For Canada order enquiries: please contact McGraw-Hill Ryerson Ltd, 300 Water St, Whitby, Ontario L1N 9B6, Canada. Telephone: 905 430 5000. Fax: 905 430 5020.

Long renowned as the authoritative source for self-guided learning – with more than 30 million copies sold worldwide – the *Teach Yourself* series includes over 300 titles in the fields of languages, crafts, hobbies, business, computing and education.

British Library Cataloguing in Publication Data: a catalogue record for this title is available from the British Library.

Library of Congress Catalog Card Number: on file.

First published in UK 2000 by Hodder Headline, 338 Euston Road, London NW1 3BH.

First published in US 2000 by Contemporary Books, a division of the McGraw-Hill Companies, 1 Prudential Plaza, 130 East Randolph Street, Chicago, IL 60601, USA.

This edition published 2004.

The 'Teach Yourself' name is a registered trade mark of Hodder & Stoughton Ltd.

Copyright © 2000, 2004 Units 1–4 and 8–12 Derek Aust; Units 5–7 Mike Zollo.

In UK: All rights reserved. No part of this publication may be reproduced or transmitted in any form or by any means, electronic or mechanical, including photocopy, recording, or any information storage and retrieval system, without permission in writing from the publisher or under licence from the Copyright Licensing Agency Limited. Further details of such licences (for reprographic reproduction) may be obtained from the Copyright Licensing Agency Limited, of 90 Tottenham Court Road, London W1T 4LP.

In US: All rights reserved. Except as permitted under the United States Copyright Act of 1976, no part of this publication may be reproduced or distributed in any form or by any means, or stored in a database or retrieval system, without the prior written permission of Contemporary Books.

Typeset by Transet Limited, Coventry, England.
Printed in Great Britain for Hodder & Stoughton Educational, a division of Hodder Headline, 338 Euston Road, London NW1 3BH, by Cox & Wyman Ltd, Reading, Berkshire.

Papers used in this book are natural, renewable and recyclable products. They are made from wood grown in sustainable forests. The logging and manufacturing processes conform to the environmental regulations of the country of origin.

Impression number   10 9 8 7 6 5 4 3 2 1
Year   2010 2009 2008 2007 2006 2005 2004

contents

acknowledgements

The authors would like to thank the following for their help in the preparation of this book: Phil Turk, the Series Editor, and Sue Hart at Hodder and Stoughton for their guidance and helpful suggestions; Loredana Polezzi for her meticulous job as Reader and students at South Devon College and Britannia Royal Naval College upon whom much of the material was tried out.

Grateful thanks also to the following friends and colleagues for their comments and invaluable help in providing and checking factual material: Daniela Becchio, Deborah Nicholas, Carole Shepherd, Novello Zoffoli, Lyndon Groves, Mrs Rita Zollo, Canon Tony Zollo, Cathi Zollo, Tony Zollo, Gill Rowe, Klyne Williams, Giusi Smith.

introduction

This book is designed to give you as full a basic overview as possible of the main aspects of Italy: the country, its languages, its people, their way of life and culture and what makes them tick.

You will find it a useful foundation if you are studying for examinations which require a knowledge of the background of Italy and its civilization, or if you are learning the language in, for example, an evening class and want to know more about the country and how it works. If your job involves travel and business relations it will provide valuable and practical information about the ways and customs of the people you are working with. Or if you simply have an interest in Italy for whatever reason, it will broaden your knowledge about the country and its inhabitants.

The book is divided into three sections.

- Units 1 and 2 deal with the forces – historical, geographical, geological, demographical and linguistic – that have brought about the formation of the country we know as Italy and the language we known as Italian. Unit 2 also takes a look at the role of Italian outside the immediate frontiers of Italy.
- Units 3–7 deal with the wealth of creative aspects of Italian culture from the beginnings to the present day. These units take a look at the main areas or works of literature, art and architecture, music, traditions and festivals, science and technology, fashion and food and drink, together with the people who have created and are still creating them.
- Units 8–11 deal with aspects of contemporary Italian society and the practicalities of living in present-day Italy: the way the political structure of the country is organized,

education, the environment, the workplace and how people spend their leisure time. The final unit looks at the country's political, economic and social relations with the wider world, and takes a glance at the future.

Taking it further

Each unit ends with a section entitled 'Taking it further', where you will find useful addresses, websites, suggested places to visit and things to see and do in order to develop your interest further and increase your knowledge.

The language

Within each unit you will encounter a number of terms in Italian, whose meaning is given in English when they are first introduced. If you wish to put your knowledge into practice, we have provided in each unit a list of useful words and phrases to enable you to talk or write about the subject in question.

We have been careful in researching and checking facts, but please be aware that sources sometimes offer differing information. Of course a book of this length cannot contain everything you may need to know on every aspect of Italy. That is why we have provided so many pointers to where you can find further information about any aspect that you may wish to pursue in more depth. We trust that you will enjoy this introductory book, and that it will provide leads to further profitable reading, listening and visiting. *Buon viaggio e buon divertimento!*

Phil Turk
Series Editor

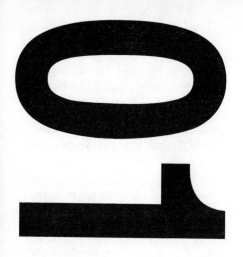

01

what made Italy?

In this unit you will learn
- about some geographical and physical features of the country
- about historical events that led to the creation of modern-day Italy

The land

Glance at the map opposite and you will see that Italy looks like *uno stivale* (a boot), which is open at the top. The toe of the boot seems to be kicking the island of Sicily (*Sicilia*) out to sea. The other main Italian island, Sardinia (*Sardegna*), is to the north-west of Sicily. This shape gives rise to the names *Italia continentale* (continental Italy = the wide part in the north), *Italia peninsulare* (mainland Italy) and *Italia insulare* (the islands of Sicily and Sardinia).

In the north, the country is bordered by France, Switzerland, Austria and the independent Republic of Slovenia (part of the former Yugoslavia). *Italia continentale* has the most extensive plain in southern Europe, along the Po Valley. It extends into five regions: Piedmont, Lombardy, Veneto and Emilia Romagna and part of Friuli-Venezia Giulia. The *River Po* runs along the whole length of this plain and numerous torrents descend into it from the Alpine mountain ranges, making this one of Italy's most fertile areas. It is a low-lying plain never more than 200 metres above sea level and in some areas towards the Adriatic it is even below sea level. It is easy to appreciate why geographical position and geological developments have favoured this part of the country. The other plains are small by comparison and are mainly situated in southern coastal areas, e.g. the *Tavoliere* in Puglia and the *Agro Pontino* in the surrounding areas of Rome.

The narrowness of the Italian peninsula is the result of thousands of years of gradual erosion by the sea. The extensive northern plain, known as the *Pianura Padana*, was formed about 10,000 years ago. Its development can be attributed to a combination of factors: a considerable drop in the sea level, the build-up of deposits from rivers and mountain torrents, and the melting and gradual withdrawal of the glaciers.

The mountains

The Alps extend in an arc from the north-west to the north-east of the country. They comprise some of the highest mountains in Europe, such as *Monte Bianco* (4,810 m) – on the borders of Italy, France and Switzerland – and *Monte Rosa* (4,634 m). To the east are the Dolomites, whose highest mountain is the *Marmolada* (3,343 m). These continuous mountain ranges no longer constitute a communications barrier between Italy and her neighbouring countries because there is a whole network of

Map drawn by Antonio Ravarino for *Teach Yourself Improve Your Italian*, reproduced by kind permission of the author, Sylvia Lymbery.

tunnels, motorways and railways which give rapid access in both directions. Italy, and particularly the north, is at the heart of Europe.

The Apennines start from Liguria in the north-west and run down through the middle of the peninsula to the toe of the 'boot'. They pass under the three-kilometre-wide Straits of Messina and re-emerge in Sicily, the Mediterranean's biggest island – a total distance of 1,350 kilometres. The highest peak in the Apennine range is *Monte Corno* (2,914 m) in the Abruzzi. Sicily is dominated by *Monte Etna* (3,340 m), Europe's biggest active volcano. Mountain ranges account for about 50 per cent of the territory, hills around 30 per cent and lowlands the remaining 20 per cent. It is not difficult to appreciate the problems facing agriculture when you consider these figures.

Both the Alps and Apennines have sprung up following movements and collisions in the Earth's crust. The numerous volcanoes, now extinct except for Vesuvius, Etna and Stromboli, are living testimony to the intensive activity beneath the surface. This is an ongoing process as Italy lies in an area of considerable seismic activity and frequent earth tremors are recorded every year. There have been many instances of severe earthquakes. The most tragic recently in terms of loss of life occurred in San Giuliano (Puglia) on 31 October 2002. The rock formation of these mountain chains is quite different: mainly granite in the Alps and in the Apennines the more crumbly clay and limestone, which are subject to greater erosion and so more likely to suffer landslides.

Rivers, lakes and seas

Italy has numerous rivers, the most important of which are in the north. The *Po* (652km) is the longest and it comes out into the Adriatic. Other important rivers, e.g. *Ticino*, *Adda*, descend from the Alpine ranges to form some of Italy's most beautiful lakes – *Maggiore*, *Como*, and the biggest, *Garda* (370 sq km). Amongst the other rivers that bathe the Po Valley are the *Adige* (410 km), *Tagliamento*, *Piave* and *Isonzo*. The rivers in the peninsula are not nearly as long because of the proximity of the Apennines to the sea. The best known are probably the *Tevere* (Tiber) (405 km), which runs through Rome and the *Arno* that runs through Pisa and Florence. These rivers empty into the Tyrrhenian Sea. The peninsular lakes are small compared to those in the north. The largest is easily *Lago Trasimeno*, situated in the heart of Umbria. The other lakes are of volcanic origin and even smaller.

Italy is in the Mediterranean and yet the seas that bathe more than 8,000 kilometres of Italian coastline and islands have different names – Ligurian, Tyrrhenian and Sardinian in the west; Adriatic in the east; Ionian in the south-east and Sicilian in the south. It is not difficult to imagine why Italy was in an ideal position to trade when the city-states began to develop in medieval times. In fact, no place in Italy is further than 230 kilometres from the coast. Apart from the two large islands of Sicily and Sardinia, the other smaller islands are mainly off the western coast of Italy and around Sicily. Perhaps the two best-known are Elba (where Napoleon was exiled), off the coast of Tuscany, and Capri, off the coast of Campania.

The climate

The further south you go the hotter it gets. However, it is not simply the latitude that determines the temperature; many other factors play their part. For example, Liguria in the north-west has a very mild climate, even in winter. The reason is that one side of the region faces the sea and the other is protected from the prevailing winds by the mountains. In Alpine regions, where the mountain peaks are covered in snow for many months of the year, the temperatures tend to be lower in winter and summer. In open, low-lying areas such as the Po Valley it can get very cold and foggy in winter and very hot and sticky in the summer. In the coastal areas the temperatures are generally a few degrees higher and there is very little snow. Further south, winters are milder and the summers very hot. Drought is a common problem and water rationing is often a feature of the summer months.

National parks

It wasn't that long ago that Italy was firmly rooted at the bottom of the European league table for the number of national parks, with just five. The area of national parkland worked out at 37 square metres per Italian citizen compared with 128 in Switzerland, 275 in England, 363 in Germany and 1,350 in Sweden. The number has now risen to 20 and they include: the *Gran Paradiso* created in 1922 and situated between the Valle d'Aosta and Piedmont; the *Stelvio* between Lombardy and Trentino-Alto Adige; the *Abruzzo* that borders the regions of

Abruzzo, Lazio and Molise; *Circeo* in Lazio, and *Sila* in Calabria. There are also plans to create more regional parks.

The regions and independent states

Italy is divided into twenty regions, the northern ones being the most populated and wealthy. The north has the majority of the biggest and most productive industries (see Unit 10), which, for trading purposes, have the added advantage of being within close proximity to other European countries.

The two independent states are *il Vaticano* (the Vatican) and San Marino. The Vatican in Rome is one of the smallest independent states in the world and the seat of the Roman Catholic Church. The Republic of San Marino is the oldest in Europe dating back, according to some historians, to the fifth century BC. Perched on a hill between Romagna and the Marche, its surface area is about 61 square kilometres. It was granted independence in 1861. This Republic survives mainly on agriculture, the craft industry, the sale of stamps and tourism. San Marino even has its own national football team, which has participated in the European championships.

GLOSSARIO	*GLOSSARY*
la carta (geografica)	*map*
nord	*north*
sud	*south*
ovest	*west*
est	*east*
nord-est	*north-east*
il confine	*border*
la Francia	*France*
la Svizzera	*Switzerland*
il fiume	*river*
scendere	*to descend*
le catene montuose	*mountain chains*
la zona	*area*
la posizione geografica	*geographical position*
favorire	*to favour*
trovarsi	*to be situated*
l'isola	*island*
il mare	*sea*
il ghiacciaio	*glacier*
le montagne	*the mountains*

le Alpi	*the Alps*
gli Appennini	*the Apennines*
la rete	*network*
iniziare	*to start*
lo stretto di Messina	*the Straits of Messina*
apprezzare	*to appreciate*
considerare	*to consider*
il vulcano	*volcano*
il terremoto	*earthquake*
il granito	*granite*
l'argilla	*clay*
il calcare	*limestone*
la frana	*landslide*
causare	*to cause*
comprendere	*to comprise, include*
il clima	*climate*
mite	*mild*
caldo	*hot*
proteggere	*to protect*
essere coperto di neve	*to be covered in snow*
la siccità	*drought*
i parchi nazionali/regionali	*national/regional parks*
sviluppare	*to develop*
risalire (a)	*to date back (to)*

History

Italy as a one-nation state is very young compared to other European countries. Unification came very late and was only completed in 1870 when Piedmontese troops entered Rome, which became the 'new' capital in 1871. (Turin was the first capital of the Kingdom of Italy in 1861, followed by Florence in 1865.) Despite her apparent youthfulness, however, Italy is really a very old lady since her origins can be traced back to Roman times, more than two thousand years ago. Even after unification, Italy remains a country of great contrast and diversity. This is reflected in the differences that exist between the individual regions, the multiplicity of political parties, the cuisine, and the language itself. A closer examination of some of the events pre-unification will help us realize why such differences permeate the social, economic and political fabric of the country.

Etruscans, Romans and Greeks

Throughout most of her history Italy has been subjected to numerous invasions and occupations, all of which have left their mark to a greater or lesser extent. Greek colonies were already established in Sicily and southern Italy as far back as the eighth century BC. Around the same time the Etruscans – some say that they originated from Asia Minor but this remains unclear – were living in central Italy, mainly the regions we know today as Tuscany and Umbria. Remarkably, almost three thousand years later, traces of these civilizations are still evident in the areas of Italy they occupied. Hardly anything is known about the Etruscan language but they were a highly cultured race and skilled at working metals such as iron, bronze and gold, which formed the basis of their trade. The Greeks called the Etruscans *Tyrrhenoi* and this gave rise both to the name of the Tyrrhenian Sea off Italy's west coast and also to Tuscany.

The Romans, who occupied the western side of central Italy, displayed great organizational skills and Rome, which hitherto had been a transition point between Greek-occupied cities in the south and the Etruscans to the north, became the focal point of political power. Gradually Rome extended its sphere of domination until it controlled the whole of the peninsula. It can therefore be argued that Italy existed as a nation during the time of the Roman Empire. There was a single central government, a common language and a framework of laws and social institutions that formed the basis of society.

During their thousand-year reign, the Romans left a legacy still much in evidence today:

- engineering, architectural and administrative skills
- road construction and irrigation schemes
- creation of many of the present-day Italian cities
- the emergence of Christianity as the State religion in AD 380

When the Western Roman Empire fell to barbarian invaders in AD 476, the Roman ideal of a united Europe was embraced by the Christian Church, which provided political and spiritual leadership for the people of the peninsula during those difficult times.

Further invasions

In the sixth century the Lombards, a Germanic tribe, controlled most of northern and central Italy and the Moors (originating from North Africa) and Byzantines (inhabitants of Byzantium, known today as Istanbul) the south. The eighth century saw the decline of Byzantine domination and the Arab conquest of the islands of Sardinia and Sicily. All of the invaders imported different cultures, attitudes and traditions to Italy and further accentuated already existing differences between the regions. In 756 King Pepin gave an undertaking to restore the states occupied by the Lombards to the Pope. This was achieved when he led the Franks to victory against the occupiers. In 774 Charlemagne, Pepin's son, played a significant part in the battles to end the Lombards' domination and was rewarded by being crowned the first Emperor of the Romans on Christmas Day AD 800. The Western Roman Empire was restored and a Papal State established.

The beginnings of feudalism

Charlemagne's death was followed by another period of instability and further invasions. The end result was the fragmentation of the kingdom he had developed. Only the popes succeeded in retaining control over their domain. The country was split up into a series of poorly run feudal regimes. Feudalism was a medieval system of land tenure with the sovereigns or overlords at the top and the vassals at the bottom. The sovereigns had powers and privileges, which increased or decreased, according to their position in the hierarchy. They were given land and property in return for loyalty and aid to their military masters. The vassals played a subservient role and were continually exploited. The south of Italy suffered greatly under this feudal regime.

When the Normans arrived some two centuries later they formed a United Kingdom of Sicily on the feudal pattern. The north of Italy was invaded by the Magyars (from Hungary) up to the middle of the tenth century. Many people abandoned the rural areas for the safety of the towns, which gradually became walled fortresses to keep out the marauding invaders. During this period not one king of Italy managed to unite the country. In 962, Otto I of Germany was crowned Emperor and a succession of German or Hapsburg (Austrian) kings was to sustain the Holy Roman Empire in some form or another until the early nineteenth century.

City-states

The eleventh century saw the decline of feudalism and the development of the *Comuni* (city-states). Cities were acquiring greater independence as trade and commerce that had begun with the Crusades flourished. The Crusades undoubtedly helped the commercial expansion of the *Repubbliche marinare* (Marine Republics) such as Venice, Genoa, Pisa and Amalfi by providing them with the opportunity to develop and intensify their trade and establish further trading bases. There were two distinct social classes: the aristocracy, who ruled the towns and cities, and the 'common' people. This period of economic and cultural revival gathered pace in the following century. Most of the cities that prospered industrially and commercially were in northern and central Italy. This process of change was halted in southern Italy by the Norman conquests and successive monarchies.

The eleventh century was dominated by the power struggles between the Papacy and the Empire, and the Church had to seek the assistance of foreign armies to retain its control. Eventually the power of the Papacy declined and at the beginning of the fourteenth century it was removed to Avignon in France (1309–1377). Its cities in central Italy came under the rule of independent princes.

Throughout the twelfth and thirteenth centuries northern Italy became increasingly prosperous whereas the south was subjected to the same kind of feudal rule as before, this time under Spanish and French overlords. Many hundreds of years later the south continues to pay the price for centuries of neglect and mismanagement. By contrast, the Marine Republics and city-states like Milan and Florence flourished. Trade with northern Europe and the East encouraged the growth of the textile, metal-processing and shipbuilding industries. It was at this time that a system of banking developed. University education was reorganized and paid posts were established and entrusted to teachers chosen by the citizens. Six universities were founded in the thirteenth century. The University of Bologna had been founded as far back as the eleventh century.

During the fourteenth and fifteenth centuries the *Comuni* were transformed into *Signorie*, i.e. towns or cities under the control of a single person or family. This happened through the consensus of the local population or by force. These walled towns and cities were mainly situated in dominant positions overlooking the valleys below. There were constant battles between rival towns that sought to extend their sphere of influence. It was a period when many rulers employed mercenary troops to fight their battles. Within the confines of the cities the rulers kept order, collected taxes and introduced a particular style to their town or city. Among the well-known families were the *Este* in Ferrara, the *Visconti* and *Sforza* in Milan, the *Medici* in Florence, the *Gonzaga* in Mantova and the *Montefeltro* in Urbino. (In the south only Naples and Palermo assumed great importance as capitals and were the only cities of any great size up to the eighteenth century.)

By the fifteenth century five main city-states had established themselves alongside a few small independent duchies (governed by a duke) and republics. The map of Italy overleaf illustrates how Italy was divided up at that time.

The Renaissance

The fourteenth and fifteenth centuries in Italy were unparalleled for their material, spiritual and artistic growth. This period marked a rebirth of interest in classical and Roman literature, art and ideas. The invention of the press at this time served to promote and spread this culture from its focal point, Florence, to other parts of Italy and Europe. Apart from the press, other factors helped lay the foundations of the *Rinascimento*: for example, Humanism, a literary movement that encapsulated this increasing interest in culture, the centre of which was the human spirit. It was also a time of great geographical discoveries, the most famous being the discovery of America in 1492 by Christopher Columbus. These discoveries brought new wealth as they encouraged the expansion of trade and commerce.

Despite this golden age, the like of which Italy may never see again, the period was one of warring and bitter strife between the powerful city-states, each striving to gain supremacy. This was at a time when in western Europe other countries such as France, England and Spain were unifying and becoming more powerful. These countries, in the wake of the geographical discoveries, were starting to develop a colonial policy. Until then the Mediterranean ports had been of paramount importance in promoting trade on a very large scale. With the discovery of America, the Atlantic Ocean became the direct route for the transportation of goods to the 'New World'. This had a tremendous impact on the Italian Marine Republics, especially Venice. Their importance rapidly declined and the maritime countries washed by the Atlantic Ocean – Spain, Portugal,

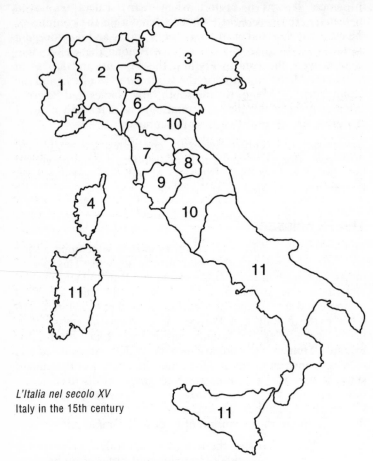

L'Italia nel secolo XV
Italy in the 15th century

Where ruled by families, the family name appears in brackets
1   Ducato di Savoia (Savoia) Duchy of Savoy
2   Ducato di Milano (Visconti, Sforza) Duchy of Milan
3   Repubblica di Venezia Republic of Venice
4   Repubblica di Genova Republic of Genoa
5   Ducato di Mantova (Gonzaga) Duchy of Mantova
6   Ducato di Ferrara e Modena (Este) Duchy of Ferrara and Modena
7   Signoria di Firenze (Medici) Territory of Florence
8   Ducato di Urbino (Montefeltro) Duchy of Urbino
9   Repubblica di Siena Republic of Siena
10 Stato della Chiesa State of the Church
11 Domini Aragonesi Kingdom of the South (under Spanish rule)

England, the Netherlands and France – were the chief beneficiaries. The economic blow to Italy was not helped by the internal fighting and the country became a much easier target for foreign conquest, particularly from the countries seeking supremacy in Europe, namely France, Spain and Austria.

Spanish occupation

The arrival of the French King Charles VIII marked the beginning of a long period of wars fought on Italian soil by the Dutch, French, Spanish and Austrians. The Treaty of Château-Cabrésis in 1559 between Francis I, King of France, and Charles V, the ruler of Spain signalled the end of the fighting but for the next century and a half the Duchy of Milan and much of southern Italy came under Spanish rule. The Spanish viceroys imposed heavy taxes and corruption amongst them was rife. They exploited the situation for their own ends, doing nothing to promote the growth or economic development of the areas they occupied. Moreover, creativity and intellectual freedom were stifled. One exception during this period of moral and economic stagnation was the development of the Savoy in the north-west of Italy, an area which acted as a buffer zone between Spanish-occupied Milan and France. The appointment of a duke led to the development of the area as a modern state.

The Wars of Succession

In the first half of the eighteenth century the so-called *guerre di successione* (Wars of Succession) radically changed the political face of Italy:

- Spanish rule came to an end
- Austria occupied Milan, Naples and Sardinia
- the House of Savoy acquired Sicily, exchanged shortly afterwards for Sardinia (1720)
- following the Polish War of Succession (1733–1738) Naples and Sicily were handed over to the Bourbon Charles III, son of the king of Spain
- the Austrian War of Succession (1740–1748) marked the end of hostilities and the beginning of a period of approximately fifty years of peace both for Europe and Italy

The arrival of Napoleon

The French revolution of 1789 had a profound political and social impact on Italy and the arrival in Italy of Napoleon Bonaparte's armies in 1796 served to reawaken in the Italians feelings of nationalism and sow the seeds of the *Risorgimento* (revival) movement. The unifying process was aided by:

- the setting up of efficiently run republics with constitutions and representative assemblies
- the construction of new roads, bridges, schools and other public buildings
- the *Code Napoléon*, a new legal system that ensured greater equality of rights, thereby destroying the privileged position of the clergy and the nobility
- the realization of Italians that they could live together as one nation, which had not been the case since the fall of Rome

Napoleon's defeat at the Battle of Waterloo in 1815 seemed initially to put a brake on this 'unifying' process. In the same year the European powers assembled at the Congress of Vienna to decide on the details of the peace settlement and their decisions put Italy into reverse rather than forward gear. The Austrian prince Metternich considered Italy as nothing more than a mere 'geographical expression'. Once again the country fell prey to different rulers, as follows:

- the Kingdom of the Two Sicilies (all of the south plus Sicily) was handed to King Ferdinand I, of Bourbon origin
- Lazio, Umbria, le Marche and the eastern part of Emilia Romagna came under the control of the popes
- Austria controlled Lombardy, Veneto and Friuli-Venezia Giulia
- Victor Emmanuel I of the House of Savoy was given Piedmont and Sardinia

Secret societies

Rule by so many different factions put a damper on more overt demonstrations of a nationalistic spirit. Consequently, sects or secret societies formed, amongst which figured the *Massoneria* (Freemasons) and *Carboneria* (Charcoal burners). The latter group, whose goal was to seek independence for the country, assumed a role of national importance. Their political influence quickly diminished, however, as attempts at insurrection failed through a general lack of organization. Another secret society, *Giovine Italia* (Young Italy), was founded in 1831 by Giuseppe Mazzini, one of the chief protagonists of the *Risorgimento*. The aims of this movement were freedom, independence, national unity and the setting up of a Republic. Mazzini was a revolutionary and he hoped to achieve a unified nation by inciting popular insurrection. The more moderate forces wanted a federal rather than centralized state, which they were prepared to realize via the diplomatic route.

The Wars of Independence

The news of the proclamation of the Second Republic in France in 1848 gave fresh impetus to the unification movement. In Naples, Rome, Turin and many other cities, people held demonstrations in the square to demand a constitution, subsequently granted by the various heads of the Italian states.

In the **First War of Independence** (1848–1849) the Kingdom of Sicily, under King Carlo Alberto, rose up against Austria. However, the insurrections in Milan, Venice and Brescia were quelled and Austria regained control of these cities. The uprising in Rome, incited by Garibaldi, another prominent figure in the *Risorgimento*, was put down by French troops summoned by Pope Pius IX. Thus thoughts of liberty and independence had once again been temporarily quashed and the constitution that had only recently been put in place was revoked.

All was not lost as Count Camillo Cavour, the Prime Minister of Victor Emmanuel II of Savoy, adopted a more patient, judicious approach through which he managed to raise the national importance of Italy in international circles. He raised the profile of his kingdom as a European power by sending troops to fight alongside Britain and France in the Crimean War. Both sides obviously appreciated this military support because Cavour was allowed to take part in the Congress of Paris in 1856 as a representative of the Italian cause. The decade 1849–1859 therefore became another preparatory phase along the road to ultimate unification.

In 1859 the **Second War of Independence**, waged against Austria with French support, gave Cavour the chance to achieve his aims. For this support Sardinia gave France Nice and Savoy. The war ended in victory for the Italian side. Lombardy united with Piedmont and the revolutionary movements in other states resulted in the annexation of Tuscany, Emilia and Romagna. This led to the proclamation of the Kingdom of Northern and Central Italy (1860).

Garibaldi

In May of the same year Giuseppe Garibaldi and his thousand volunteers in *camicie rosse* (red shirts) set off from Quarto near Genoa for Marsala in western Sicily. After a series of battles Garibaldi's troops managed to overthrow the resistance of the Bourbon army before rapidly moving up to Naples, capital of the Kingdom of the Two Sicilies. They entered Naples on 7 September 1860. Meanwhile Cavour, who wanted Italy to be united under a Piedmontese monarch, realized that it was essential to send troops to central and southern Italy to liberate those areas. This he did and his army defeated the Papal forces in September 1860. The final outcome of this second War of Independence was the proclamation of the Kingdom of Italy on 17 March 1861 and Turin, capital of Piedmont, became Italy's first capital and Victor Emmanuel II her first king. The jigsaw puzzle was not yet complete, however. The missing pieces were the Austrian-controlled regions of Veneto, Trentino, Venezia Giulia, the Lombard city of Mantova (liberated in 1866) and Lazio, or the Papal State.

It proved a very difficult task to bring the other remaining regions under the one umbrella. The **Third War of Independence** of 1866 solved part of the problem:

- Italy teamed up with the Prussia (formerly a subdivision of northern Germany) of Bismarck against Austria and gained control of Veneto, except for Trento and Trieste
- the French Empire collapsed following the defeat by the Prussians at Sédan in 1870. Napoleon III's position as a strong defender of the Papacy, *Italia agli italiani, ma Roma al Papa* (Italy to the Italians, but Rome to the Pope), was subsequently weakened and the Italian troops occupied Rome on 20 September 1870

Pope Pius IX reacted to this situation by shutting himself in the Vatican. This gave rise to a conflict between the Catholic Church and the Italian State that lasted until 1929, when the Vatican City was granted independence. On setting up an Italian Parliament, in May 1871, a law inspired by Cavour was approved: *libera Chiesa in libero stato* (a free Church in a free State). This law ensured that the Pope had certain guarantees and privileges to exercise freely his spiritual authority.

Political developments post-*Risorgimento*

As a result of the numerous battles fought on Italian soil, the new government's first task was to try and improve the rather disastrous conditions that most of the country found itself in. The lack of natural resources such as iron and coal hindered industrial development and, on a political level, the centuries of foreign domination were not an ideal preparation for self-government. However, the first government, the *Destra* (literally, 'Right'), adopted Cavour's policies and set about the task:

- schools were opened
- a programme of public works was started
- financial and administrative systems were put in place
- heavy taxes were imposed to finance this programme
- the armed forces were expanded through obligatory conscription

Cavour's untimely and premature death at the age of 50 in 1861 was a major blow because his diplomatic, practical style of leadership might well have smoothed the path leading to final unification and helped Italy develop a democratic parliamentary system. However, it has to be borne in mind that the three key figures in the *Risorgimento* were northerners – Mazzini was born in Genoa, Cavour in Turin and Garibaldi in Nice – and the north was keen to impose its ideas on the remainder of the territory. The north and south were poles apart, as much of the south had been neglected and underdeveloped for centuries.

In 1876 power passed to the *Sinistra* (literally, 'Left') who implemented various reforms such as free compulsory elementary education and passed laws to safeguard the workers. However, poverty was widespread and this was the most worrying problem that the Left failed to solve. The increase in the population from about 18 million at the beginning of the century to about 36 million by the end of the nineteenth century made the situation worse. It was at this time that a significant increase in emigration was recorded as people sought to escape poverty for a better existence elsewhere. Emigration became an important factor in Italy's development, serving two purposes: the reduction of the population and a solution to the unemployment problem.

Ironically, unification did nothing to unite the north and south. In fact, 50 years after unification the gap had widened. The southern regions seemed remote to successive governments, which continued to impose unsuitable structures and policies, failing to recognize the need for a different approach to their problems. The landowners and ruling classes went along with these ideas and the State, in return, safeguarded their privileges. Everything seemed to benefit northern interests and the south always played second fiddle.

The 40 or so years after unification saw a period of relative stability in Europe and the development of two powers, Germany and Italy. Italy became a part of the Triple Alliance with Germany and Austria in 1882. Towards the end of the nineteenth century Italy's socialist government began to entertain ideas of becoming more powerful and embarked on a policy of colonial expansionism. Africa was the targeted area. Italy first took possession of Eritrea, followed by Somalia, and then (in 1911) Libya. These colonial wars were a drain on the financial resources of the country and cost thousands of lives but they were seen as a way of resolving Italy's overpopulation problem.

The First World War (1914–1918)

The nineteenth century ended in social unrest and in many parts of the country there were uprisings and strikes, ultimately put down by military force. This military repression prompted an anarchist to assassinate King Umberto (1900). His son, Vittorio Emmanuele III, succeeded him and the country moved towards a period of stability up to 1914, under the political leadership and prudent statesmanship of Giovanni Giolitti. The year 1914 marked the start of the First World War. Italy remained neutral in the early stages but finally entered on the side of the Allies (France, Britain and Russia) on 24 May 1915. In return she was promised the Austrian-held provinces of Trieste and Trento in the north-east of Italy as well as some territories along the coast of what was later to become Yugoslavia. During the period 1915–1918, Italy was engaged in many bitter, costly battles in the north-east and along her borders. Despite many defeats she achieved a crucial and decisive victory at Vittorio Veneto on 24 October 1918 that led to the surrender of Austria-Hungary. At the beginning of November Trento and Trieste were returned to Italy.

The rise of Fascism

The aftermath of the war was another difficult period for Italy both economically and politically. The economic price for her involvement caused a budget deficit, devaluation, price increases and high unemployment. There were strikes and uncertainty reigned amongst the ruling class. The time was ripe for strong, authoritarian leadership and the opportunist Benito Mussolini saw his chance to seize power. It was the beginning of Fascism, founded in Milan in 1919 by Mussolini, a former socialist. His fervent nationalism won him great support and the country was in such chaos that he met with little opposition. The Monarchy put up no resistance either and, following the march on Rome with his black-shirted *fascisti* on 28 October 1922, Mussolini was duly appointed leader by the king. He was to assume the title of *Duce* – the title given to a 'commander' in Roman times. (The word *fascista* also originated from the Roman period. It comes from *fascio* = a bunch of elm or birch rods with an axe in the middle, carried by those who walked in front of the Roman magistrates as a symbol of their punitive power. It became the symbol of the Fascist Party.)

Mussolini's promises to restore Italy to her former greatness meant dictatorship, i.e:

- a totalitarian regime in which all forms of opposition were gradually destroyed
- censorship of the press
- imprisonment or exile for political activists
- the swearing of allegiance to the Fascist Party by all and sundry
- state control of industry and labour

There were positive contributions too:

- intervention in agriculture made the sector more self-sufficient in food production, thus eliminating dependence on food imports
- land reclamation by means of draining marshlands and making them cultivable
- tourism was encouraged
- the trains ran on time
- the solution to the *questione romana* (Roman question), the long-standing problem between Church and State that had gone on since the time of unification. In 1929, Mussolini and the then Pope Pius XI signed the Lateran Pacts, a treaty which recognized the Holy Church and gave the Vatican City its own independence. In return, the Church legally recognized the Kingdom of Italy. Catholicism became the accepted religion of the Italian people.

One of Mussolini's objectives was to boost the Italian population and emigration was discouraged. He felt that to be a powerful nation Italy needed 60 million inhabitants. Tax incentives were introduced to encourage families to have more children. It was a reversal of an earlier policy when emigration had been encouraged to solve overpopulation and economic problems. The policy was not a success, however, and this 'magic' figure has not been reached even to this day.

Foreign policy

Mussolini embarked on a policy of further colonial expansion in Africa and in 1935–1936 he conquered Ethiopia. He thought that the acquisition of additional territories would help solve Italy's economic problems, a policy of previous liberal governments that had ended in failure. Mussolini's colonialist policy was equally disastrous. Moreover, it incurred the wrath of the *Società delle Nazioni* (League of Nations) – which imposed economic sanctions, weakening Italy's position even more. Mussolini's subsequent decision to align himself with Germany and the Fascist dictator Adolf Hitler was to have even more disastrous repercussions. In 1939 Italy and Germany joined in *il patto d'acciaio* (the Pact of Steel), which meant that they were prepared to fight alongside each other in the coming world war. In this same year Italy invaded Albania, so Vittorio Emmanuele III was King of Italy and Emperor of Ethiopia (1936–1941) and Albania (1939–1945).

The Second World War (1939–1945)

Italy, despite being totally unprepared, entered the conflict on the side of Germany on 10 June 1940. She lacked the military resources to fight a war on two fronts, i.e. at home and abroad. The sending of troops to more distant lands weakened the internal defences of the country which had such a massive coastline to protect. Thousands of Italian troops lost their lives in Greece, North Africa and particularly on the Russian front. Italy proved no match for the combined forces of Britain, Russia and the United States. After numerous heavy defeats the Italians were becoming sick of war and disillusioned with Mussolini's Fascist regime and its false promises. These feelings had intensified by the time of the British and American landings in Sicily in the summer of 1943. Even Mussolini's party and military leaders lost confidence in his leadership. A vote of no confidence was passed by the Fascist Grand Council between 24 and 25 July 1943 and Mussolini was forced to resign by the king and subsequently arrested.

The newly formed government lasted in office from 26 July 1943 to 11 February 1944. In September 1943, an armistice of 'unconditional surrender' was signed with the Allied Forces and shortly afterwards Italy declared war on Germany. However, no adequate arrangements were in place to prevent German troops entering and occupying northern Italy. They were obviously not too pleased by the Italian U-turn and were bent on seeking revenge. German troops managed to rescue Mussolini from his 'house arrest' and return him to Lake Garda in Italy, where he set up his new Fascist republican government. However, his influence until his final downfall was minimal. The Germans meanwhile moved down through Italy, seizing control of the central part and blocking the Allied Forces between Rome and Naples. Because of the German threat the king and government abandoned Rome and sought refuge in Brindisi.

This proved to be a most difficult period for Italy, one characterized by fierce fighting between the Germans and the Allied Forces, civil strife and mass destruction. In the German-occupied Italy a well-organized resistance movement, *i partigiani* (the partisans), began to develop, doing its utmost to sabotage and obstruct the German forces. On 4 June 1944 the Allies entered the capital city of Rome and this signified the steady advance up through Italy. On 25 April 1945 the northern cities rose up, bringing an end to the war and resulting in the fall of the Fascist republic. Other significant developments quickly followed:

- Italy became a Republic in June 1946 (see also Unit 8)
- the signing of the peace treaty in Paris on 10 February 1947. Italy had to give up some of her colonial territories, the African colonies of Libya and Eritrea, although Somalia was to remain under Italian administration until she achieved independence in 1961. Briga and Tenda on Italy's western border became part of French territory. The Dodecanese islands were restored to Greece, and Istria, Zara, Fiume and some islands in the Adriatic were handed back to Yugoslavia. Trieste was set up as a free territory and only came under Italian control in 1954.

The setting up of a republic

The fall of Fascism, the signing of the armistice with the Allied Forces and the abdication of Vittorio Emmanuele III all paved the way for the restoration of a democratic system and the eventual setting up of a republic. The people voted for a Constituent Assembly, which would be responsible for drawing up a new constitution. The election for this Assembly was held in June 1946 and was the first free election in Italy since Mussolini's rise to power and also the first time that women were allowed to vote. The first parliamentary elections were held on 18 April 1948. They marked the dawn of a new era in the history of Italy.

GLOSSARIO	GLOSSARY
la storia	history
rispetto a	compared to
l'unificazione	unification
la capitale	capital (city)
i tempi romani	Roman times
gli etruschi	the Etruscans
i greci	the Greeks
occupare	to occupy
i longobardi	the Lombards
il secolo	century
restituire	to give something back
riuscire (a)	to manage (to), succeed (in)
dividere	to divide
invadere	to invade
lo sviluppo	development
il commercio	trade
la chiesa	the church
le città fortificate	walled cities
la scoperta	discovery
la politica	policy, politics
trasportare	to transport
le guerre di indipendenza	the wars of independence
sfruttare	to exploit
risvegliare	to reawaken
mettere fine a	to put an end to
lo scopo	aim
sconfiggere	to defeat
la sconfitta	defeat
realizzare	to realize, achieve
il divario	gap
il Papa	Pope

risolvere un problema	*to solve a problem*
indire le elezioni	*to hold elections*
il fascismo	*Fascism*
la monarchia	*monarchy*
incoraggiare	*to encourage*
la sovrappopolazione	*overpopulation*
la caduta	*fall*

Taking it further

Suggested reading

Contemporary Italy – Politics, Economy and Society since 1945 (Second Edition), Donald Sassoon, Addison Wesley 1997

Italy, Russell King, Harper and Row Publishers 1987

A History of Contemporary Italy: Society and Politics 1943–1948, Paul Ginsborg, Penguin 1990

Modern Italy 1871–1995 (Second Edition), Martin Clark, Longman 1996

A Concise History of Italy, Christopher Duggan, CUP 1994

The Italian Renaissance (in its historical background) (Second Edition), Denys Hay, CUP 1994

Italy since 1800, Roger Absalom, Longman 1995

The Italians, Luigi Barzini, Penguin 1964

Piccola Storia d'Italia, Gianluigi Ugo, Guerra Edizioni 1994

L'Italia contemporanea 1943–1998, Giuseppe Mammarella, Il Mulino 1998

Appunti di storia della Prima Repubblica, Francesco Di Natale, Guerra Edizioni 1994

See also a recent edition of the **Microsoft Encarta Encyclopedia** on CD ROM.

Most good guide books on Italy usually have a summary of the key developments of Italian history.

Websites

www.lonelyplanet.com/dest/eur/ita.htm#facts (information on history, church, etc.)

www.initaly.com (ancient Italy, regions, etc.)

http://web.uccs.edu/~history/index/Italy.html

For information in English or Italian try the search engine www.google.com

For information in Italian try the search engines
www.google.it
www.libero.it
www.yahoo.it

You can use the above search engines for information on all topics in this book. Make sure you type in the minimal number of words that apply to your specific interest.

02

the language

In this unit you will learn
- about the origins of the
  Italian language
- about the various forms of
  Italian
- about more recent influences
  on the language

Italy is a country of great contrast and variety and the same can be said for the language. Indeed if variety is the spice of life then Italian has spice in abundance. In their book *La Lingua Italiana*, Maurizio Dardano and Pietro Trifone mention four categories of Italian. These are:

- *italiano comune* or 'standard Italian', which is the language used for official purposes, administration, education, etc.
- *italiano regionale*, which is peculiar to each individual region and has differences in pronunciation and some vocabulary from standard Italian
- *dialetto regionale*, the dialect of the region as a whole, e.g. *siciliano* (Sicilian)
- *dialetto locale*, which is limited to smaller geographical areas and their inhabitants. In other words, within the same region the regional dialect subdivides into other dialects. The bigger the area, the greater the number of dialects. There are many similarities between the regional dialect and the local variations but there are also many differences. *Sardo*, for example, is the regional dialect of Sardinia. The indigenous inhabitants would almost certainly understand it but, for everyday purposes, would tend to use one of the four main dialects spoken on the different parts of the island.

The most marked difference is between dialect and standard Italian, as will become evident during this chapter. Students of Italian need not despair, however, because the standard Italian they are learning will be understood everywhere! There's more encouraging news later in the unit, but first the basics.

Latin roots

Italian derives mainly from *latino volgare* (vulgar, i.e. popular – not rude! – Latin), which was the language spoken by the ordinary, less educated citizens of ancient Rome. The other form, *latino classico* (classical Latin) was used for literary purposes. Many words currently used in everyday written and spoken Italian are taken directly from the Latin of two thousand years ago. The examples below should be obvious to those who have not studied Latin and either have no knowledge or a very limited knowledge of Italian. They are: *causa, gloria, poeta, memoria, medicina, simile, offendere.*

The use of Latin spread as a result of the Roman conquests and the extension of the Roman Empire. As a spoken language,

Latin probably dates back to the eighth century BC and would have survived until somewhere between AD 800 and 600 – the period of the emergence of the Romance languages. The Romance languages developed over a period of time from vulgar Latin to form a series of different languages that include Portuguese, Spanish, French, Romanian and, of course, Italian.

After the fall of the Roman Empire and the political fragmentation that ensued, the early development of Italian took the form of a multiplicity of different dialects. These dialects tended to retain their separate identity because there was very little population movement. In the Middle Ages, for example, travel opportunities were restricted mainly to merchant traders, the nobility, and important public servants such as ambassadors. *Fiorentino* (Florentine) was the one dialect to gain wider exposure in Italy among the more educated classes, through Dante, Petrarch and Boccaccio, whose literary works gave it great prestige and prominence.

It was Dante who was considered the key figure in the development of Italian on a national scale. His renowned *Divine Comedy* (*La Divina Commedia*) was written in the fourteenth century in a language that was accessible to the ordinary people – the local language of his native Florence. This masterpiece became immensely popular and consequently the language in which it was written eventually became the adopted language of the Italian people, i.e. *italiano comune*.

Some other major influences on Italian

Latin might be the leading player in the development of Italian but it would be wrong to underestimate the significant contributions made by 'foreign invaders', many of whom occupied Italy for centuries before its unification. (Refer back to Unit 1 as a reminder.) Little wonder that Italian has such regional variations and a plethora of dialects.

The German-speaking tribes, particularly the Lombards, had a considerable influence on the language. Their occupation spanned more than two centuries. *Longobardo* actually gave rise to the name of the region Lombardy. From these people Italian has inherited a number of general words that are in current use, e.g. *guancia* (cheek), *schiena* (back), *scherzare* (to joke).

Other early important contributions were a direct result of the commercial contacts with the Arab and Byzantine traders who exported vocabulary as well as goods to Italy! Not surprisingly, this vocabulary includes many commercial terms. Some examples originating from Arabic are: *dogana* (customs), *tariffa* (tarif) and *magazzino* (warehouse); other terms are linked to plants and products, such as *arancia* (orange), *limone* (lemon) and *cotone* (cotton). From the Byzantines Italian acquired a number of words of Greek origin. Again these terms are linked to the sea or trade: *gondola, molo* (jetty/pier), *anguria* (water melon), *basilico* (basil).

The French influence has also been considerable. Following Charlemagne's conquest in AD 774, 'old French' began to make its mark on Italian. The French-speaking Normans occupied southern Italy for two centuries. French and Provençal literature was highly regarded and this again helps to explain why a lot of French words found their way across the Alps and into the Italian language.

The importance of French culture was also much in evidence in the eighteenth century, when the French language was spoken by the educated classes throughout Europe. It became the vehicle of expression for new philosophical and intellectual ideas and this resulted in the spread of the culture of *Illuminismo* (Enlightenment). In more recent times some of the influences of French on Italian have been in the field of fashion and cooking – *prêt-à-porter* (ready-to-wear), *garbardine, maionese, omelette, ragù.*

The emergence of standard Italian

After unification, Florentine, which had hitherto only been spoken in Tuscany and by the educated classes in other parts of Italy, began to spread to the whole of the population as a result of the following:

- the introduction of compulsory elementary education
- the migration of unemployed workers in search of work – the north was particularly attractive as this was the area of major industrial expansion in Italy
- the development of the big cities and increase in population as a result of an exodus from the countryside
- the conscription of young people to do their military service, often in other parts of the country
- the need for a 'common' language in order to understand new State laws, regulations, etc.

This was the real launch in a sense of an official Italian language. Prior to unification, in 1861, a survey revealed that 78 per cent of the population was *analfabeta* (illiterate). Most people, including the literate, tended to communicate in their own dialect. It was estimated that only 2.5 per cent of Italians spoke Italian. The first king of Italy, Vittorio Emmanuele II, and his Prime Minister, Count Camillo Cavour, were much more at home speaking French or *dialetto piemontese* (the dialect spoken in Piedmont) than Italian – which, in actual fact, they spoke rather badly. By the turn of the twentieth century, the percentage of those who spoke Italian was still quite low.

The diffusion of standard Italian gathered real momentum from 1950 onwards, when about 34 per cent spoke Italian and the remainder dialect. Why has the development been so marked since 1950? The following factors played a part:

- the ever-increasing use of radio and television in homes throughout Italy, even in the remoter areas
- the diffusion of other forms of mass media such as newspapers, magazines and the cinema
- a better-educated population with the development of secondary education and a rapid increase in the numbers of university students from the 1960s onwards
- an increase in the mobility of the population in search of employment – particularly from the south to the rapidly developing cities of Genoa, Turin and Milan, known as *il triangolo industriale* (the industrial triangle)

In order to carry out many essential everyday activities – a hospital appointment, a visit to public offices or schools – people had to resort to a common language in order to be understood. Standard Italian became the vehicle of communication for these essential transactions. A dialect would have had a more restrictive application. However, standard Italian did retain regional variations, so that every region has its own 'brand' of Italian.

Regional Italian

Italians, as is usual when people of the same nationality speak together, are generally able to tell from which part of the country their compatriots originate. Firstly, those from the north, centre and south have markedly different accents and secondly, the vocabulary used in different regions can vary. These differences are attributable to the numerous occupations and invasions of the country alluded to previously. Happily, regional variations as such do not normally represent a barrier to communication. The fact that a northerner would use *anguria* and a Tuscan *cocomero* for 'water melon' does not pose a problem for anyone, neither would the fact that 'now' is expressed by *adesso* in the north, *ora* in Tuscany and *mo'* in the south.

These regional variations are usually the result of differences that exist between the vast number of dialects. This is particularly true when it comes to pronunciation. In the north there is a general tendency not to pronounce the double consonant so that *bello* (beautiful) and *rotto* (broken) become *belo* and *roto*. (In standard Italian it is important to pronounce clearly the double consonant to avoid misunderstandings, e.g. *nono* = ninth, whereas *nonno* = grandfather). Conversely, in the south single consonants are pronounced as double consonants so that the correct dialect and spoken standard Italian forms of *subito* (immediately) and *rubare* (to steal) become *subbito* and *rubbare*. This is particularly noticeable in words ending in *-abile*, *-obile* and *-ibile*, such as *abbile* (clever), *nobbile* (noble), *terribbile* (terrible).

Inevitably, there are also variations in grammatical and structural usage. In the south particularly, and in some parts of central Italy, the past definite is used in speech in place of the present perfect, which is now the norm for the vast majority of Italians. *Sono arrivati ieri sera* (They arrived last night) would be said by the vast majority of Italians; *arrivarono ieri sera* would be more common in the south. There are other variations, such as the avoidance of the subjunctive after certain expressions, which illustrate the way the language is evolving.

Dialects – what are they?

A dialect is a form of language spoken by a particular region or by a locality within that region. It is in no way a corruption of the national language but rather an autonomous language that has its own vocabulary and system of grammar. As local dialects can vary, even from one village to the next, it is easy to understand why there must be literally hundreds of dialects spoken in Italy, each with its own peculiarities. If two Italians, one from Piedmont and the other from Sicily, spoke in their respective regional dialects, *piemontese* and *siciliano*, they would almost certainly not understand each other. Thus the only way for these people to communicate is through standard Italian (or appropriate gestures!). Dialect of necessity is a vehicle of communication for a select minority who understand it, i.e. family, friends and inhabitants of the local community.

The vast majority of dialects are spoken rather than written forms of communication. There are some exceptions: Carlo Goldoni, the Venetian playwright, wrote some of his works in the Venetian dialect. Many well-known Neapolitan folk songs are sung in dialect. In fact folk music is an important art form that helps to preserve the dialect, its culture and traditions.

As *ladino* and *sardo* are so different from standard Italian many people consider them languages in their own right. The inhabitants of these regions would almost certainly go along with this view. *Ladino*, spoken by about 40,000 inhabitants in Trentino-Alto Adige, has recently been officially recognized by the Italian authorities. There is a newspaper in the language as well as some radio broadcasts and it is taught in schools. *Sardo* is also taught in schools in Sardinia alongside standard Italian.

The survival of dialects

Over the past 30 or 40 years many young people have abandoned their local village communities for the greater job opportunities and more attractive social scene in the nearby cities. Here they are obliged to communicate in standard Italian, which has inevitably led to a declining use of dialect. There is a

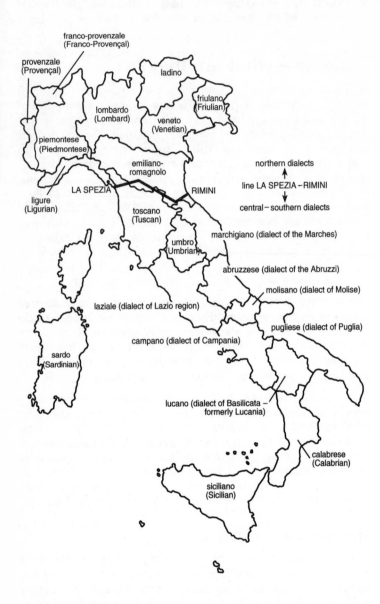

Map of Italy showing some of the main dialects

whole generation of younger people growing up who will no longer be exposed to their local dialects and so will be unable to preserve the traditional language of their ancestors.

The mass exodus of thousands of southern Italians to the northern cities of Turin, Milan and Genoa has also meant the migrants are less likely to speak in their local dialect, which has become more and more the preserve of small villages or remoter areas. Within these local communities the survival of the dialect equates to the survival of the local culture and traditions. Moreover, these dialects have enriched the national language, with vocabulary that is linked particularly to areas such as trade, professions, food, and traditions. For example, the coastal cities have deposited *laguna* (lagoon), *lido* (beach/shore), *traghetto* (ferry) into standard Italian.

Some clear divisions!

If a line were drawn on a map from La Spezia (Liguria) in the west across to Rimini on the Adriatic coast, it would mark the rough point of division between the northern and southern dialects. The northern dialects are of Celtic origin and bear many similarities to French. One of the main features has already been mentioned, namely the pronunciation of a single instead of the double consonant. The Florentine dialect is an exception, in that it retains the double consonant between two vowels. It also:

- retains the 'o', *aceto* (vinegar) whereas many of the central and southern dialects have 'u' at the end of a word, *acetu*
- keeps the diphthongs 'ie', 'uo' – *piede* (foot), *buono* (good) – whereas other dialects drop the first vowel and the words are pronounced as *pede*, *bono*
- has *-iamo* in all the first person plural conjugations – *andiamo* (we go/let's go). In Umbria this becomes *anamo*, in Veneto *andemo*, and in Piedmont *anduma*.

Despite the fact that the Florentine dialect became Italy's 'official' language, it has a feature that clearly marks it out from all other dialects and that is the pronunciation of the hard 'c' as an aspirate 'h' in front of the vowels a/o/u. A Florentine has to watch his Cs and Hs, not his Ps and Qs! Look at the cartoon on p. 34 and work out the message in *italiano comune*.

So where is the best Italian spoken? The majority of impartial Italians would probably say that the Italian spoken in central Italy is the most acceptable model. Those who want to narrow

una hoha hola
e una hannuccia

down the area would logically plump for Florence. After all the
Florentine dialect did become the official national language. The
inhabitants of Siena would almost certainly disagree, as there is
still a lot of rivalry between the cities of Florence and Siena that
dates back to the time of the city-states (see Unit 1).

Linguistic minorities

There are approximately 2.5 million Italian inhabitants who
speak languages other than Italian. During the Fascist era it was
forbidden to speak a language other than Italian and this
resulted in some people leaving Italy in order to preserve their
linguistic independence. The Constitution of 1948 tried to
repair the damage that had been done during this period by
stating that *'La Repubblica tutela con apposite norme le
minoranze linguistiche'* (The Republic will through appropriate
laws safeguard the existence of linguistic minorities). Two such
minorities were given official recognition by the Italian State at
an early stage and they were the German-speaking people of
Alto Adige and the French-speaking inhabitants of Valle
d'Aosta. Each of these regions must respect its 'own' language
and local traditions alongside the language and laws of the
Italian State. Thus road signs in Valle d'Aosta are written in
both languages; in the valleys of the province of Bolzano, where
both *ladino* and German are spoken, they are written in three.
Certain information in the telephone directory is in the
respective languages. The same applies to shop signs.
Newspapers are available in two languages or part in one
language and part in another.

Other linguistic and/or ethnic minorities include the following:

- Slovene, spoken in the areas that border Slovenia – now an independent republic of the former Yugoslavia
- Catalan, spoken in Alghero (Sardinia) – originates from the fourteenth century, when Spanish prisoners served their time there reclaiming the marshlands
- Greek, spoken by certain communities in Calabria and Puglia; its origin can be traced back to the Greek occupations in ancient times (800 BC)
- Albanian, spoken by the descendants of those who emigrated to the south of Italy as early as the fifteenth century (see also Unit 11)

Italian outside Italy

Italian is more widely spoken outside Italy than many people realize. There are more than half a million Italian speakers in the Swiss canton of Ticino. Italian was, moreover, exported to a number of European countries and other continents during the periods of mass emigration after the unification of Italy and at the turn of the twentieth century. Italians left in their thousands for America at the time of the *caccia all'oro* (gold rush), thinking they were going to make their fortune there. Now there are more than 5 million Italians working abroad who have retained their Italian citizenship.

The following countries are the most popular:

Germany	698,799
Argentina	601,658
France	379,749
Brazil	300,323
Belgium	281,017
USA	214,676
Great Britain	156,776
Venezuela	134,678
Canada	137,324
Australia	122,843

There are over 100,000 in Africa, mainly in the former Italian colonies where Italian continues to be taught, e.g. Asmara in Eritrea.

Also to be added to the final total are the emigrants or children of emigrants who have taken the nationality of their adopted country. They number about 2.5 million in the USA alone. In all of the above-mentioned countries there are Italian-speaking communities. The Italian Government sends consular teachers to these countries to teach Italian to children of Italian nationals and promote the Italian language and culture.

Slang *gergo*

Slang is a form of language that is used and usually only understood by a limited group of people, e.g. soldiers, students, prisoners or drug users. It makes sense that in certain circumstances such a group wishes to communicate in a private language not readily understood by either superiors or peers. It is perhaps not surprising that the most interesting variety of slang is used by members of the underworld and criminal society.

Slang is different from dialect, as the latter would normally be comprehensible to all the inhabitants of a locality or area. There are occasions where slang becomes an integral part of the national language and the vehicle for its diffusion is again the mass media. Young people in the 14–20 age bracket are strongly influenced by television and they quickly absorb into their linguistic baggage the slang employed, for example, by comedians. Here is just a brief insight into the world of slang, bearing in mind, however, that even slang is subject to geographical variation:

- in the underworld: *malloppo* (loot), *palo* (look-out), *cantare* (to talk, confess)
- drug-related: *maria* (marijuana), *cannone* (joint), *farsi* (to inject oneself)
- general use: *un cesso* (an ugly person), *gasato* (big-headed), *broda* (petrol)

An expressive language that needs no words!

Italian has another form of language that is most communicative and at times extremely effective, yet is a language that needs no words. It is of course the language of *i gesti* (gestures). Southern

Italians are purported to use gesture far more than their northern counterparts. This is probably true, as southerners in general are inclined to be much more expressive. When you see Italians in full flow it is indeed a wonderful sight to behold but it can be rather bewildering to the foreigner. As the conversation becomes more animated and intense, the variety of hand movements gathers pace. However, to the 'informed', the non-verbal form of language is as communicative as the verbal variety and often much more economical and interesting.

It is most important that students of the language learn the meaning of various gestures. It is moreover important to learn them correctly, as a movement in the wrong direction or an over-exaggerated gesture in some cases could prove very offensive. In the 'Taking it further' section at the end of this unit there is a reference to a very good book on the subject, appropriately named *Senza Parole* (Without Words). Those who perfect the art will be surprised how much they will be able to communicate without actually saying anything!

Meaning of gesture: *Me ne frego* (I don't give a damn)

More recent influences on the Italian language

The biggest influx of words into the Italian language in recent times has undoubtedly been from Britain or America. After the end of the Second World War Italy underwent a radical transformation from an agricultural economy to a rapidly expanding industrial one. Changes and advances in technology came thick and fast and Italian has in the main borrowed numerous English and American words rather than creating new Italian ones.

Italy does have an organization (*Accademia della Crusca*, founded in Florence in the second half of the sixteenth century) which is supposed to 'oversee' the language and safeguard its standard. However, it does not appear to have the influence of, for example, the *Académie française*, which is perhaps more rigid in its attempts to protect the French language from too many foreign imports. In any event, Italian is very susceptible to accepting foreign words.

The field of journalism has certainly had a profound influence and it has become very fashionable to use English terms even when there are Italian equivalents (e.g. *rete* for 'goal' or *tassì* for 'taxi'). Some fields of influence include:

- sport: *football, tennis, golf, hockey, rugby, sport, goal*
- transport: *(auto-) bus, ferry-boat, yacht, charter*
- food and drink: *picnic, sandwich, whisky, cocktail, gin*
- clothing: *nylon, blue-jeans, smoking (jacket), pullover*
- entertainment: *film, sketch, jazz, night, folk, bar*
- technology and commerce: *computer, mouse, e-mail, software, market, compact disc*
- general vocabulary: *hobby, handicap, VIP, weekend, tunnel, relax, okay, quiz, partner*

It is interesting to note that most of the above words end in a consonant and do not have a plural form if used in Italian. Italian words end in vowels and the number of vowels is a key feature of the Italian language. A good word for practising these sounds is the plural of *aiuola* (flower-bed), *aiuole*, as it contains all five vowels. The vowel sounds give the language its attractive lilting, musical quality.

A considerable number of foreign words used in Italian retain their original form (*boutique, goal, part-time, computer*). Others are Italianized in some way such as *vagone* (railway carriage), from the French *wagon*. Sometimes an Italian word is coined by means of a direct translation of the foreign original – *autocontrollo* (self-control), *grattacielo* (skyscraper), *fotocopiare* (to photocopy). 'New' verbs, incidentally, tend to belong to the regular group ending in *-are* rather than those in *-ere* or *-ire*, e.g. *cliccare* (to click on the mouse) and *surfare* (to surf the net). It would be impossible to Italianize all 'borrowed' words (e.g. jazz, quiz).

Many *neologismi* (new words) are inevitably introduced via the mass media. The advertising world is constantly looking for new publicity slogans and frequently resorts to the creation of new words to convey its message. *Neologismi* could in theory be considered the term for any foreign words used in Italian but the specialists in linguistics would rather label those words *prestiti* (borrowed) and use the term *neologismi* for new words created only from Italian words, e.g. *prepensionamento* (early retirement), which is a combination of the prefix *'pre'* and the word *pensionamento* (retirement).

A fairly recent *neologismo* is *tangentopoli* which derives from *tangente* 'protection money/bribe'. *Tangentopoli* is used to convey the corruption scandal involving businessmen, industrialists and government ministers that started in Milan in 1992. As a consequence Milan was dubbed *Tangentopoli* (Bribesville).

This very creative use of the language does not always respect grammatical rules. A radio advert once used *regalissimi* for *regali* (presents). Thus a superlative was created from a noun, i.e. 'very presents', which is grammatically impossible. Advertising slogans rely a lot on *giochi di parole* (puns), such as *cin contriamo con Cin Soda*. The verb *contriamo* does not exist, the word *cin* is used for 'cheers' so the effect is created by splitting up the Italian verb *c'incontriamo* 'we meet'. Publicity takes advantage of a kind of poetic licence for its own ends. Some newly coined words and expressions catch on and enter into everyday Italian but most are quickly forgotten as others are created. This reflects the ever-changing linguistic face of the advertising world.

What of the future?

There is no doubt that the use of standard Italian has progressed rapidly since the 1950s. Today it is estimated that 90 per cent of people in Italy communicate in *italiano comune* and the use of dialects in general is declining. Dialects will probably continue to flourish in local village communities but their long-term survival will depend on the younger generations.

Standard Italian itself continues to evolve but not in a form acceptable to many of the purists. Like everywhere else, there is a growing tendency to simplify the language. People in the main are using less vocabulary and ignoring grammatical structures;

for example, the subjunctive is tending to disappear after certain verbs expressing opinion. Students of the language may not be dismayed by this but teachers of Italian probably will be! It is the spoken language that changes the most, as the written form still tends to adhere more closely to the accepted rules.

Obviously there will always be variations in both written and spoken Italian depending on the education and social background of the person speaking or writing. The various social classes can be distinguished according to certain criteria: income and standard of living; their way of thinking; and also the language they speak. The upper classes are those who read newspapers, travel, have a higher standard of education, mix with people of similar background and are therefore considered to speak *un buon italiano* (good Italian). The less educated members of society speak the more simplified form of the language referred to above. In general, the latter are far more at ease with their local dialect than with Italian.

Encouragement for present and future learners

Italian is one of the four official languages of the European Union. Italy is one of the leading industrial nations in the world. Italian was the language of the first operas. For lovers of opera and music Italian is a must. How can you sing or learn to read music without some knowledge of terms such as *allegro, vivace, moderato, adagio*? For lovers of art, architecture and history Italian is the vehicle to their greater appreciation.

The Italians are delighted to hear foreigners speaking their language and are generally most helpful. However, they do tend to assume that the production of two or more words by the foreigner means fluency and they then proceed to utter the next 50 words or so without taking a breath. *Parli più lentamente per favore* (Please speak more slowly) is a useful expression to know.

The language is very accessible particularly to those who have studied another Romance language, such as French or Spanish, or to the diminishing few who have a knowledge of Latin. English speakers also have a head start because so many Italian words are similar to their English equivalents; for example, *intelligente, diligente, interessante, timido, terribile, industriale, politico, democratico*. The application of a few 'general' rules will lead to the immediate recognition of many more words:

- **ct** in English becomes **tt** in Italian: *fatto, patto, atto, intatto*
- **x** in English becomes **s** in Italian: *espressione, esame, esatto, esclusione*
- **ph** in English becomes **f** in Italian: *telefono, foto, farmacista*
- **ti** in English becomes **zi** in Italian: *nazione, creazione, stazione, informazione*
- **ns** in English becomes **s** in Italian: *trasformazione, trasfusione, trasmissione, trasparente, costruzione, istruzione*

As you can see, *è facile come bere un bicchiere d'acqua* (= it's a piece of cake). Why not try some? *Buon appetito* (Enjoy your meal).

GLOSSARIO	GLOSSARY
l'albanese	Albanian
capire	to understand
il catalano	Catalan
comunicare	to communicate
la comunicazione	communication
la conoscenza	knowledge
conservare	to preserve
la cultura	culture
i dialetti settentrionali	northern dialects
i dialetti meridionali	southern dialects
la differenza	difference
la doppia consonante	double consonant
l'esodo	exodus
l'espressione	expression
il francese	French
la grammatica	grammar
il greco	Greek
l'italiano scritto	written Italian
l'italiano parlato	spoken Italian
parlare	to speak
la parola	word
la percentuale	percentage
la pronuncia	pronunciation
scrivere	to write
il secolo	century
il significato	meaning
lo sloveno	Slovene
la struttura	structure

lo sviluppo	*development*
il tedesco	*German*
la tradizione	*tradition*
il vocabolario	*vocabulary*

Taking it further

Suggested reading

The Italian Language Today (Second Edition), Anna and Giulio Lepschy, Routledge 1996

A Linguistic History of Italian, Martin Maidan, Longman 1995

Storia linguistica dell'Italia unitá, Tullio De Mauro, Laterza 1996

La Lingua Italiana, Maurizio Dardano and Pietro Trifone, Zanichelli 1985

Senza Parole, Pierangela Diadori, Bonacci 1990

There is a good range of Italian texts available for anyone wishing to take up the language. Most of the books come with CDs or cassettes.

Language courses

For courses in Italy, the Italian Institute will usually provide an information booklet with addresses and some information about the centres. The Italian Institute in London is at 39 Belgrave Square, SW1X 8NX (**www.italcultur.org.uk**). The two most famous Universities for foreigners in Italy are in Siena (Tuscany) and Perugia (Umbria). See also **www.Italian. about.com**.

Websites

For those with a knowledge of Italian here is a website address to get up-to-date information on the slang, colloquialisms, etc. used by young people in different parts of Italy. Explanations of the terms are given in standard Italian.

www.maldura.unipd.it/giov/index.shtml

For information in English on different Italian dialects:
www.sil.org/ethnologue/countries/ital.html

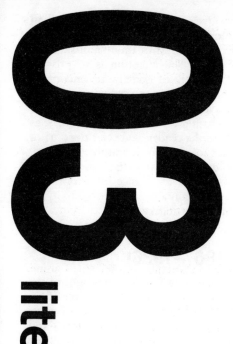

03

literature

In this unit you will learn
- about some contemporary Italian writers
- about some of the great names of early Italian literature

It is not the aim of this unit to give a complete overview of Italian literature from its early beginnings to the present day. Were it to be so, the reader would have the briefest of thumbnail sketches or the bare bones with no flesh. The intention is to provide enough information on a selection of writers to encourage further research into the works of anyone who particularly attracts the reader's literary eye. Another break with tradition will be to devote most of the chapter to the twentieth century, as this period is more accessible to the reader, and refer to some of the 'older' household names of Italian literature – Dante, Petrarch, Boccaccio and Goldoni – towards the end. There is perhaps an inevitable subjectivity in the choice of authors but some attempt has been made to attain a degree of objectivity by sounding out the opinions of Italian colleagues.

Luigi Pirandello (1867–1936)

Pirandello is recognized as the leading Italian playwright of the twentieth century. His three highly acclaimed masterpieces *Così è (se vi pare)* (Right You Are – if you think so), *Sei personaggi in cerca d'autore* (Six Characters in Search of an Author) and *Enrico IV* (Henry IV) have been played on stages throughout the world. Acknowledgement of his achievement was the award of the Nobel prize in 1934, two years before his death.

Pirandello, born in Agrigento in Sicily, started his working life as a secondary-school teacher but soon combined this profession with writing poetry and narrative. He wrote his most successful novel in 1904, *Il fu Mattia Pascal* (The Late Mattia Pascal). However, it was only when he turned his attention to playwriting in 1910 that he managed to become sufficiently successful in the literary sphere to be able to relinquish his teaching post.

Così è (se vi pare)

The very title of this play embodies one of Pirandello's central themes, i.e. truth versus reality. The following lines from Act 1 Scene 2 underline the key message.

> *Signora Sirelli: Ma secondo lei allora non si potrà mai sapere la verità?*
> *Signora Cini: Se non dobbiamo più credere neppure a ciò che si vede e si tocca.*
> *Laudisi: Ma sì, ci creda signora! Però le dico: rispetti ciò che vedono e toccano gli altri, anche se sia il contrario di ciò che vede e tocca lei.*

(Signora Sirelli: So in your opinion we shall never be able
to know the truth?

Signora Cini: If we must no longer believe not even what
we see and touch.

Laudisi: But of course believe it, madame! However, I am
saying to you: respect what others see and touch even if
it is the opposite to what you see and touch.)

This is very much on a par with the saying 'Beauty is in the eye
of the beholder' but in this case substitute 'truth' for 'beauty'.
The crux of the message is that the truth is whatever each of us
believes it to be; there can be no absolute truth and the whole
concept becomes relative. This theme pervades Pirandello's three
great plays. It is intriguing but also frightening and frustrating in
many ways, especially for those looking for definite answers and
never finding solutions. Throughout *Così è*, Laudisi, one of the
protagonists, is constantly reminding the characters investigating
the lives of others of the futility of trying to arrive at the truth.
As the play unfolds his advice is borne out by the fact that every
revelation of the supposed truth cannot be substantiated by any
tangible proof. What is truth? What is reality? The suspense
mounts but the answer is not forthcoming. It is like holding up a
mirror to life and trying to interpret the reflections. There are
many instances in the play that use this mirror image. In Act 3
Scene 3, Laudisi conducts a lively and very comical conversation
with his reflection in the mirror, posing the question: 'Which one
of us is mad?'

The play has many comic moments as well as the darker and
more pessimistic reflections on the absurdity of life and its utter
meaninglessness. A prelude to this theme can be found in the
novel *Il fu Mattia Pascal* when Mattia comes to the sad
conclusion that *'la vita è una triste buffoneria'*, which conveys

the idea that life is a cruel joke. This reflects Pirandello's own view of life. There are episodes in his personal life that profoundly influenced him and perhaps resulted in this rather bleak and pessimistic outlook. In 1916 his son Stefano was captured and made a prisoner of war and his wife's mental health deteriorated to such an extent that he eventually had to commit her to a mental institution.

Così è works on a number of levels: a thriller that is full of suspense, a social comedy, an intellectual drama, and a tragedy in which there are underlying feelings of sympathy and compassion for those caught up in it. After *Così è* Pirandello embarked on his most prolific period, writing ten plays between 1917 and 1921.

Enrico IV

The theme of reality and illusion is again central both to *Enrico IV* and the other play in the famous trilogy, *Sei personaggi in cerca d'autore*. Other characteristic features of these plays include:

- the juxtaposition of two groups of people, a technique used in Greek tragedy
- the play within a play, which is not an innovation in itself
- the use of masks
- the contrast between art, in this case acting, and real life

Enrico IV contains the whole gamut of common Pirandellian themes, which evolve quite naturally through a range of situations. There is moreover an added dimension in *Enrico IV*, namely, the theme of sanity and madness, of which Pirandello had first-hand experience through his wife's affliction. The story revolves around *un gentiluomo* (a gentleman) who becomes mad following a riding accident and lives for years believing himself to be Enrico IV. When he recovers his sanity, he continues to feign madness. This conscious decision to shun a 'normal' life is a radical denouncement of existence, an escape from the absurdity and futility of life. So he prefers to hide behind a mask. There are times in life when we all either intentionally or unintentionally hide behind a mask because we wish to hide from the truth. In the mind of Pirandello, life makes puppets of us all. The reality–illusion theme is one that many of us would rather not consider too deeply for it would require an examination of the inner self in an attempt to discover the truth. Pirandello's three plays have survived the test of time because they raise pertinent questions that are universal and relevant to us all.

Eugenio Montale (1896–1981)

Montale, born in Genoa, spent much of his childhood further down the Ligurian coast in the *Cinque Terre*. His poetry contains numerous references to the sea and landscape of this area. He wrote his first collection of poems, *Ossi di seppia* (Cuttle-fish Bones) in 1925 after moving to Turin. He subsequently shifted his roots to Florence. It was here that he became involved in a cultural group that met up in the now famous café *Giubbe Rosse* in Piazza della Repubblica. The café itself is worth a visit and, while sipping your drink, you can look at photographs on the walls of these literary figures. Montale eventually lost his job in Florence because he refused to become a Fascist Party member.

He published his second collection of poems *Le occasioni* (Occasions) in 1939 and after the war moved to Milan to work for a leading national newspaper, *Corriere della Sera*, for which he wrote cultural articles. In 1956 he published his third collection of poetry *La bufera e altro* (The Storm and Others). In 1967 he was nominated *senatore a vita* (life senator) and was awarded the Nobel prize for literature in 1975.

His poetry

Montale belonged to a group of so-called hermetic poets. The term 'hermetic' originates from a Greek word literally meaning 'closed'. In English we talk about something being hermetically sealed and this fits the description of his poetry, which is full of symbolism and references that need to be uncovered if they are to be meaningful to the reader. We have to remember that Montale was writing during a time of oppression, the Fascist period, under a totalitarian regime in which criticism of the system brought the risk of being imprisoned or exiled. The writer Carlo Levi, for example, was packed off to southern Italy out of harm's way and his novel *Cristo si è fermato a Eboli* (Christ Stopped at Eboli) records this experience. Montale, therefore, had to ensure that unfavourable references to this period were couched in a 'secret code'.

In the poem *A Liuba che parte* (To Liuba who is Leaving) there are several examples of these 'secret messages'. Liuba is a typical female Jewish name. During the time of Fascism the Jews were persecuted and many fled to escape being deported to the concentration camps in Germany. There is a reference in this poem to the *dispersa tua famiglia* (your family that has 'scattered' = fled). Shortly afterwards Montale alludes to *i ciechi tempi* (literally, 'the blind times') but this is his way of defining this dark, oppressive period of 'Fascism and Nazism'. It is understandable in the circumstances that his early work especially is full of gloom and pessimism, and throughout *Ossi di seppia* his aversion to Fascism lies behind many of the coded messages. However, beyond this rather painful vision of the world there are a few glimmers of hope. In *A Liuba che parte*, the *gatto* (cat) is the symbol of salvation, the continuation of life, a reference that once again underlines how almost every word is loaded with meaning and symbolism. The 'cat' assumed godlike status in countries like Egypt. A cat has 'nine lives' and herein maybe lies the note of optimism.

Man and time

The relationship between man and time was a common theme in Montale's poetry. He talks about the vulnerability of life, the struggles, the loneliness, and the road to eventual extinction. Montale's vision of the world was said to be '*una visione senza sorriso*' (a vision without a smile). Even the description of the Ligurian landscape seems dark and threatening. However, it is in his later works that time assumes greater significance when he can see his own life ebbing away. For a closer examination of this theme refer to *Poiché la vita fugge* (As Life is Fleeing). The image in this poem of '*ricacciare la vita indietro*' (driving life backwards) is an attempt to cling on by halting the flow of time. There is more to this poem than the question of the temporality of man: there is a preoccupation with the destiny of art and this image is conveyed by the '*piccolo scaffale che viaggiava con Clizia*' (the little bookcase that travelled with Clizia) which:

avesse la virtù di galleggiare	had the virtue of floating
sulla cresta delle onde	on the crest of the waves
quando il diluvio avrà	when the flood will have
sommerso tutto	submerged everything

The *piccolo scaffale* is the embodiment of man's creative activities, which resist time and last for ever. If Montale was hoping that his poetry would outlive him then thus far he can rest in peace.

In another of his famous poems, *L'anguilla* (The Eel) from *La bufera e altro*, there is now greater optimism than before. The war is over, Fascism is no more and there is fresh hope in democracy and the birth of the Republic. The disillusionment and sense of hopelessness have been replaced by a sense of joy. Perhaps this coded message is conveyed by the eel leaving the cold of the Baltic for the warmer climes of Italy.

L'anguilla, la sirena
dei mari freddi che lascia il
Baltico per giungere ai nostri
mari

The eel, the siren
of cold seas that leaves the
Baltic to reach our seas

It will wend its way upstream to the spawning grounds, where its journey ends but a new journey begins for the baby eels. These are the hope, the continuation of life.

Leonardo Sciascia (1921–1989)

Leonardo Sciascia, like Pirandello, was born in Sicily and his writings are very much based on his native land. However, Sciascia deals with the reality of society whereas Pirandello was concerned with themes of a more philosophical nature. Sciascia embarked on his writing career at a time of great social, political, and economic change. It was a period that provided so many writers with events to comment on and allude to in their works: Fascism, the Second World War, the partisan movement, a return to democracy, the economic miracle, etc. To find out about Sciascia's main concerns a good starting point would be *Le parrocchie di Regalpetra* (1956), which comprises a series of documentary essays about Sciascia's home town and refers to his chief preoccupations – Fascism, the Mafia, the Church, Sicilian and Italian society, history and politics. These issues crop up at different points in his later writings.

Il giorno della civetta (1961)

Il giorno della civetta (The Day of the Owl) is one of Sciascia's best-known novels and it is centred on the Mafia. It is a concise, detective-style story about the investigation by an officer of the *Carabinieri* (military police) from Parma (northern Italy), into the murder of a man shot while boarding an early morning bus. The officer eventually manages to extract confessions from the suspects but the case remains unresolved. It is obviously a Mafia contract job but, because of involvement at government level, it is not surprising that the perpetrator of the crime goes unpunished.

Although the crime, which happens in the opening paragraph, is the crux of the novel, Sciascia at varying intervals gives the reader an insight into a number of interesting aspects that serve to form a picture of both Sicilian and Italian society:

- the silence of the Sicilian people as if they wish to deny the very existence of the Mafia. After the killing '*Il bigliettaio guardò tutte quelle facce che sembravano facce di ciechi*' (The bus conductor looked at all those faces which seemed like faces of blind people). A little later on we are told '*Di quelli che stavano sull'autobus, nessuno ha visto niente*' (Of those on the bus, no-one saw anything). The passengers may genuinely have known nothing but those who may have known something preferred to turn a blind eye. In this 'honoured society' the informer, once discovered, usually joins the fish at the bottom of the sea.

- the resentment that Sicilians feel for people from the north, who have no understanding of their society. This ill-feeling is also born out of northern neglect for their region. Perhaps that is why Sicilian communities are so closely knit and the family assumes even greater importance than elsewhere. They view the State as a remote entity that does nothing to help their cause. '*La famiglia è lo Stato del siciliano. Lo Stato...impone le tasse, il servizio militare, la guerra...*' (The family is the State of the Sicilian. The State... imposes taxes, military service, war...).

- the violent, criminal society where people are forced to pay protection money or face likely reprisals for not doing so

- the corruption that pervades much of Italian society

- the northern misconception that Sicily is synonymous with the Mafia and nothing else: '*Questo qui, caro amico, è uno che vede mafia da ogni parte: uno di quei settentrionali con la testa piena di pregiudizi*' (This one here, dear friend, is someone who sees Mafia everywhere: one of those northerners with his head full of prejudices). Another misconception is that Sicilians are lazy and have no initiative: '*E non è vero che i siciliani sono pigri. E non è vero che non hanno iniziativa*' (And it's not true that Sicilians are lazy. And it's not true that they don't have initiative).

Through this novel, as with so much of his work, Sciascia displays a social commitment by deliberately pinpointing serious problems that affect Italian society as a whole. Within Italy there is an entire network of complicity that extends to those who hold positions of great responsibility and the country has had to endure a number of corruption and political scandals over the years. *Il giorno della civetta*, as much as any of Sciascia's novels, alludes to a whole range of issues that throw light on both Sicily and Italian society. Other novels worth referring to are *A ciascuno il suo* (To Each his Own) (1966) and *Il contesto* (1971). In all these works there are few sparks of humour and much serious criticism of Italians and Italy today.

Elsa Morante (1912–1985)

Elsa Morante was born in Rome. She married Alberto Moravia in 1941 and soon afterwards they moved to the south because her husband had been accused of being involved in anti-Fascist activities. Throughout her life Morante seems to have been a very private person who shunned the spotlight and preferred to let her work do the talking for her. Her work is such that in fact it would be difficult to attempt to place her into some kind of category of writers. She separated from Moravia 21 years after they married and, following a long illness, committed suicide in 1985.

Morante, like many other writers of her time, experienced Fascism and all its rhetoric so that reality and truth were pushed into the background. Freed from the shackles of an undemocratic regime Morante felt the need to bring reality to the foreground and recount events in an honest, uninhibited way. In the post-war years her preoccupations lay with the rapid industrialization of Italy, the process of urbanization and the creation of a consumer society. Good human values were being relegated to second place in the rush for progress.

La storia (1974)

La storia (History: a novel) is one of Morante's greatest successes and it provides a well-documented picture of Italian life from 1941 to 1947. It is a protest against '*uno scandalo che dura da diecimila anni*' (a scandal that has gone on for ten thousand years). The scandal is the violence and oppression which have defiled our history. Her way of expressing opposition to what has gone on is through the innocence of a small boy. She places her faith in childhood as a symbol of hope in the fight against the rising tide of materialism and greed. This idea that only children can be our protection from destruction is evident in *Il mondo salvato dai ragazzini* (1968). Two of Morante's other well-known works are *Menzogna e sortileggio* (1948) and *L'isola di Arturo* (Arturo's Island) (1957). The former is the dramatic story of a family from the south of Italy, whereas the latter is a blend of the real and the fairy-tale and narrates the memories of a young boy growing up on an island. It is an initiation to the discovery of life and the episodes relate to *l'amore* (love), *l'amicizia* (friendship), *il dolore* (pain) and *la disperazione* (desperation).

Natalia Ginzburg (1916–1991)

During the period since the Second World War women writers in Italy have grown in stature and Natalia Ginzburg figures prominently among this group of highly acclaimed authors. She grew up in Turin and was an ardent anti-Fascist. Her first husband Leone Ginzburg died at the hands of the Fascists. She subsequently remarried and moved to Rome. She remains one of the most respected and popular twentieth-century novelists. One of her main themes is family life and human relationships and she is not afraid to depict harsh reality.

> We cannot lie in our books and we cannot lie in any of the things that we do. And perhaps this is the only good thing to have come to us out of the war...We are close to things as they really are. (from *Mai devi domandarmi*)

Her work displays a strong sense of social and political commitment, which is conveyed in a straightforward, uncomplicated, very descriptive and, at times, almost poetic style. It is this clarity of style that makes her novels so accessible and readable. Some of the best known are: *Tutti i nostri ieri* (All our Yesterdays)(1952), *Le voci della sera* (Voices in the Evening) (1961) and *Lessico famigliare* (Family Saying) (1963). She also wrote extensively for the theatre.

È stato così (1947)

This novel exemplifies one of Ginzburg's central themes, as it tells the story of a woman caught up in a real-life situation that she cannot fully grasp or comprehend. It is about a desperate and jealous love that you feel from the outset is never going to have a happy ending. The leading female protagonist has a clear picture of her ideal marriage to someone she can trust, love and lead a normal family life with. Ginzburg, however, shows us that life does not usually run that smoothly and simply. Life has its complexities and can be full of contradictions. We see the contrast with the more orthodox traditional family life of the girl's parents and the more liberal changing attitude of the post-war generation. The father says:

> *Le ragazze moderne hanno perso il rispetto e non dicono neanche una parola di quello che fanno.* (Modern young girls have lost their respect and don't even say a word about what they are doing.)

Although the young woman does marry Alberto their relationship is destined to fail because he has always loved someone else, Giovanna, who is already married. The marriage for both partners to some extent becomes one of convenience, although the wife desperately wants it to work. '*Ma dopo un mese che eravamo sposati se n'è andato. È stato via dieci giorni.*' (But a month after we had got married he went off. He was away for ten days.) Despite his love for another woman Alberto thought perhaps it would work:

> *Credevo che l'avrei dimenticata, credevo che fosse semplice e invece quando abbiamo cominciato a vivere insieme noi due, soffrivo terribilmente perché eri tu e non lei con me.* (I thought that I would have forgotten her, I thought that it was simple and instead when we began to live together, I suffered terribly because it was you and not her with me.)

The wife throughout the novel constantly tortures herself with jealousy and self-doubt. She admits on more than one occasion that '*il matrimonio era un disastro*' (the marriage was a disaster). Her life and state of mind is in complete contrast to the way her friend Francesca sees life. Francesca adopts a nonchalant, carefree attitude and sees herself as a free spirit. She doesn't want to be tied down by marriage.

The self-doubt, the fear, the inner torture are destined to go on. The young wife resigns herself to the fact that she had never been capable of living a different life and it is now too late to change:

> *Adesso certo era troppo tardi per imparare, pensavo che nella mia vita non avevo mai fatto altro che guardare fisso fisso nel pozzo buio che avevo dentro di me.* (Now certainly it was too late to learn, I thought that in my life I had never done anything but stare into the dark well that I had inside me.)

It is all rather sad and tragic and the death of their child is a further blow. The feeling of empathy also extends to Alberto, who never realizes his main hope of being with the woman he really loves. These are the harsh realities of life, which people have to try and make sense of and which Ginzburg manages to communicate so unambiguously in this novel.

Italo Calvino (1923–1985)

Some biographical details

- born in Cuba of Italian parents but spent his childhood in Liguria
- became a member of the Communist Party
- participated in the Resistance movement during the Second World War
- worked both as a writer and editorial consultant for the publishing company Einaudi
- considered one of the fundamental roles of the writer to be a communicator of the real problems confronting people in a rapidly changing world
- recognized as one of the great post-war writers and figures in the category of some other neorealist writers of the period, Cesare Pavese, Beppe Fenoglio, Pier Paolo Pasolini and Mario Soldati. Neorealism was a term applied to literature, the cinema and art forms in general that gave a realistic picture of the society of the time.
- later moved from neorealism to fantasy

Il sentiero dei nidi di ragno (1947)

The post-war period signalled a revival in the arts – literature and the cinema – as, not surprisingly, those involved in the period of conflict had their story to tell. Calvino, Beppe Fenoglio and Primo Levi, amongst others, used the medium of literature to record and express such events. The Resistance movement was the source of inspiration for Calvino's first novel *Il sentiero dei nidi di ragno* (The Path to the Nest of Spiders). This movement, which symbolized the spirit of fraternity and the road to eventual freedom, is seen through the eyes of a child. Thus we have the contrast between the innocence of youth and the violent conduct of adults caught up in the atrocities of war.

A characteristic feature running through much of Calvino's writing is the association with the fairy-tale. He was *un appassionato di fiabe* (a fairy-tale enthusiast) and this tendency is evident in his choice of the child to mirror the events of the novel. Calvino himself wrote that by doing this he managed to '*osservare la vita partigiana, come una favola di bosco*' (observe the partisan life as a fairy-tale in the woods). This affinity with the fairy-tale is present in later works such as *Il barone rampante* (The Baron in the Trees) (1956), *Il cavaliere inesistente* (The Non-Existent Knight) (1959) and *Marcovaldo* (1963). However, the fantasy world created by Calvino is not intended simply to be what some would classify as escapism, as the link between the reality of his time and its problems is always present.

La speculazione edilizia (1957)

This novel portrays very well the rapidly changing world mentioned earlier. It is set at the time of the economic boom of the 1950s and the building of characterless blocks of flats along the Ligurian coast to accommodate the wealthier middle classes from northern cities such as Milan. The flats will serve mainly as 'second homes' by the sea but their construction will be at the expense of the natural beauty of the area where Calvino spent much of his childhood. This economic boom bred unscrupulous profiteers, represented in the novel by Caisotti, a building speculator, and the materialism and selfishness that are usually associated with such people.

The story also underlines Calvino's concern with the problem of man's alienation in this rapidly changing society. Quinto, one of the protagonists of the novel, epitomizes the theme of isolation from the world in which he has grown up. He too becomes ensnared in the *speculazione edilizia* (building speculation) with the decision to sell off part of his mother's garden for the development of a block of flats: '*Se tutti costruiscono perché non costruiamo anche noi*' (If everyone else is building why don't we build as well). The new development will inevitably disfigure the old surroundings, an act which equates to man's alienation from nature: '*Quinto lo considerava un'appendice accessoria della villa e nemmeno v'era legato da memorie dell'infanzia perché tutto quel che lui ricordava di quel luogo era scomparso*' (Quinto considered the garden an unimportant addition to the villa, and he was not even attached to it by memories of childhood because all that he remembered about that place had gone/disappeared). Quinto's decision further alienates him from those he once knew although, since he had abandoned his home town, he had isolated himself anyway. Money and profit are now the symbols of the new order replacing the good old values of the past.

Another insight into that society is how the honest folk face the burden of taxation while the *grossi* (literally, 'the bigwigs/the important people') get away without paying their fair share. Calvino is striking a moral note and we must always remember that he is a Communist who is working for the improvement of society for all and not a select band. The point he makes here about taxation, however, still holds true to this day. In Chapter Fourteen he presents a picture of post-war development – the return to democracy – and highlights very clearly the economic imbalance that exists between different parts of Italy. In this novel there is the dichotomy between the need for advancement and economic progress on the one hand and, on the other, the effect that such progress can have on human beings especially when confronted by the lure of materialism.

A look at the past

Many of the works of the contemporary writers mentioned in the first section have been studied and widely read, either in the original version or in translation, not only in Italy but in countries throughout the world. The four writers in this next section have also been very influential in their different ways and reference to their impact on the literary world is made under each author. What about the intervening years, especially from the time of Boccaccio to the start of the twentieth century? Here is the briefest of overviews.

- The literature in the first half of the sixteenth century tended to reflect the Renaissance idealism and desire to create something perfect. In Castiglione's *Il libro del Cortegiano* there is this attempt to depict the perfect courtesan, physically, intellectually and morally.
- Ludovico Ariosto's masterpiece *Orlando furioso* (1532), an epic tale of chivalry, inspired the works of other great authors, e.g. *Don Quixote* by Cervantes and Shakespeare's *Tempest* and *Midsummer Night's Dream*.
- Niccolò Macchiavelli's *Il Principe* (The Prince) (1513) was also closely scrutinized by later writers in Italy and abroad, to

gain an insight into the Renaissance and to understand the development of modern thought.

• The early period of the nineteenth century was marked by the *romanzo storico* (historical novel), the most famous of which was Alessandro Manzoni's *I promessi sposi* (The Betrothed). This novel is studied by all Italian students. It is important partly for the language in which it was written. Manzoni wanted the literary language to be identified with the spoken language of the people. For this reason he went to Tuscany because here *nel fiorentino* (in Florentine) he would find the kind of language he required. Manzoni is regarded as a highly important figure in the development of modern spoken and written Italian in the same way as Dante was before him.

The poets Giacomo Leopardi (1798–1837) and Ugo Foscolo (1778–1827), who wrote at this time, are also significant.

Carlo Goldoni (1707–1793)

Goldoni was born in Venice. Son of a doctor, he had no great inclination to study himself, much to his father's regret. However, on the death of his father, Goldoni settled down. He got married and graduated in law from the University of Padua. He developed a fascination for the theatre at an early age and this became the focus of his future career. He was a prolific playwright and wrote 120 plays in Italian, French or Venetian dialect. What he achieved for the theatre can best be gauged by the fact that in the *Ottocento* (nineteenth century) his plays were represented and imitated and in the *Novecento* (twentieth century) they were still performed successfully on stages throughout the world.

The theatre for Goldoni was an honest form of entertainment. Through his plays he wanted to make people happy while painting a picture of the real world. In so doing Goldoni was detaching himself from the *commedia dell'arte* where the tradition was for the actors to wear masks to represent particular characters. As we shall see when we look briefly at one of his most famous plays, *La Locandiera*, in Goldoni's works there are no masks but real people with whom the audience can identify.

The real world for Goldoni was eighteenth-century Venice, one of the important Marine Republics and the city of merchants, nobility, and the bourgeoisie, although he does not forget the 'ordinary' working-class folk. The 1750s onwards witnessed the decline of the merchant middle class and this is recorded in *La Locandiera*. Here are some of the main features of his plays:

- a good-natured humour
- a sympathetic and appreciative attitude to the virtues of the old merchant class
- an appreciation of the vitality and spontaneity of the lower classes
- an uncomplicated style that incorporates elements of everyday spoken language – slang, colloquialisms, etc.
- a detached, affable, non-critical presentation of the facts of life as he sees them

La Locandiera (1753)

This play manages to blend together harmoniously the above-mentioned features to paint a picture of *la vita settecentesca* (eighteenth-century life). We have the contrasting characters of the working-class Mirandolina, the innkeeper; the proud but penniless Marquis of Forlipopoli, the Count of Albafiorita who has secured this title through his wealth; and the Knight of Ripafratta, who loathes women. The whole plot revolves around Mirandolina, manoeuvring her way rather mockingly around her two suitors, the Marquis and the Count, as she sets her sights on the 'woman hater'. She eventually wins him over but then decides to marry the waiter, which is nothing more than a marriage of convenience, as she is seeking someone to protect her without domineering her. This act is also her way of showing that money cannot buy everything. Mirandolina has her own ideas about what she wants.

> *Tutto il mio piacere consiste in vedermi servita, vagheggiata, adorata. Questa è la mia debolezza, e questa è la debolezza di quasi tutte le donne. A maritarmi non ci penso nemmeno; non ho bisogno di nessuno; vivo onestamente, e godo la mia libertà. Tratto con tutti ma non m'innamoro di nessuno.* (All my pleasure consists in seeing myself served, longed for, adored. This is my weakness, and this is the weakness of almost all women. I don't even think about getting married; I don't need anyone; I live honestly, and I enjoy my freedom. I deal with everyone but I fall in love with no-one.)

It is now time to turn the clock back and consider the three founding fathers of Italian literature.

Giovanni Boccaccio (1313–1375)

Boccaccio was probably born in Certaldo, Tuscany. In his youth he spent some time in Naples, supposedly to get experience of working in a bank, but he gained greater insight into the social life surrounding the Court of the Angioini than into the world of work. Boccaccio had a yearning to study and he began to read Dante, Petrarch and the works of French poets. To his regret he had to leave Naples in 1340 and return to Florence. In his eyes Naples was '*lieta, pacifica, magnifica*' (happy, peaceful, magnificent) whereas Florence was '*noiosa*' (boring) and its people '*superba, avara, invidiosa*' (arrogant, mean, envious). His experience in Naples probably served him well when he wrote the *Decameron*, which gave him world-wide fame and marked him out as the first Italian novelist.

The *Decameron*

The setting for the *Decameron* was a villa in Fiesole overlooking Florence in which a group of seven young women and three young men sought refuge from the pestilence sweeping the city in 1348. Here they indulged in revelry but dedicated part of the day to recounting tales. For this purpose *il re* (king) or *la regina* (queen) was selected from the group and their task for that day was to choose a theme around which everyone then had to relate a tale. The topic was 'open-ended' on the first and ninth days, and Friday and Saturday were exempt from story-telling. The hundred stories that make up the *Decameron* were related over ten days, hence the title, which in Greek means 'ten days'. Among the themes are the happy and the less fortunate experiences of love. The *Decameron* has many similarities with the later *Canterbury Tales* of Chaucer from the point of view of the story-telling technique.

The following points are intended to create a picture of Boccaccio himself and provide a framework for an examination of this major work. Boccaccio:

- depicts the world and people as he sees them. He is a *cronista* (reporter) of everyday events and the people and life of his day. The stories are about people from all walks of life – aristocracy, bourgeoisie, merchants and working classes
- takes a detached view of the people and events; he does not cast moral judgement
- realizes that nature and fortune set before us a series of obstacles but overcoming the obstacles is an essential part of

the learning process. A good example is the *Tale of Andreuccio da Perugia*

- is endowed with great imagination to be able to create all these tales – but his life's experience has served him well
- has his thoughts fixed firmly on Earth and doesn't look to the spiritual and the world beyond (compare Petrarch)
- is a contented, sociable being who enjoys the good things in life – love, good food and wine, entertainment – and wants to entertain others
- does not intend examining others too deeply, neither does he want to indulge in any kind of self-examination

Boccaccio's tales and his style of writing had a profound influence on writers both in Italy (Pulci, Ariosto) and elsewhere in Europe (Chaucer, Cervantes, Shakespeare, Molière) and provided the comedy plots for many works in sixteenth-century Italian theatre.

Francesco Petrarca (1304–1374)

Petrarca (Petrarch) was born in Arezzo in Tuscany but moved to Avignon in France in 1312. Subsequently he travelled a great deal around Italy. He studied law at the universities of Montpellier and Bologna but his main interest was the study of the classics, especially Virgil and Cicero. A significant moment in his life was when he met Laura in the church of Santa Chiara in Avignon on *venerdì santo* (Good Friday), 6 April 1327. She became the inspiration for one of his major works, *Il Canzoniere*. In fact, such was her influence on him that she is immortalized in this collection of lyrical poems.

Il Canzoniere

This collection of 366 poems, 317 of which are sonnets, assured Petrarch of a permanent position in the hall of fame of Italian literature. It is divided into two sections, the first dedicated to Laura's life and the second to her death. Petrarch is not married to Laura and the sonnets tell of a platonic, unrequited love, with all the accompanying pangs of emotion – pain, anguish, joy, hope. The beauty of Laura is mirrored by the beauty of the sonnets themselves. The careful choice of words that always have a precise meaning in the given context and the musicality of the rhymes create a tremendous feeling of sensitivity. As you journey through the various sonnets and experience the range of emotions, you sense a soul torn between the reality of a terrestrial world, in which beauty, happiness, etc. are but ephemeral, and the spiritual world where you can find peace. The transience of beauty is evoked in the last three lines of a famous sonnet of exquisite charm and elegance: '*Quel rosigniuol che sì soave piagne*' (That nightingale that is so softly weeping).

Or cognosco io che mia fera	Now I know that my savage
ventura vuol che vivendo e	fate is to make me learn
lagrimando impari come nulla	living and weeping, that nothing
qua giù diletta e dura	here below delights and lasts.

This conflict between Heaven and Earth was characteristic of the medieval conscience. Petrarch feels torn between the two, hence his melancholic state. There is anguish at Laura's passing whereas for Dante there would have been joy. Laura is a human being, whereas the Beatrice of Dante is a divine figure and his philosophy is linked to the theology of the Middle Ages. A short span of time separated Dante and Petrarch yet the poetry of the latter tended more towards Humanism which, together with his interest in classical studies, marked him out as a forerunner of the later Renaissance period.

Not all the poems in the collection are dedicated to Laura. The following lines have political overtones and reflect the conflicts that raged during the Middle Ages.

Che fan qui tante pellegrine spade?	What are so many alien swords doing here?
Perché 'l verde terreno del barbarico sangue si depinga?	Why is the green earth painted with barbarian blood?

Petrarch exhorts the rulers of the time to refrain from war. He ends up by saying:

I'vo gridando: Pace, pace pace.	I keep on shouting: Peace, peace, peace.

The influence of the *Canzoniere* was felt both in Italy and Europe. The poems were acclaimed for their stylistic perfection, their images and metaphors. They were carefully studied and became a model for many later poets, giving rise to *petrarchismo* (imitation of his style) in the fifteenth and sixteenth centuries.

Dante Alighieri (1265–1321)

Dante Alighieri was born in Florence, where he received a typical medieval diet of literature, philosophy and theology. At the age of nine he met Beatrice, a source of inspiration for much of his work, e.g. *Vita Nuova* (1292–1294), and an important figure in his famous *capolavoro* (masterpiece) *La Commedia*, later to become *La Divina Commedia* (The Divine Comedy). The addition of *Divina* is significant because this symbolizes Beatrice, who to Dante is 'divine'.

La Divina Commedia

Structure

The poem is divided into three canticles, each of which represents a different phase on Dante's imaginary journey: *Inferno* (Hell) = damnation; *Purgatorio* (Purgatory) = atonement; *Paradiso* (Paradise) = bliss. Each canticle has thirty-three sections. Dante here is respecting medieval tradition, which acknowledged the significance of certain numbers, particularly the three and the multiples of three. Three is the perfect number because it symbolizes *Trinità* (Trinity) = *Padre, Figlio e Spirito Santo* (Father, Son and Holy Spirit), so important in Christian theology. Consider the structure of the work: *three* canticles, *thirty-three* sections, *three* lines in each verse.

Story

The *Commedia* is an allegorical poem which aims to reawaken man's conscience so that, through the light of reason, he will hopefully turn his back on sin and find purity and thus salvation. Through the various characters we are made aware of the vices of the world and the temptations before us that can inevitably lead to sin and eventual damnation. There is the contrast between life on Earth with all its pitfalls and the beauty of the life beyond. In the first canticle, Dante finds himself in the *selva oscura* (dark wood), which symbolizes sin. Virgil, who represents *ragione* (reason), comes to his rescue and will act as his guide through Hell and Purgatory. At this point Beatrice, who is all purity, will guide him along his final journey through Heaven, which is *pura luce* (pure light), and to the vision of God.

This work is an expression of medieval life and culture. In the society of the time discord, violence, corruption and power struggles (the Papacy versus the Empire) were much in evidence. Dante himself had been exiled from his beloved Florence, something that was always to rankle with him. He is hoping for a regeneration of society that will purge itself of its evil ways. It highlights the fragility of man but there is hope and a place in *Paradiso* for all those who pursue righteousness. The question of the Papacy and the Empire, i.e. Church and State, temporal and spiritual power, is interesting as it has continued up to the present day (see Unit 1).

Dante's epic poem has exerted a tremendous influence on both Italian and European literature. It is widely studied almost seven hundred years later and Dante Alighieri societies have been set up throughout the world. It was written in the language spoken by the people because he wanted to reach out to the public at large. Had it been written in Latin the work would have remained within the confines of a select band of intellectuals. For further details on Dante's influence on the Italian language see Unit 2. To end, let us go back to the beginning and the opening two verses:

Nel mezzo del cammin di nostra vita mi ritrovai per una selva oscura, che la diritta via era smarrita.	In the middle of the journey of our life I found myself in a dark wood where the straight way was lost.
Ahi quanto a dir qual era è cosa dura questa selva selvaggia ed aspra e forte, che nel pensier rinnova la paura.	Ah! how hard a thing it is to tell what a wild, rough and stubborn wood this was, which in my thought renews the fear.

This mini-tour of Italian literature is at an end but for you, the reader, let's hope it is just the beginning. Now it remains simply to invoke poetic licence and invent a new Italian phrase, '*felice lettura*' (happy reading).

GLOSSARIO	GLOSSARY
l'attore, l'attrice	actor, actress
il capolavoro	masterpiece
comico	comical
comunicare	to communicate
descrivere	to describe
la descrizione	description
ermetico	hermetic
esaminare	to examine
esprimere	to express

la fiaba	*fairy-tale*
influire su	*to influence*
la letteratura	*literature*
la memoria	*memory*
il messaggio	*message*
mettere in rilievo	*to emphasize*
la narrativa	*narrative*
narrare	*to narrate*
il Novecento	*twentieth century*
la novella	*short story*
il palcoscenico	*stage*
la poesia	*poetry*
il/la poeta	*poet*
la raccolta	*collection*
raccontare	*to relate, tell*
rappresentare	*to represent*
la realtà	*reality*
recitare	*to perform, play*
rendersi conto	*to realize*
rispecchiare	*to mirror*
il romanzo	*novel*
la scena	*scene*
scoprire	*to discover*
lo scrittore, la scrittrice	*writer*
scrivere	*to write*
il significato	*meaning*
il simbolo	*symbol*
la società	*society*
lo stile	*style*
la tecnica	*technique*
la tragedia	*tragedy*
tragico	*tragic*
la trama	*plot*
triste	*sad*
la verità	*truth*

Taking it further

Suggested reading

Many of the works of the writers covered in this unit have been translated into English.

The Italian Text series published by Manchester University Press has introductions in English. The texts focus on the twentieth century and include the following:

The Italian Resistance, ed. Phillip Cooke
Pirandello Three Plays, ed. Felicity Firth
Morte accidentale di un anarchico, Dario Fo, ed. Jennifer Lorch
Fontamara, Ignazio Silone, ed. Judy Rawson
A selection from the Decameron, Boccaccio, ed. Kathleen Speight
La luna e il falò, Cesare Pavese, ed. Doug Thompson
Italian women writing, ed. Sharon Wood
Il giorno della civetta, Leonardo Sciascia, ed. G.W. Slowey

There are a number of Penguin Parallel Texts available that have *Racconti italiani* (Italian short stories) written by a range of twentieth-century authors – Alberto Moravia, Cesare Pavese, Carlo Emilio Gadda, Natalia Ginzburg, Carlo Cassola, Italo Calvino, Mario Soldati and many more.

A selection of short stories by contemporary authors is also available in *The Quality of Light: Modern Italian Short Stories*, ed. Ann and Michael Caesar, Serpent's Tail 1993.

The Italian publisher Guerra has a range of simplified literary texts.

Some other suggested authors not already mentioned:

- the poets Pascoli, Quasimodo and Ungaretti
- in narrative: Primo Levi; Umberto Eco, who wrote *Il nome della rosa* (The Name of the Rose), turned into a film starring Sean Connery; Tomasi di Lampedusa, who wrote the classic *Il Gattopardo* (The Leopard), which was also a film starring Burt Lancaster; Antonio Tabucchi

The **Microsoft Encarta Encyclopedia** available on CD ROM will provide some useful background information on numerous Italian writers.

Websites

Use one of the search engines mentioned at the end of Unit 1, e.g. **www.google.com**, and type in the name of the writer, e.g. 'Leonardo Sciascia'.

For information on Italian publications, publishers, bookshops, etc. try: **www.Alice.it**
   www.amazon.co.uk

The following books in Italian are also worth investigating for an overview of Italian literature and its historical setting:

La letteratura italiana del Novecento (Second Edition), Cesare Sergi, Editori Laterza 1999

Breve storia della letteratura italiana – dalle origini a oggi, Giorgio De Renzo, Bompiani 1997

Letteratura italiana, Raouletta Baroni and Piero Cigada, A. Vallardi 1997

In English see *The Cambridge History of Italian Literature*, ed. Peth Brand and Lino Pertile, CUP 1996

04

art and architecture

In this unit you will learn
- about great artists through the ages
- about the golden age of the Renaissance
- about Italy's wealth of artistic, architectural and archaeological treasures

Italy has probably the biggest outdoor art museum in the world. To appreciate the vast array of invaluable treasures – Greek temples, Roman arches and amphitheatres, Byzantine basilicas, medieval castles and towers, fountains, statues, churches and cathedrals, public buildings – the millions of visitors who flock to see them every year just have to take a good look around them. Many Italians seem to display an almost nonchalant indifference to their artistic patrimony, perhaps because they are surrounded by it and see it every day, whereas the cultural-minded tourists are generally enthralled by what they see.

Some of the most ancient treasures go back 2,000 years or so yet they have influenced the works of artists throughout the centuries, and no more so than during the golden age of Italian art – the Renaissance – some 1,500 years later. Italy has always retained a close affinity with its ancient past and the classical style of that time has remained the dominant architectural force in secular and religious buildings. However, Italy has been subject to a mixture of styles that can, for the most part, be attributed to the influence of successive invaders and settlers mentioned in Unit 1. Here are some examples.

- Venice is a blend of different architectural styles, a good example being the Byzantine, Romanesque and Renaissance Basilica in St Mark's square. Many of the *palazzi* (palaces/homes) along the Grand Canal mirror the Byzantine and Gothic influence.
- Lombardy was important as a centre of Romanesque and Gothic architecture, Milan Cathedral being a superb example of the latter style. Milan also figured prominently during the later Neo-Classical period.
- The Adriatic town of Ravenna has one of the world's best collections of Byzantine mosaics, which decorate its churches and monuments in 'a symphony of colour', as Dante put it.
- Rome, apart from its many ancient buildings, embodies elements of the Gothic, Renaissance, Baroque, post-*Risorgimento* and Fascist periods. Rome has been described as 'an archaeological archive' of Western culture.
- Greek temples and theatres are prevalent in southern Italy and Sicily – Paestum (Campania), Metaponte, Agrigento, Taormina, Siracusa and Selinunte (Sicily).
- Buildings in the south also bear testimony to Norman and Arab influence.
- The Aosta region, which was the crossing point from the Alps into Italy from the time of Hannibal to Napoleon, has numerous castles. Military architecture was not particularly

inventive and most castles date back to the feudal period and the development of the city-states.

Although this unit will deal with the modern, ancient art and architecture has to be the starting point, as it was the springboard for much of Italy's enduring artistic success.

Greek and Roman art

As early as 700 BC the first Greek colonies were founded in southern Italy and Sicily and these regions still preserve priceless remains of that period. Of particular importance are the Doric-style Greek temples with steps and columns on all four sides. Columns were also a feature of important secular buildings. Construction techniques showed a great awareness of symmetry and geometry, which Renaissance artists studied and developed. Greek sculpture, like that of the Etruscans, portrayed human figures in such a way as to show a natural range of emotions.

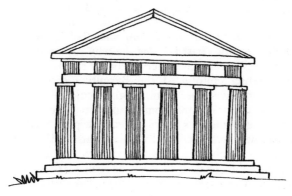

Doric temple

From the second century BC Roman influence predominated. The Romans were renowned for their engineering skills and they adopted some of the key features of Greek architecture and added another dimension, the dome. The Pantheon in Rome was an excellent example of this new feature. The Romans have left a legacy of their achievements throughout their vast Empire but Italy, their homeland, has been the principal beneficiary. They constructed roads, aqueducts, public baths, amphitheatres (the amphitheatre in Verona is still used for a season of opera during the summer), temples and monumental arches. The latter commemorated individuals and important historic events, e.g. the

Arch of Constantine (the first Christian Roman Emperor) in Rome and the Arch of Augustus in Aosta.

Chief characteristics of Roman architecture were regularity and symmetry, semi-circular arches and, as mentioned above, the dome. The semi-circular arch technique was used in the construction of vaulted roofs, bridges and aqueducts. Equestrian statues figured prominently in Roman art and the Romans even had statues made of themselves in the form of heroes or Greek gods. During this era public buildings and villas were decorated with frescos and mosaics.

Roman remains abound throughout Italy. A visit to Rome and its ancient port of Ostia Antica, followed by a trip to Pompeii near Naples, would certainly whet the appetite.

The Byzantine influence

The Roman era was followed in the fifth and sixth centuries by the construction of Byzantine basilicas. Byzantium, the present-day Istanbul, accommodated the Roman Emperors from the fall of the Roman Empire in AD 330 until 1453. Ravenna on the northern Adriatic coast became the new capital of the Western Roman Empire and was under Byzantine rule from AD 540 to AD 751. Ravenna epitomized the Byzantine style, whose chief characteristics were beautiful, brightly coloured mosaics, solid brick structures and the dome rising up from a square base. Many of the mosaics were of saints portrayed in a very expressionless manner. The Byzantines also influenced parts of south-eastern Italy and Sicily, over which they ruled at varying times until the eleventh century, as well as the major Marine Republics of Pisa and Venice, which traded with the East during the height of their economic and political power.

The Dark Ages

From about AD 500 to AD 1000, the period commonly known as the Dark Ages, many castles, churches and monasteries were built. Of architectural interest was the evolving design of churches and basilicas. As Christianity spread, these buildings were built to be used by people to gather and worship in, unlike the ancient Greek and Roman temples, which just served as shrines to a god. Thus religious buildings resembled large assembly halls and their interior was shaped in the form of a cross.

Romanesque
(c.1050–1200)

- rounded arches
- tall, high buildings
- simple, basic structure
- plain façades
- heavy, high pillars
- little window space
- use of huge stone blocks
- austere

Gothic
(c.1200–1400)

- pointed arches
- tall pointed spires
- less wall and more windows (stained glass)
- gables and niches with statues on the façades of buildings
- importance of verticality
- flying buttresses
- ribbed vaults
- slender columns (to give the idea of weightlessness)
- ornate and decorative

Renaissance
(c.1400–1600)

- rejection of the ornate decorative features of the Gothic and a return to the simple classical style of the Romans – harmony and symmetry
- domes
- vaults and arches
- triangular pediments above doors
- colonnades

The architectural design of both religious and secular buildings gathered pace from the eleventh century onwards. The table on p. 71 highlights some of the key words and features that characterized successive architectural styles for about the next 600 years.

Romanesque

Early Romanesque started in the Dark Ages but it assumed greater prominence in the twelfth century, the time when many of the towns and cities as we know them today developed. Romanesque evolved from the classical style of the Greeks and Romans and was concentrated almost entirely in religious buildings whose size and structure resembled those built by the Romans. This was a most creative and inventive period in architectural history and it paved the way for the later Renaissance architecture.

The political and economic independence of the leading Italian cities was reflected in the different architectural styles they adopted. Pisa, for example, produced its own brand of Romanesque architecture, a stunning example of which is the *Campo dei Miracoli* (literally, 'Field of Miracles'). This world-famous square contains the decorative green and white marble

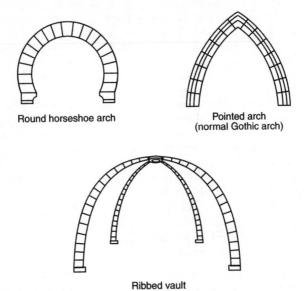

Round horseshoe arch

Pointed arch
(normal Gothic arch)

Ribbed vault

Duomo (Cathedral), the *Battistero* (Baptistery) – baptism preceded entry into the church and was carried out in a separate building – and the free-standing *Campanile* (Bell Tower). The latter is of course the unmistakable *Torre Pendente* (Leaning Tower), one of the seven wonders of the world and the subject of great concern for many years in the latter half of the last century, as engineers from different countries were engaged in projects to stop it toppling over. Fortunately they succeeded and it has now been re-opened to the public. Pisan Romanesque spread to other Tuscan towns, such as Lucca and Arezzo, and also to churches in Sardinia.

During the twelfth century, towers designed like castle keeps were constructed in many Italian towns that fought each other for political supremacy. In some towns noble families competed with each other to construct the tallest tower. The taller the tower, the greater the prestige. San Gimignano in Tuscany is famous for its towers. It had seventy during the Middle Ages; now there are just thirteen.

Gothic

As so much Italian art and architecture had close links with its ancient past, Gothic art did not have the same influence in Italy as it had in countries north of the Alps. There were also political reasons for this as the Goths figured among the barbarous invaders of Italy and were blamed for destroying much of Italy's classical art. 'Gothic' therefore was used as a derogatory term. Gothic architecture was, however, used to embellish buildings, e.g. cathedrals and churches, that in some cases took centuries to complete due to redesigning or restoration work or to parts being added on. This is why we see so many buildings that embody a mixture of different architectural styles. Unlike the heavy, blank stone walls and massive pillars that were required to support the weight of the Romanesque structures, Gothic churches were a blend of stone and glass. The structures took on a lighter appearance with their slim pillars. The combination of pointed arches and ribbed vaults held the two sides of the building together. The slender columns on the façades of the buildings were typical of this style and created a feeling of grace and weightlessness. The sculptures were also more life-like in contrast to the more solid Romanesque figures.

An excellent example of Gothic architecture is Milan Cathedral, with its numerous pinnacles and spires reaching heavenwards, illustrating the importance of height to this style. Siena Cathedral is a good example of the adaptation of the Gothic style. It started off in the thirteenth century as a Romanesque church in the Pisan style – semi-circular arches, black and white striped façades – but the façade was remodelled by Pisano in 1284 in the Gothic style: deep doorways beneath gables, pointed towers with piers and pinnacles and lots of sculptures. In secular buildings a striking example of Gothic architecture is the *Ca' d'oro* (Golden House) on the Venice Grand Canal, built between 1420 and 1434. Many of the buildings along the canal reflect the Gothic-Byzantine influence.

In sculpture, the thirteenth-century pulpits by Nicola Pisano in Pisa and Siena cathedrals bear the hallmarks of later Renaissance works – harmony, naturalism and depth. These very intricate and beautifully decorative marble reliefs were undoubtedly two of Pisano's masterpieces.

In painting, the work of the Florentine artist Cimabue (1240–1302) also had the stamp of the imminent Renaissance movement – the importance of perspective, the search for beauty and a more perfect environment, and a greater sense of humanity in the facial expressions of the figures.

Giotto (c.1266–1337) was another forerunner of the Renaissance. He took things a stage further by painting whole scenes, not just the Madonna (Virgin Mary) and Child, and his search for reality was evident in the sense of movement and expression in his works, e.g. the frescos narrating the life of St Francis in Santa Croce, Florence. His *affreschi* (frescos) were his most famous works, so called because they were painted on the wall while the plaster was still fresh. Giotto had discovered the art of creating the illusion of depth on a flat surface.

The Renaissance

This was the most illustrious and creative period in the history of Italian art in all its forms, the highest peak of which was in the *Cinquecento* (sixteenth century), known as the High Renaissance. *Renaissance* means 'rebirth' and it signified at the time the revival of the grandeur of Rome's illustrious past, sparked off by a renewed interest in antiquity, classical literature and the classical styles of architecture. The great artists of the Renaissance were interested in humanity and in the human form, and they studied anatomy to learn about the human body.

Also prevalent was a belief in God combined with a respect for the pagan mythology. Some artists preferred religious scenes, the most common being the Madonna and baby Jesus. The paintings and frescos of Perugino (1445–1523), who belonged to the Umbrian school, were religion-based. Others like Botticelli (1445–1510) preferred pagan or allegorical subjects, as in *Primavera* (Spring) and *Venere* (Venus) in the Uffizi Gallery, Florence.

The interest in classical Roman architecture was illustrated by the fact that artists like Michelangelo (1475–1564), Brunelleschi (1377–1446), Donatello (1386–1466) and Bramante (1444–1514) went to Rome to study the techniques of design and geometry. In Rome there was no shortage of buildings, ruins and statues to observe, the Pantheon and Colosseum being two prime examples. The Pantheon was the best-preserved building of ancient Rome and its dome was probably the finest architectural achievement of that time. Artists like Brunelleschi were able to develop the design techniques into a more refined artistic form. The massive *cupola* (dome) of Florence Cathedral could not have been built without a great appreciation of symmetry and geometry, important aspects in the design of religious and public buildings as well as in town planning. Architects recognized that all buildings, and even statues, had to harmonize with their surroundings.

Brunelleschi was the founder of modern architecture, basing his designs on plans and not merely on his experience as a master mason. He gave the artists the mathematical means to create the illusion of depth, i.e. perspective, so that objects appear to diminish in size as they recede from the viewer. Artists turned to mathematics to study the laws of perspective in the same way as they had turned to anatomy to study the human body. It was artists like Botticelli and Raffaello (Raphael 1483–1520) in Florence, and Tiziano (Titian c.1485–1576) in Venice, who perfected the use of perspective. Raphael was a pupil of Perugino from whose style he would have learnt about purity, simplicity and the importance of symmetry of composition.

The birthplace of the Renaissance was the city of Florence but the movement touched the whole of Tuscany. From there it spread to other Italian regions and eventually was influential in architectural development in other western European countries. This period in fact left an artistic legacy that is still felt to this day, such were the standards it set. The Renaissance took off at a time when the communes (see Unit 1) were flourishing economically and politically and cities like Florence were leading the way. In the 1400s Florence was the Bank of Europe. It was a city run by bankers, merchants and shop owners, who invested in the arts, sponsoring and commissioning many of the great artists of the time. The Church was also a great patron of the arts. It was probably no coincidence that many of the celebrated artists – Michelangelo, Raffaello, Botticelli, Donatello, Masaccio, Brunelleschi – were born in Florence and lived very close to one another. They were multi-talented. Michelangelo Buonarotti, widely acclaimed as the greatest and most influential of them all, was a sculptor, painter, architect and poet. Giotto was an artist, architect and town planner and Leonardo da Vinci a painter, sculptor, engraver, architect, engineer, musician and poet.

Masaccio (1401–1428)

Masaccio developed the technique of space and depth in his works. This was achieved by painting figures in the foreground and the use of light from one direction, creating a *chiaroscuro* (light and shade) effect. It was a characteristic of his frescos, giving life-like realism to his figures, and set a pattern that was to greatly influence future Renaissance painters.

Piero della Francesca (c.1416–1492)

Piero della Francesca was an exceptional painter who researched the theory of perspective, with the help of Masaccio, who taught him its links with geometry. The technique was so important to him that he devoted much of his later life to writing two treatises on perspective and geometry. Artists like Piero marked a major turning point in the history of art, replacing the anonymous art of the medieval period. He worked on the fresco cycle in the church of San Francesco (Arezzo). The frescos depicted the Legend of the Holy Cross, a typical theme in Franciscan churches and friaries in the Middle Ages. The harmonious colours and accurate drawing gave the work its realism.

The fresco technique flourished during the Renaissance and was used to cover entire walls as well as vaults and ceilings. Frescos were very common in churches but were also used to decorate public buildings, e.g. the *Palazzo Pubblico* (Town Hall) in Siena, and private homes, e.g. the Medici Palace in Florence. Artists had to be very skilful to use this technique successfully, as it required them to have an overall view of what the scene should portray and then work swiftly to produce it. Revisions the next day were not possible. Tuscany reveals the full richness of fresco painting.

Michelangelo (1475–1564)

Michelangelo's favourite art form was sculpture, using the famous Carrara (Tuscany) marble for his *capolavori* (masterpieces). Two of his most celebrated yet contrasting works were *Pietà* (Pity), in St Peter's, Rome, and *Davide* (David) in the Accademia in Florence. The former is rather small and shows the young Mary seated holding the body of Christ across her lap. The grace and elegance are the work of a master craftsman. The latter is a towering colossus of over four metres. This massive figure of a youthful, muscular male nude portrays great realism through David's emotional intensity, which was characteristic of many of Michelangelo's figures. David, however, does not display the perfect beauty of most Renaissance works, as the head and hands are rather too large and the muscular features of the body are rather over-exaggerated. It is nevertheless a magnificent work of art and to fully appreciate it – a tip from an Italian History of Art teacher – you should approach the figure with head bowed and only look up at the last moment. The surrounding works of art just pale into insignificance by comparison. Visitors gaze in sheer wonderment. The David outside the Palazzo della Signoria in Florence, by the way, is only a copy. You must see the real thing.

Another of Michelangelo's outstanding achievements was his series of fresco paintings on the ceiling of the *Cappella Sistina* (Sistine Chapel) in St Peter's, Rome. They took four years to complete and have just recently been restored. The five large and four small scenes are from the book of Genesis. There are other biblical scenes and figures around the edges of the ceiling and the whole is a wonderful creation of harmony.

Michelangelo's most impressive architectural project in Rome was St Peter's Basilica, whose rebuilding had been started by Donato Bramante in around 1508 and was continued by a number of architects over the decades. The regularity and harmony of this massive building exemplify Renaissance design.

Michelangelo had a profound influence on his contemporaries as well as on later generations of artists. The Renaissance poet Ludovico Ariosto wrote of him: 'Michael more than immortal, divine angel'.

Leonardo da Vinci (1452–1519)

A supreme artist, Leonardo da Vinci is known the world over for his painting of the *Mona Lisa* housed in the Louvre in Paris. The entire painting is one of perfect beauty. There are none of nature's imperfections and Mona Lisa's eyes are bright and alive and seem to be looking at you even if you change your position to gaze at her. Another among his many famous works is the *Last Supper* (1495–1498), a wall painting in the refectory of the monastery of Santa Maria delle Grazie in Milan.

Tiziano (c.1485–1576)

Second in importance to Florence, as a centre of Italian art, was Venice. The Venetian artists placed great emphasis on the use of colour to give their paintings their special effect. Venice with its canals, lagoons, brilliant light and unique atmosphere inspired the painters of this city to use colour in a more deliberate, observant and sensual way than those elsewhere in Italy. Tiziano Vecelli (Titian) is considered one of the greatest Italian painters. His subjects ranged from the allegorical – legends and myths of the past – to portraits or religious scenes such as the *Assunta* in the Chiesa dei Frati in Venice.

Other important artists were Tintoretto (1518–1594), real name Jacopo Robusti, and Veronese (1528–1588).

Secular architecture

Michelangelo also designed grand secular buildings in Rome during the last phase of his career, e.g. the Farnese Palace, and redesigned the *Campidoglio* (Capitol) on the Capitoline Hill, the civic and political heart of the city. In the field of secular architecture this period saw the building of mansions in towns and cities and villas in the country. Cities vied with each other to secure the services of the greatest artists to beautify their buildings and create works of lasting fame. Thus palaces were created for the beauty of their proportions, the spaciousness of their interiors and the imposing grandeur of the ensemble. The entrances to many of the more lavish residences were designed like an ancient Roman temple, and they often had well-planned gardens all around adorned by fountains and statues.

The architect Andrea Palladio (1508–1580) applied ancient Roman temple design to the façades of his churches in Venice and also to his villas in the Veneto region – steps leading up to the entrance and columns holding up the temple façade. During this period many of the developing towns and cities acquired their own special character through the construction of grand buildings such as *palazzi* (*palazzo* means 'home' as well as 'palace'), which were symbols of family success. Renaissance-style buildings were well proportioned, highlighting once again the importance of symmetry, and often embellished with classical columns.

Sixteenth and seventeenth centuries: Baroque

Baroque, meaning 'absurd' or 'grotesque', was a development of Renaissance art. However, it was a sharp contrast to the more austere Romanesque, Gothic and Renaissance styles. It flourished particularly in the Catholic churches – the Church was a patron of this art form – in the late sixteenth and seventeenth centuries, although its influence extended to sculpture, painting and furniture design, e.g. tables and chairs with spiral legs. It was a grand, pompous and ceremonious art form, whose characteristic features were the spiral, twisting effect that conjured up the image of a curtain billowing in the wind. It was considered a joyous style of architecture – the sculptures were certainly lively and full of movement – and one that suited the Italian temperament. Baroque was used extensively to decorate the interior of churches so that they became very much like showpieces.

Baroque style

Two great Baroque artists were Francesco Borromini (1599–1667) and Gian Lorenzo Bernini (1598–1680). In Rome, city of Baroque churches and fountains, are some of Bernini's most dramatic and celebrated sculptures: the twisting figures of Apollo pursuing Daphne in the gallery of the Villa Borghese and the *Fontana dei Quattro Fiumi* (Fountain of Four Rivers) in Piazza Navona. Borromini placed a spiral bell tower on the church of Sant'Ivo della Sapienza and his considerable contribution to Baroque art can still be seen today in many of Rome's buildings and churches.

As the political importance of Florence waned in the sixteenth century so did its importance as an art centre. In the seventeenth, and particularly the eighteenth, century the spotlight fell more on the Venetian painters, like Caravaggio (1573–1610) and Canaletto (1697–1768). Caravaggio painted more realistic scenes, the truth as he saw it. His figures, e.g. the painting of St Thomas, were very realistic portrayals as opposed to the idealism of the Renaissance figures. Canaletto gave us views of Venice, especially those memorable scenes of the buildings and boats along the Grand Canal, using the colour and light to masterful effect.

Nineteenth century: Neo-Classical

After the peak of the Renaissance period perhaps a lull was almost inevitable. In the 1800s the sphere of artistic influence passed to France while the Italians tended to underestimate the quality of their achievements, a fact underlined by the number of foreign artists who flocked to cities like Rome and Naples to study models of the Neo-Classical style of architecture. Neo-Classical was a rejection of Baroque and a return once again to Italian roots embedded in the classical heritage of Rome. Thus, many public buildings throughout Italy adopted classical designs that harked back to the Pantheon of Rome. A highly regarded exponent of this art in sculpture was Antonio Canova (1757–1822) and a famous example of his work is the figure of Paolina Borghese (Napoleon's sister) as Venus in the Villa Borghese in Rome.

During the first half of the nineteenth century the seemingly innate talent Italians have for architectural design was demonstrated by their town-planning projects and civic schemes in Turin, Trieste, Naples and later on in Rome. The symmetry and harmony of the layout, the well-proportioned façades, the long, wide, straight avenues reflected the Roman influence. The *portici* (arcades) were another feature of this period. Turin is worth a visit to observe the neat geometric aspect of these developments.

In the latter half of the nineteenth century Italy contributed to the advancement of architectural design through her railway stations and galleries. A notable example was the Porta Nuova railway station in Turin (architect Carlo Ceppi), with its round arched arcades and windows. The station displayed a combination of the classical trait of proportion with a new development, the use of iron supports and glass cover. This technique signalled a move to a more modern kind of architecture, represented by the iron and glass-roofed shopping galleries, the most famous of which was Giuseppe Mengoni's Galleria Vittorio Emmanuele in Milan (1865–1878). This immense structure was the Roman Forum of its day where people, protected from the rain and sun, could shop in comfort or sit outside cafés. Were the Italians the precursors of the present-day shopping precinct?

Rome had a mixture of architectural styles and this was especially evident once it became the capital city in 1871. Residential and public-building work was intensified. Major public works included the *Palazzo di Giustizia* (Palace of Justice), *Palazzo delle Esposizioni* (Exhibition Hall) and the massive, richly sculpted white marble monument to King Victor Emmanuel II in Piazza Venezia. The monument was built to celebrate Italian unity, the theme of most monuments from then onwards. Because of its appearance it was nicknamed the 'typewriter' by the Romans and it already bore all the hallmarks of the future grandiose architectural structures of the twentieth-century Fascist era, which were hard and mechanical-looking, and symbols of power, menace and self-confidence.

Twentieth century: the Futurists

Italy made a significant contribution to the development of European art through the Futurist movement and metaphysical painting. The Futurist manifesto was written by Filippo Tommaso Marinetti in 1909 and signed a year later by artists such as Umberto Boccioni (1882–1916), Carlo Carrà (1881–1966), Giacomo Balla (1871–1958) and Gino Severini (1883–1966). The manifesto was a proclamation of a new dynamism that aimed to capture the technological and scientific developments of a modern changing world. The car, industrialization and urbanism had arrived. These artists were inspired by the idea of progress and concerned with the future not the past. The paintings therefore were not static but full of movement and excitement. Buildings, for example, were no longer perpendicular and straight but portrayed with jagged, angular shapes as if they had been struck by an earthquake. It became difficult in most cases to distinguish individual forms, which merged into an interlocking mass.

Metaphysical painters

Another important movement that coincided with Futurism was *la pittura metafisica* (metaphysical painting), instigated by Giorgio de Chirico (1888–1978) around 1911–1912. The word 'metaphysical' was chosen to convey the deeper, mysterious meaning of the world around us. Carlo Carrà was also a leading exponent of this art form that was characterized by:

- precise geometric arrangement of the figures, objects and landscapes
- allusions to classical antiquity
- distorted shapes
- painters deliberately working out of perspective
- the light casting deep shadows

Giorgio Morandi (1890–1964) was another important artist of this period and known for his paintings of still life – flowers, objects and landscapes.

Modern architecture

Antonio Sant'Elia (1880–1916) was an imaginative architect whose designs and drawings envisaged the cities of the future with their skyscrapers, pedestrian precincts and flyovers. Despite his premature death his visionary plans came to fruition in later building developments.

Some of the leading figures of the modern era are:

- Giovanni Michelucci (1891–1990) architect of the long, low railway station of Santa Maria Novella in Florence
- Gio Ponti (1897–1979), designer of the 1955 elegant Pirelli skyscraper in Milan
- the engineer Pietro Nervi (1891–1979) who developed the use of reinforced concrete in a creative, varied and original way, as is evident from some of his major works: in Rome, the *Palazzetto dello Sport* (Sports Arena) and the *Palazzo dello Sport* and *Stadio Olimpico* built for the 1960 Olympic Games; in Turin, the Exhibition Hall

Domestic architecture

Italian houses reflect a variety of styles that have much to do with geographical position. In the northern Alpine regions there is the chalet type of home, constructed from local stone and timber. Chalets have sloping roofs and overhanging eaves as a form of protection against the heavy snowfalls. In the German-speaking Bolzano, in the north-east, the Austrian influence is evident in the architectural design of many of the buildings.

In the northern plains the *cascine* (big farmhouses) were once very common. They were rectangular in shape with one- or two-storey buildings along the edges of the rectangle and a big courtyard area in the middle. The owners or landlords lived in the main building and the farm workers, animals, machines, etc. occupied the outbuildings. The *cascine* were like self-contained villages. With the advent of mechanization fewer people were needed to work the land and the present-day *fattoria* (farm) is more like a villa.

Characteristic features of many houses around the northern lakes, Maggiore and Como, are the turrets, towers and brightly coloured, painted walls. Turrets and towers are in fact features of many houses in hillside towns. In southern Italy the Mediterranean-style homes have whitewashed exteriors as protection against the intense heat. In the south-east you can also see Arabic influence in house design. In the south-eastern part of the Murge, in Puglia, there are rural homes that stand out for their distinctive shape: they are called *trulli*. They are built of local limestone, are circular or rectangular in shape and the main distinguishing feature is the conical slate roof. Originally they were the homes of the farm workers but most have now been converted into holiday homes for tourists. In Alberobello entire districts are full of these distinctive dwellings.

A *trullo*

In city areas the vast majority of the population has always lived in flats, for two main reasons: space is at a premium and house prices are extortionate. In the 1950s and 1960s blocks of flats sprang up like mushrooms in the suburbs of cities such as Milan and Turin. Construction companies often ignored building plans and regulations, and the net result was a jungle of multi-storey nondescript blocks that in no way blended with the architecture of the buildings in the nearby cities. The older *palazzi* (blocks) are more solid and generally have more style and character. The structural design of more recent housing developments has shown greater inventiveness, combining functional importance with the aesthetic.

GLOSSARIO	GLOSSARY
il museo	*museum*
visitare	*to visit*
apprezzare	*to appreciate*
l'opera d'arte	*work of art*
il capolavoro	*masterpiece*
il patrimonio artistico	*artistic heritage*
greco	*Greek*
romano	*Roman*
i resti	*remains*
gotico	*Gothic*
bizantino	*Byzantine*
barocco	*Baroque*
il duomo	*cathedral*
la basilica	*basìlica*
disegnare	*to design, draw*
risalire a	*to date back to*
lo stile	*style*
l'architettura	*architecture*
l'affresco	*fresco*
i mosaici	*mosaics*
archeologico	*archaeological*
conservare	*to preserve*
caratterizzare	*to characterize*
la facciata	*façade*
l'edificio	*building*
il secolo	*century*
il Duecento/Trecento, ecc.	*thirteenth/fourteenth century, etc.*
costruire	*to build*

la struttura	structure
studiare	to study
sviluppare	to develop
l'architetto	architect
lo scultore	sculptor
la scultura	sculpture
restaurare	to restore
il colore	colour
la luce	light
la tecnica	technique
rispecchiare	to reflect

Taking it further

Places to visit

The richest collections of Etruscan art are in the National Museum (Naples), Villa Giulia, the Gregoriano Museum in the Vatican (Rome), and the Archaeological Museum in Florence. There is also a good collection of Etruscan art in the museum in Volterra. Tuscany and Umbria are the regions to visit for those interested in the Etruscan civilization.

The largest collections of Greek art are in Taranto (Puglia), Palermo (Sicily) and the Vatican.

Important art museums: the Uffizi Gallery (Florence) for paintings of so many great Renaissance artists, the National Museum (Naples), the Villa Giulia Museum, the Galleria Borghese, the National Gallery of Modern Art and the Vatican Museums (Rome). The largest collection of Roman sculptures is in the Vatican Museums. There are also a good number of Roman statues in the Archaeological Museum in Naples.

For Italian painting and sculpture since unification, visit the National Gallery of Modern Art in Rome. There are also Galleries of Modern Art in Milan and Turin. There is the Estorick collection of Italian Futurist Art in London, with paintings by some of the main protagonists of this movement – Giacomo Balla, Umberto Boccioni, Carlo Carrà, Gino Severini. The museum is at 39a Canonbury Square, Islington, London N1 2AN.

Leading cities that provide a good overall insight into Italian art are Rome, Florence and Venice.

Urbino (le Marche) is a small town and a real jewel of the Italian Renaissance. In Florence you will find many splendid Renaissance buildings, e.g. Palazzo Pitti, Palazzo Vecchio and Palazzo Strozzi.

Siena in Tuscany has the best medieval centre in Italy.

Suggested reading

The Story of Art, E.H. Gombrich, Phaidon-Oxford (15th Edition 1989)

Italy, David Gentleman, Hodder and Stoughton 1997

Roman Art and Architecture, Sir Mortimer Wheeler, Thames and Hudson 1964

The Architecture of the Italian Renaissance, Peter Murray, Thames and Hudson (Revised Edition 1984)

Architecture in Britain and Europe, Bruce Allsopp, Country Life Books 1985

See also the most recent edition of the **Microsoft Encarta Encyclopedia** on CD ROM.

General guide books on Italy or on individual regions can be very good for those interested in more detailed descriptions of works of art and their respective artists, e.g the Michelin Tourist Guides, the Lonely Planet book entitled *Italy*, which has a special colour guide to Italian art and architecture (5th Edition published 2002), or *The Rough Guide to Italy* (6th Edition 2003).

Websites

The Italian Cultural Institute, London

www.italcultur.org.uk

www.estorickcollection.com

www.lonelyplanet.com

www.roughguides.com

www.arte.it

www.artonline.it

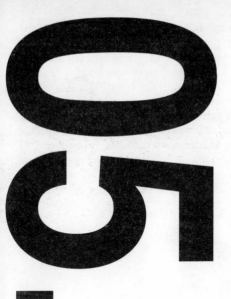

05

Italian music

In this unit you will learn
- about Italy's musical heritage
- about traditional and ecclesiastical music
- about Renaissance, Baroque and Romantic eras
- about opera and pop music

Think of a musical country, and you probably think of Italy. Equally, think of an Italian personality and the first who springs to mind is Luciano Pavarotti. Think of a typical caricature of Italy or the Italians, and music will probably feature somewhere. Read a road-test report of the latest Alfa-Romeo or Ferrari: almost always the test-driver refers to the 'musical note' of the engine! There is no getting away from the fact that Italy and music go hand in hand. However, the most significant fact is often forgotten, which is that musicians throughout the world are familiar with the Italian language, not only because it is one of the two or three languages most suited to and most used in opera, but also because Italian provides almost all musical terminology.

'Big' Luciano

Luciano Pavarotti

The best-known one-third of the 'Three Tenors' is a veritable giant in every sense of the word, and undoubtedly the most famous tenor of his age. The young Pavarotti was destined to be a professional footballer, but fortunately for us he decided on a musical career after his experience as a young member of the amateur choir of Modena at the Welsh Eisteddfod at Llangollen, where he was greatly impressed and uplifted by the quality of the music and the atmosphere.

Pavarotti has gained the following of the public at large, bringing operatic and classical vocal music to the realm of popular taste. Given his earlier footballing exploits, it is appropriate that his rendition of *Nessun Dorma* from Puccini's opera *Turandot*, used as the theme tune for the 1990 football World Cup, has become an international sporting anthem, forever associated with Pavarotti and football. (See 'Name that tune', p. 103.)

This success led in turn to another: the 'Three Tenors'. Joining with the two great Spanish tenors, José Carreras and Plácido Domingo, Pavarotti broadened his popular appeal still further. The trio have performed together regularly over the last few years in venues such as Hyde Park (London), Central Park (New York) and so on, usually in association with a sporting event or special occasion. More recently, Pavarotti has apparently taken seriously the business of being an international superstar. An essential attribute of such a personage is to be involved in 'gossip magazine' scandal: Luciano did so by leaving his wife for his much younger secretary and constant companion, Nicoletta Mantovani (34 years his junior). They married in December 2003. The Italians are even more scandalized when Pavarotti takes risks with his precious voice or, worse, sings on stage when it is less than perfect, or makes mistakes. Apparently it is only the perfectionist opera fans of Italy who have the right – and have dared – to boo him off the stage!

In spite of this, the affection in which Pavarotti is held has enabled him to achieve something few have managed: he has bridged the gulf between classical and pop music. Operatic purists will no doubt have winced at his performing with the Spice Girls, but Pavarotti has shown a great talent for bringing musical performers together for altruistic purposes. Capitalizing on his broad appeal and on his contacts in the wider realms of music, he has starred since 1995 at several concerts under the heading 'Pavarotti and Friends' (sometimes known affectionately in the Italian press as 'Big Luciano and Friends'!). Thanks to the organizational skills of Nicoletta Mantovani many of these concerts have been staged in aid of charity. The 1999 edition, for example, held in July in Sanremo was a sell-out even at prices as high as 600,000 lire (about £200). 14,000 Italians applied for these tickets, as well as much larger numbers for the cheaper places: artists as varied as B.B. King, Joe Cocker, Boyzone, Gloria Estefan, Ricky Martin, Lionel Richie, Zucchero and many others helped Pavarotti raise *4 miliardi di lire* (*un miliardo* = one thousand million, i.e. one billion) for the international children's charity War Child.

Luciano Pavarotti is undoubtedly one of Italy's and the world's greatest tenors, yet he has arguably achieved something even more significant: he has attracted millions of fans to opera, bringing classical music to the people to a degree seldom seen before. At the same time, of course, he has reminded us of what a great musical nation the Italians are.

The heritage

So, what musical heritage has produced such a figure as Pavarotti? As with so many other aspects of Italian culture, we need to go back to the Romans to consider the heritage that has produced what we can enjoy in the present day. The Romans were undoubtedly fond of music, as evidenced by frequent references in Roman literature and the frequent depiction of musicians and instruments in Roman art: groups of musicians often figure in the mosaics of Pompeii and Herculaneum. However, although there is plenty of archaeological evidence of Roman instruments, we can only guess what the actual music sounded like from the sound of modern instruments that have evolved from them.

Instruments

Many musical instruments were developed in Italy and have Italian names. Here are some examples:

- *piano* – one of various evolutions of the keyboard instrument; the piano strikes strings rather than plucking them as others do. The *pianoforte*, to give it its full name, was so called because the volume can be varied by changing the pressure with which one hits the keys, or by applying the soft (*piano*) pedal or the sustain/loud (*forte*) pedal.

- *piccolo* – a small flute (*piccolo* = small).

- *viola/violino/cello* (= violoncello) all of these are variations on the word *viola*. The best or most valuable ever made came from Italian craftsmen: we have all heard of Stradivarius. No other violin can ever better a Stradivarius for tone and quality of sound, not to mention value.

Traditional music

Like any country with a long history, Italy has many traditional forms of music – usually associated with dance – which have survived down the ages. Here are a few different types of traditional music to give you the taste:

The *tarantella* is a dance originating in southern Italy, the name possibly deriving from the port of Taranto. The couple generally dance together to the music of castanets and a tambourine, at an increasing speed. It used to be thought that frenetic solo dancing of the *tarantella* could cure insanity from the bite of the tarantula spider...which may be an alternative reason for its name.

Given the importance to Italians of children and family, the *ninnananna* (lullaby) is very important to the Italian mother and, perhaps in this age of working mothers, even more important to *la nonna* (granny). There are different versions of the same lullabies, varying according to region or even families. Here are a few lines of the Neapolitan versions of a couple of lullabies:

Nonna, nonna bebè,	Go to sleep, go to sleep, baby,
che ora viene papà,	here comes Daddy,
e ti porta la pappa,	and he's bringing you your babyfood
fai la nonna bebè	go to sleep, baby.
Miciè, miciè, vattene,	Pussycat, pussycat, go away,
ninuccio vuole dormire,	baby wants to go to sleep,
vattene lontano lontano,	go a long way away,
e non tornare più.	and don't come back again.

In Italy, as elsewhere, children sing as they play. Some of the songs are sung with particular gestures for events such as seeing a new moon. Others are more widely sung, such as this verse of a southern Italian equivalent to 'Ring-a-Ring o' Roses', sung to a similar tune:

Giro, girotondo,	Turn and turn around,
com'è bello il mondo,	how beautiful the world is,
ci son' tanti bambini,	there are so many children,
fiori e uccellini,	flowers and little birds,
gira di quà, gira di là,	turn this way, turn that way
e tutti cadiamo a terra!	and we all fall down!

Of course, Italy has Christmas carols (carol = *un canto di Natale*), and they tend to be livelier than Anglo-Saxon carols. In southern Italy, even recently, shepherds from the Abruzzi mountains would come down to towns to play carols on their *cornamusa* (a sort of bagpipe), busking in the street in return for money. Here is a verse of a typical example in which the nativity message is clear:

Tu scendi dalle stelle,	You come down from the stars,
o re del cielo,	O King of Heaven,
e vieni in una grotta,	and you go into a cave,
al freddo e gelo.	in the cold and ice.
O bambino mio divino,	O my Divine Child,
tu ci vieni a liberare.	You come to set us free.

Any area or city with a strong identity has its musical traditions: typical is Venice. The songs of the *gondoliere* (gondolier), traditional Venetian songs, have been sung for perhaps hundreds of years. Nowadays many *gondoliere* songs are of operatic or Neapolitan origin, being popular and well-known to tourists. However, Venice's rich heritage of traditional song and instrumental music is kept alive by amateurs and musical academics.

The *Palio* in the Tuscan hilltop city of Siena stands out among the various festivals (see Unit 6) which feature special music. In preparation for the horse racing around the Piazza del Campo, the supporters of each horse parade through the city waving

Il Gondoliere

their flags and drumming, using battle rhythms dating back to the Middle Ages: not very tuneful, but the noise is certainly intimidating!

The strongest regional tradition of music is that of *Neapolitan songs*. Many of these have actually become part of the wider musical heritage. Several elements characterize Neapolitan songs: love, the beauty of the Naples area, and nostalgia for the place left behind (especially related to the emigrations which have occurred since the middle of the nineteenth century). The names of singers from the past like Enrico Murolo and songwriters like De Curtis are well-known to Neapolitans, but in fact many of the songs are heard around the world. Here is a small selection of Neapolitan songs, some of which you might recognize:

Song	Composer	Theme
Funicolì funicolà	Denza	The funicular railway, which takes me up the hill
Mamma	Bixio	A devoted son sings to his beloved mother
Marechiare	Tosti	The 'window of love' at Marechiare, Posillipo in Naples
Non ti scordar di mi	De Curtis	Do not forget me, my absent love
*O sole mio**	Di Capua	To look at your face is like looking at the Sun
Santa Lucia	Longo	The silver moonlight shimmers on the sea in Santa Lucia
Torna a Surriento	De Curtis	Girl begs boy to return to beautiful Sorrento…and to her!
Tu, ca nun chiagne	De Curtis	You who do not weep, where are you? I want to be with you

Used for a TV 'Cornetto' ice-cream advertisement in the UK

The Italian *inno nazionale* (national anthem) is stirring and almost operatic compared to most; football and Formula One fans are familiar with it.

An element of military music unique to Italy is that of the *Bersaglieri*, the mountain rifle regiment, who play music on the run. Their music typically has a galloping rhythm, and to see the

Bersaglieri running in their almost 'operatic' uniforms with feathered hats, and their alpine horns blaring, is quite an experience!

Ecclesiastical music

The influence of the Church on music in a Catholic country like Italy is to be expected, just as the importance of music to religious ritual cannot be understated. Indeed, many great Italian composers have composed at least some church music, and almost all great performers, certainly singers, include religious works in their repertoire. In past centuries influential church figures were patrons of composers and performers alike; many Italian composers earned their living as church choirmasters or composers of church music first and foremost. Classical Italian music, particularly as in the styles of opera singing, therefore owes much to church music. A look at the great names among Italian composers confirms this close connection between church and secular music.

Composers of the Renaissance era

Giovanni da Palestrina (1525–1594)

Born in Palestrina near Rome, this master of plain-chant and polyphony studied singing in the great basilicas of Rome, becoming organist and choirmaster in the cathedral of his home town in 1544. He was choirmaster at several basilicas in turn, including St Peter's. He was also for a time master of music at a Jesuit seminary and musical director to a cardinal. Palestrina was, then, very much a composer of church music. His music has a mystical, often ethereal quality, and he set standards for other church composers to follow.

Recommended listening: Almost any mass, motet or whatever you can get hold of, but especially *Missae Papae Marcelli* and *Missa Aeterna Christi Munera*: prepare yourself for an uplifting experience!

Claudio Monteverdi (1567–1643)

Monteverdi was the composer who bridged the transition from the Renaissance to the Baroque period. Born in Cremona he began composing at the age of 15. As well as church music, he composed secular music, and thanks to his works *Orfeo* and *Arianna* opera began to be considered a serious musical genre.

In 1613 he was appointed choirmaster and conductor at St Mark's cathedral in Venice. Among his later operas are *Il ritorno d'Ulisse in patria* (The Return of Ulysses to his Homeland). This most influential composer of early opera died in Venice in 1643.

Recommended listening: any of the works mentioned.

The Baroque period

Antonio Vivaldi (1678–1741)

Very much the Venetian composer, Vivaldi's father was a violinist at St Mark's cathedral, and he himself became a priest in 1703. He established an international reputation while teaching music at the Ospedale della Pietà, a music school for girls; there he composed concertos and oratorios for weekly performance and special events. Producing operas from 1713 onwards, he also travelled to Rome and other cities to oversee their production. From 1740, he was a court composer in Vienna where he died.

Vivaldi wrote over 500 concertos, 70 sonatas and 45 operas. His religious music has operatic qualities, and he was a great influence on J.S. Bach, who was slightly younger; he established norms that others followed in various aspects of solo concertos and the *concerto grosso* (for solo instrument(s) with full orchestra). In particular he perfected the *ritornello*, the interplay between soloist and orchestra.

Recommended listening: We are all too familiar with his concertos *Le quattro stagioni* (The Four Seasons); similar, and strongly recommended is *L'estro armonico*. Also, well worth listening to if you enjoy classical guitar: *Concerto in A Major* (also in mandolin version) and *Concerto in D Major*. If you like church music, his *Gloria* is highly recommended.

Domenico Scarlatti (1685–1757)

If you like listening to the harpsichord, Scarlatti is your man! Born in Naples, this brilliant harpsichordist and composer was greatly influenced by his composer father Alessandro, who established the Neapolitan style of opera, with an overture in three movements. Living first in Rome, then Naples and Lisbon, Scarlatti travelled Europe as a virtuoso performer; he was summoned to the Madrid court in 1729 and remained there, as a result of which much of his music displays a Spanish influence. Most of his compositions are for keyboard, and he made keyboard technique what it is today. Scarlatti composed operas, cantatas and over 550 sonatas, all of which are well worth listening to; sonatas 287, 288 and 328 are officially organ sonatas, though they are also played on harpsichord.

Recommended listening: Sonatas nos. 13, 82, 184, 287, 288, 328, 421, 430, 450, 487, 523, 531, 533, 544.

Giovanni Battista Sammartini (1701–1775)

One of a pair of musical brothers, Sammartini began as an organist, choirmaster and church music composer in Milan. He composed almost 300 works, mostly sonatas, and had a strong influence on Mozart, Haydn and Gluck.

Mauro Giuliani (1780–1832)

The foremost guitarist of his time, Giuliani started out playing the violin and flute and then favoured the guitar. Although self-taught, he had an extraordinary talent and soon had a tremendous reputation and a successful concert career. At the age of 27 he settled in Vienna and associated there with the likes of Haydn and Beethoven. He wrote 300 guitar pieces: his style combines the classical with the melodiousness of the opera. He died in 1832 during a concert season in London.

Recommended listening: *Concerto in A Major for Guitar*, often recorded with the Vivaldi guitar concertos.

The Romantic era

Gioacchino Rossini (1792–1868)

The most successful opera composer of his day, Rossini was born in Pesaro, and trained at the Conservatorio di Bologna. A leading exponent of *bel canto* (literally, 'beautiful singing'), emphasizing melody rather than drama and emotion, his style is light and lively; he composed 37 operas, some of which are *opera buffa* – comic operas. He composed *Il Barbiere di Siviglia* (The Barber of Seville) in 1816 and in 1842 the beautiful *Stabat Mater* (the lament of Mary standing before her crucified son). In particular, the overtures of many of his operas are often performed as separate items, notably:

• *L'Italiana in Algeri* (The Italian Girl in Algiers)
• *Il Turco in Italia* (The Turk in Italy)
• *La Cenerentola* (Cinderella)

- *Guglielmo Tell* (William Tell) Overture (used as the theme tune for *The Lone Ranger!* – see 'Name that tune', p. 103).

Recommended listening: the Overtures of all the above.

Giuseppe Verdi (1813–1901)

Verdi, as other Italian composers before him, began his career writing church music, his *Requiem* (1874) being especially well-known: it is particularly operatic in style. However, he is most widely known as an operatic composer: his works are among the best in Italian opera.

He was born in Roncole near Parma; after studying music in nearby Busseto, he applied for entry to the Milan Conservatory at the age of only 19, but was rejected. Instead, he studied with the Milanese composer Vincenzo Lavigna. His first opera was produced at La Scala (see p. 100) in 1839, but his next was a failure, and Verdi, who had also just lost his wife and two children, gave up composing. However, the director of La Scala persuaded him to write *Nabucco* (1842), which was a sensational success; it told the story of the Jews in captivity in Babylon, and the *Chorus of the Hebrew Slaves* is a popular part of the repertoire of many choirs today.

Many other operas followed, including *Macbeth* (1847), but it was *Rigoletto* (1851), *Il Trovatore* (1853) and *La Traviata* (1853) which brought him international fame and enduring popularity. *La forza del destino* (The Force of Destiny, 1862), based on a Spanish play, stands out for musical characterization and for the way the orchestra is used. *Aida* (1871), his most popular opera, was commissioned by the Egyptians to celebrate the opening of the Suez Canal and was first performed in Cairo. In his seventies, Verdi produced a brilliant pair of operas based on Shakespearean plays: the tragic opera *Otello* (1887) and the comic opera *Falstaff* (1893).

Verdi's non-operatic compositions include the dramatic cantata *Inno delle nazioni* (Hymn of the Nations, 1862) and the *String Quartet in E Minor* (1873).

Verdi's works are noted for their emotional intensity, tuneful melodies, and dramatic characterizations. He transformed Italian opera, until then rather formulaic, into a vibrant and coherent art form.

Recommended listening: *Chorus of the Hebrew Slaves, Aida, Rigoletto, Il Trovatore, La Traviata.*

Listen out for: *Rigoletto, La donna è mobile* (Woman is Fickle); *La Traviata, Libiamo* (Let's Drink), Overture to *La forza del destino* (all well-known tunes).

Giacomo Puccini (1856–1924)

Born in Lucca, near Pisa and Florence, Puccini came from a long line of local church musicians. He wrote *Messa di Gloria* (Mass of Glory) at the age of just 24, attracting attention and sponsorship. After studying at the Milan Conservatory (1880–1883), Puccini began his opera-composing career in earnest. Following on from Verdi, Puccini's operas blend intense emotion and theatricality with tender lyricism, colourful orchestration and rich vocals. Among his best and most popular works are:

- *Manon Lescaut* (1893), an early work of genius based on a French novel
- *La Bohème* (The Bohemian, 1896), with several well-known and memorable melodies
- *Tosca* (1900)
- *Madama Butterfly* (1904), the story of a Japanese lady's love for an American seaman
- *Turandot* (1924) – Puccini died while composing this opera, which then had to be finished by Franco Alfano; its première was in 1926.

Puccini gave the world *Nessun Dorma*, theme tune of the Italian World Cup in 1990

Recommended listening: *La Bohème, Madama Butterfly, Turandot.*

Listen out for: *Turandot, Nessun Dorma* (Let Nobody Sleep).

Pietro Mascagni (1863–1945)

Born in Livorno (Leghorn), he studied with composer Alfredo Soffredini. Mascagni's most important work is the opera *Cavalleria rusticana* (1890), the story of a rural love triangle which ends in tragedy. Although his other 16 operas are not well-known, the *Intermezzo* from *Cavalleria rusticana* is one of the better known classic orchestral pieces, though few know what it is!

Recommended listening: *Intermezzo* from *Cavalleria rusticana*.

Gian Carlo Menotti (1911–)

Menotti was born in Cadegliano and educated at the Milan Conservatory and the Curtis Institute of Music, Philadelphia, USA. Although considered an Italian-American composer, he follows very much in the tradition of early twentieth-century Italian opera. He has written his own librettos, and one of his operatic compositions won him the Pulitzer Prize. In other senses he is very much a modern composer writing for the new age and the new world, and one of his best-known operas was the first ever composed for television: *Amahl and the Night Visitors* (1951). Often broadcast at Christmas, being based on the story of the Magi or Three Wise Men, it tells of a little crippled shepherd boy: meeting the Three Kings, who ask him the way to Bethlehem, he learns of the birth of Jesus, and joins them in their journey to adore the newly born Saviour.

Recommended listening: *Amahl and the Night Visitors*.

Opera

So, what exactly is opera? Essentially, a musical play – indeed, many are based on well-known plays as in examples above – but one governed by several conventions. The basic ingredients are a central figure with a problem (who will be one of several solo singers), plus strong characterization, a chorus and an orchestra. Whatever the plot, it must allow for several *arias*, an essential ingredient of any opera. An *aria* (air) is a song composed for solo voice with orchestral backing. *Arias* originated in Italy in the sixteenth century, and they often feature in an *oratorio* or *cantata*. They are very lyrical, providing relief from the dramatic action of an opera, a sort of pause for (musical) reflection and comment on an aspect of the plot or another character, equivalent to a soliloquy in a play. They are often a considerable test of the skills of the singer, and many famous *arias* are often performed as set pieces.

Some would say that Italian is the 'proper' language of opera; many non-Italians (e.g. Mozart) wrote some of their *libretti* in Italian, and all professional classical singers learn Italian pronunciation! Besides, the Italian language lends itself to the rhythm and intonation of opera, and English translations tend to lose out in terms of passion and impact.

There are several great opera houses in Italy, including some whose names are well-known abroad:

- *La Scala* in Milan, one of the foremost opera houses in the world; *scala* means 'ladder' or 'staircase'
- *La Fenice* in Venice, 'The Phoenix', an appropriate name in view of the fire which destroyed it a few years ago and, yes, it has now risen from the ashes; restored and reopened in 2003
- *San Carlo* in Naples, one of the true homes of Italian opera and, to genuine Italian opera fans, one of the holy places of Italian opera
- *Baths of Caracalla*, the ancient Roman baths in Rome, in the ruins of which open-air operas are performed – when weather permits
- *Roman arena*, Verona. Also an open-air venue, but this time in spectacular surroundings which in the past saw a different sort of drama!

The great tenors

Given the Italian operatic tradition, it is no surprise that Italy traditionally produces great tenors who have seemed able to transcend the bounds of their musical sphere, generally opera, and to become well loved by the public at home and abroad. Many will be familiar with the names *Caruso, Gigli, Tito Gobbi*, as well as their successor *Pavarotti*.

Enrico Caruso (1873–1921) was born in Naples and made his debut there in 1894. He quickly became established both in Italy and abroad. In addition to his successful stage career, he was one of the first singers to make records and become universally famous.

Beniamino Gigli (1890–1957) was the greatest tenor of his day, and some would say of all time. Born at Recanati in 1890, he was a choirboy in his local church; he learnt to sing from the lullabies sung by his mother. In 1914, he began his career at various opera houses around Italy, and within five years was touring abroad, principally in the USA and Latin America. He performed operas and concerts abroad for fifteen years before returning to live and work mostly in Italy, by now well established. He gave his farewell performance in 1955 and died in 1957.

A curious anecdote concerning this great man gives a flavour of the times he lived in: during the Second World War one of his greatest fans was a young British corporal based in Naples with the Royal Electrical and Mechanical Engineers. This opera fan, later a talented amateur tenor himself, was a frequent member of Gigli's audience at the San Carlo opera house, often seeing the same opera several times over. Having met Gigli at the stage door, he became a friend of the family, often being invited to dine with Beniamino, his wife Costanza and his daughter Rina, also a singer. Nowadays it would be considered less than appropriate that he also used to give Gigli cigarettes – difficult for an Italian tenor to come by in wartime, but not the best thing for his voice!

Tito Gobbi (1913–1984) was born at Bassano del Grappa (Vicenza). He began his very successful career in Rome in 1938; often performing on the new medium of television, his career in Italy and abroad spanned 40 years.

So, who will be the next in this unbroken chain of great Italian tenors? The current favourite is the blind tenor **Andrea Bocelli**. This rising star, destined perhaps to be even more of an international star than Pavarotti, is particularly popular in Germany, France, Belgium, Holland, Spain, Latin America, New Zealand and the USA. One of his records, *Sogno*, was a Number One hit in six countries and had phenomenal sales throughout the western world. Even more than Pavarotti – and of a much younger generation – he is a pop superstar, mixing the singing of classical and operatic favourites with music of a more overtly popular type...

It is interesting to note how modern these enterprising Italian tenors are in terms of being prepared to go way beyond the sphere of opera into other media and other musical contexts – and how in so doing they have brought their type of music onto the world stage, making it popular even with relatively young music lovers.

Pop music

The Italian pop song best known outside Italy is probably *Volare*, with which **Domenico Modugno** won the Sanremo Festival in 1958, and which has been sung since then by singers as diverse as Pavarotti, Sinatra and the Gypsy Kings. Another success on an international scale was **Gigliola Cinquetti**, who won the Eurovision Song Contest in 1964 at the age of 16 with *Non ho l'età (per amarti)* (I am not Old Enough [To Love You]), a sort of romantic ballad, later followed by *Ti amo* (I Love You).

Although the Italian pop music scene in the 1960s and 1970s was characterized by adulation and imitation of British/ American pop music and performers, notably the Beatles, a particularly Italian feature of the 1960s onwards have been the many *cantautori* (singer-songwriters), writing and performing their own songs, mostly in ballad style. The most popular in Italy have been: **Luigi Tenco** and **Gino Paoli** (both from the early 1960s to the mid 1980s); **Fabrizio De André** (from mid 1960s until his untimely death in 1997); **Lucio Battisti** (early 1970s to mid 1990s); and **Lucio Dalla** (mid 1960s to present) whose best-known song *Dallamericacaruso* (1986) sold over eight million copies, including a version by Luciano Pavarotti.

A *cantautore* who recently performed in London is **Paolo Conte** (mid 1970s to present). Among other Italian pop singers of the late 1990s, with examples of their songs, are:

- **Luciano Ligabue**, *Certe Notti* (Certain Nights), a sort of Italian 'soft rock', a bit like Bon Jovi
- **Litfiba**, *Spirito* (Spirit), Mediterranean teeny-bop rock
- **Edoardo Bennato**, *Le ragazze fanno grandi sogni* (Girls Have Big Dreams), a sort of funky rock style, with instrumental undertones of Oasis

A singer of enduring popularity in Italy and abroad for the last couple of decades, is **Zucchero (Sugar) Fornaciari**, who is one of the very few Italian pop singers to have gained a following abroad. He has performed and made recordings in the UK and in the USA with well-known artists in both countries, such as *Senza una donna* (Without a Woman), recorded with the British singer Paul Young. His styles range from ballad to heavy rock, so most people will find something to appeal to them.

Current Italian pop stars to listen out for include Biaggio Antonacci, Gigi d'Alessio, Alessandro Safina, Alex Britti, Daniele Silverstri, Luca Carboni, Irene Grandi, Negrita, Giorgia, Pino Daniele and Sergio Cammariere; among groups, Articolo 31 and Gemelli Division.

GLOSSARIO MUSICALE	GLOSSARY OF MUSICAL TERMS
adagio	slowly
al fine	to the end
allegro (ma non troppo)	lively (but not too much)
andante	at walking pace
cadenza	falling cadence (literally), often a solo section
cantabile	melodic (literally, 'singable')
con brio	with liveliness
crescendo	growing (getting louder)
da capo	from the beginning
decrescendo	decreasing in loudness
diminuendo	decreasing
dolce	sweet
forte/fortissimo	loud/very loud
legato	linked, tied, smooth
leggero	light
moderato	moderate
molto...	very...
mosso	full of movement
piano/pianissimo	soft/very soft
rallentando	slowing down
staccato	disjointed, jerky
tranquillo	tranquil
vivace	lively
vivo	animated

Name that tune

Here is a list of some of the best known Italian tunes and their composers. In the Appendix (p. 252) you will find the transcriptions of these tunes: can you read music well enough to match them up? The answers are printed at the bottom of p. 104.

A   De Curtis: *Torna a Surriento*

B   Denza: *Funiculì Funicolà*

C   Di Capua: *O sole mio*

D   Puccini: *La tua manina è fredda* (Your tiny hand is frozen), from the opera *La Bohème*

E **Puccini:** *Nessun Dorma*, from the opera *Turandot*

F **Mascagni:** the *Intermezzo* from the opera *Cavalleria rusticana*

G **Rossini:** the overture from the opera *William Tell*

H **Verdi:** *La donna è mobile* (Woman is Fickle), from the opera *Rigoletto*

I **Verdi:** *Chorus of the Hebrew Slaves*, from the opera *Nabucco*

J **Vivaldi:** *Spring*, from *The Four Seasons*

GLOSSARIO	GLOSSARY
la musica (classica) (pop)	*(classical) (pop) music*
mi piace … (molto)	*I like… (very much)*
non mi piace … (per niente)	*I don't like… (at all)*
preferisco	*I prefer*
ascoltare	*to listen to*
il compositore	*composer*
la sinfonia	*symphony*
il concerto	*concerto*
la cantata	*cantata*
l'opera	*opera*
l'aria	*aria, air*
la canzone	*song*
la melodia	*tune, melody*
il/la cantante	*singer*
l'orchestra	*orchestra*
il gruppo, il complesso	*(pop) group*
lo strumento	*instrument*
suonare	*to play*
(non) so suonare…	*I (don't) know how to play…*
la cassetta	*cassette*
il registratore a cassetta	*tape-player*
il CD	*CD, compact disc*
il lettore (di) CD	*CD player*

Answers

A 3; B 5; C 10; D 8; E 2; F 1; G 9; H 4; I 6; J 7.

Taking it further

Suggested reading

Music and Menus from Italy (Great Italian Arias and Classic Italian Recipes), Antonio Carluccio, Pavilion Books 1996

Italian Opera Since 1945, Raymond Fearn, Harwood Academic 1998

Enjoying Italian Opera (with cassette), Dale Harris, Highbridge Audio 1995

Joy of Italian Melodies, Agay and Metis, Music Sales Corporation 1998

To listen to Italian pop music, if you have access to the Hotbird satellites, on radio try *Radio Italia (solo musica italiana)*, or on TV *Video Italia (solo musica italiana)* and *Italian Music*.

Websites

There are many websites available on the music and composers covered in this unit; choose your composer and do a search with the appropriate name according to your interest, and using your favourite search engine. It may be best to specify Italian websites if you can cope with the Italian; look out for the word *discografia* (list of records made); other terms like *CD*, *45 giri* and *33 giri* should not cause you problems. On some websites, you will even be offered a snatch of the composer's or singer's best tunes!

For the Italian national anthem:

www.italyguide.com

06

festivals, customs and traditions

In this unit you will learn
- about Italy's festivals
- about customs and folklore
- about traditions and superstitions

Although a young nation politically, Italy has been inhabited since ancient times thanks to its kind Mediterranean climate, and is therefore rich in tradition, customs and festivals dating back centuries. Most Italians are still religious in the sense of 'gut religion', although some are atheists and agnostics. Even those who do not attend church often practise an instinctive observance of Catholic rituals and follow practices of religious origin: religion has a strong influence upon the way of life of all Italians.

Festivals

Every town, village and region in Italy celebrates festivals, local as well as national ones, often with a religious connection. The church calendar is perhaps even more important in Italy than in the rest of Europe: most ordinary days of the year are a 'feast day', dedicated either to a saint or to the Virgin Mary (as seen in examples on the calendar on pp. 108–110). This has an impact on Italians and their calendar in two ways:

- Most Italians are named after a saint, and some have the name of the saint on whose day they were born. Families often have a tradition of giving the same names to children of successive generations. Some Italians celebrate their *onomastico* (saint's day) in a similar way to their birthday, and they receive presents from relatives and friends.
- Every town or village has its patron saint, and holds a festival on the saint's day; many last for a few days before and after it. Typically there is a solemn religious procession to the church or shrine dedicated to the saint, followed by fireworks and general festivities according to local tradition.

Il Calendario

Here is a selection of the more important national and local festivals and holidays:

Date	Place	Festival
1º gennaio (January) (national holiday)	Italy	*Capodanno* (New Year): fireworks; in some areas people throw old crockery into the street
6 gennaio (national holiday)	Italy	*La Befana* (Epiphany): children hang stockings on their beds on the 5th and *La Befana* (a sort of witch or female Santa Claus) fills them with gifts, or coal if the child has been naughty;
	Rome	in Rome, a special toy fair is held in Piazza Navona
2 febbraio (February)	Italy	*Candelora* (Candlemas): a special mass is celebrated; members of congregation hold candles
19 marzo (March)	Italy Rome	*San Giuseppe* (St Joseph): people eat *zeppole* (sugared doughnuts) and other special cakes; in Rome stalls sell *frittelle* (fried sweets)
movable	Italy	*Carnevale/Martedì Grasso* (Shrove Tuesday): children wear fancy dress; in many areas traditionally lasagne is eaten on Shrove Tuesday
	Venice	*Carnevale*: Venice celebrates during ten days up to Shrove Tuesday (see p. 110)
movable	Italy	*Giovedì Santo* (Maundy Thursday): people dress up and visit churches; one chapel is decorated with statues
movable	Italy	*Venerdì Santo* (Good Friday): special church services (the Way of the Cross) to commemorate Christ's suffering and death; many people attend
movable	Italy	*Vigilia di Pasqua* (Easter Saturday): procession with the statue of suffering Mary; Catholics attend the Easter Vigil Mass at midnight
movable	Italy	*Pasqua* (Easter Sunday): processions; traditional food – lamb and special cakes such as the *colomba*, a dove-shaped cake; Pope gives *Urbi et Orbi* blessing ('to the city and the world')
movable (national holiday)	Italy	*Pasquetta* (Easter Monday): family outings to country or seaside; eating in a *trattoria* (restaurant)

25 aprile (April) (national holiday)	Italy	*La Liberazione* (National Liberation Day): celebrates liberation of Italy in 1945
1º maggio (May) (national holiday)	Italy	*Labour Day*: a highly politicized lay feast, but also traditionally associated with St Joseph the Worker (*San Giuseppe*)
First Sunday in May	Naples	*San Gennaro*: the blood of San Gennaro, in a phial kept with his relics in the *Duomo* (cathedral) in Naples, is displayed in a special ceremony and liquefies
40 days after Easter	Italy	*Pasqua dei Fiori* (Easter of Flowers): flower festivals, food similar to Easter
13 giugno (June)	Italy	*Sant' Antonio* (St Anthony of Padua): prayed to when you have lost something
24 giugno	Genoa Rome	*San Giovanni*: in Genoa, major processions and festivities; in Rome, outdoor festival, people eat snails and roast suckling-pig
luglio (July)/agosto (August)	Siena	*Palio* (horse race) in Siena (see p. 110)
15 agosto (national holiday)	Italy	*Ferragosto – Assunta* (Assumption of the Blessed Virgin Mary into Heaven): traditional holiday period
1º–10 settembre (September)	Naples	*Piedigrotta*: fireworks, Neapolitan song contests
settembre	Venice	*Film Festival*
19 settembre	Naples	*San Gennaro*: the blood of San Gennaro liquefies again; if not, it is a sign of impending disaster
ottobre (October)	Venice Italy	*Festa del Mosto* (Feast of the Must): ritual grape-pressing by foot on island of Sant' Erasmo, Venice; also *Vendemmia* (grape-harvest festival) in Bardolino wine-producing area and many others
1º novembre (November) (national holiday) 2 novembre	Italy	*Ognissanti* (All Saints)/*Giorno dei Morti* (All Souls' Day): people visit cemeteries to take flowers to deceased relatives, then have a meal out
8 dicembre (December)	Italy Rome	*Immacolata* (Mary of the Immaculate Conception): veneration of Our Lady, and *presepe* (Crib/Nativity Scene) prepared for Christmas season; in Rome, floral garland placed on statue of Our Lady in Piazza di Spagna

25 dicembre	Italy	*Natale* (Christmas): most Italians attend Midnight Mass; children write a special letter or card to their father, apologizing for being naughty, promising to be good for the next year, hide it under his plate; presents exchanged; *Babbo Natale* (Santa Claus) now becoming popular; beautiful nativity scenes in churches. Food: fish on Christmas Eve, pasta, poultry, fish, salads, cakes

A *carnevale* mask

There are so many and varied local festivals that it would be impossible to describe all of the main ones, and difficult to draw the line. To give you a flavour, here are details of a couple of major festivals, followed by a typical village *festa*:

Carnevale – Venice

This pre-Lent festival (*Carnevale* means 'farewell to meat') dates from the eleventh century, but it has been revived and revitalized since 1979. During the ten days of the festival, Venice is full of revellers wearing fancy costumes and the colourful masks one sees on sale throughout the year. All over the city colourful events are organized, including concerts, exhibitions and gondola races, culminating in the water-borne parade on the *Canal Grande* (Grand Canal).

Palio – Siena

This festival in the Tuscan hilltop city of Siena is held on 2 July and 16 August every year. Each district of the city has a *contrada* (a sort of guild) which takes part in a horse race around the Piazza del Campo in the city centre (the 'track' consists of sand laid over the cobbled road-surface). The supporters of each *contrada* and its horse parade through the city waving the flags of their district – the flag-waving is skilled and spectacular and the drumming which accompanies the parade is intended to intimidate the opposition (see Unit 5). Places on the grandstand in the Piazza del Campo are limited and expensive, only available to locals and VIPs, but the race is always televised. It is spectacular and perilous, and the winning team wins the *Palio*, a prize banner.

The *Palio*

Sant' Antonino – Viticuso

By contrast, the *festa* of this mountain village near Cassino, founded by Benedictine monks from the order's headquarters in Montecassino, is typical of innumerable village festivals all over Italy. The patron saint of Viticuso is St Antonino of Pamiers (in France), who is believed to have lived in the village for a while. On 2 September, the parish priest leads the faithful from the village up the steep hill to the shrine of St Antonino, the statue of the saint being carried by men who have bid large sums of money for the privilege. As usual, later in the day there are fireworks and a *festa*, and a good time is had by all. Some families who have left Viticuso to work in the cities of northern Italy or abroad return each year for this village festival. Needless to say, a high proportion of boys in the village are called Antonino, a tradition continued through generations of descendants living abroad.

Shop-closing dates

Visitors should be aware that Italians enjoy their leisure time so much that there are times when everything seems to be closed; shops, banks and petrol stations usually close for two or three hours in the middle of the day. In addition to the national holidays shown in the calendar on the preceding pages, all shops are closed on Sundays and in addition on a handful of religious feasts as follows:

- *19 March* – St Joseph's Day
- *Ascension Thursday* – celebration of the Resurrected Christ ascending into Heaven
- *Corpus Christi* – celebration of the Holy Eucharist
- *29 June* – St Peter and St Paul
- *14/15 August* and often a week or two either side, especially in the Mezzogiorno (south)!
- *1 November* – All Saints' Day
- *8 December* – Immaculate Conception of the Blessed Virgin Mary
- *26 December* – Santo Stefano – St Stephen's Day

The Italian life-cycle

Il battesimo

For Italians the birth of a child is a very major event, celebrated by the extended family. In most families the *battesimo* (baptism) follows soon afterwards, with large numbers of family and friends attending the church. *Il padrino* and *la madrina* (godparents) take their role very seriously, promising at the baptismal font to ensure the child is brought up in the true Christian way. The beautiful white lace christening gowns of Italian babies have to be seen to be believed. A party ensues, naturally, at which *confetti* are distributed to each guest in a *bomboniera* – a 'presentation pack' of *confetti* (sugared almonds) wrapped in lace, blue for a boy, pink for a girl, usually acccompanied by a little china statuette or something similar.

La prima comunione

Most Italian children make their First Holy Communion at some stage between the ages of 8 and 12. This is a special occasion for the whole family. Boys dress smartly, usually in white, and girls dress as brides. After the Mass there is a party, usually at a restaurant, and *bomboniere* are distributed to guests, friends and family.

Cresima

In their early teens Catholic children are confirmed in a special church service by the local bishop; boys have a male sponsor (*padrino*), girls have a female sponsor (*madrina*). Celebrations afterwards are as for a christening.

Le nozze

Marriages and weddings are also important to Italians and, again, most have a proper church wedding, usually with a Nuptial Mass at which bride and groom receive the Host in Holy Communion, kneeling in front of the congregation. As the couple leave the church, the guests throw rice over them. The celebration which follows invariably involves much eating and drinking, and usually dancing, often to the sound of the local traditional music; bride and groom always lead the dancing. The bride and groom take around a silver bowl to distribute *confetti* to the guests, and once again *bomboniere* are distributed to guests and those friends and family unable to attend. In some places bride and groom are taken to some suitable local statue or monument so that their wedding photographs can be taken against an illustrious background. Nowadays, as elsewhere, it is a must to have the wedding recorded on video.

La morte

In Italy, death is regarded by surviving relatives as deprivation of the presence of their departed loved ones. One important aspect of death in Italy is that it tends to arrive later than elsewhere, since Italians have a very long life-expectancy. The *funerale* starts with a Requiem Mass; Italians are not generally people who hide their emotions, and it is perfectly acceptable for Italian men to show their grief by weeping as they walk behind the funeral cortège. Italian hearses are ornate, rather Baroque affairs, of a similar style to the splendid black funeral carriages drawn by jet-black horses with feather plumes, which used to be used before the days of motorized transport. In most cemeteries, families have what almost amount to mini-chapels with niches. After the *funerale*, only close family return to the house for a muted gathering.

Le vacanze

On a brighter note, Italians not only believe in enjoying life every day, but also love to get away from the city for their holidays. As detailed in the calendar on pp. 108–10, there are favourite holiday periods when most cities become almost ghost towns. A lot of Italians abandon their home for a month or more in summer: for many, a flat at the seaside or a cottage in the mountains is home from home, or for the less affluent perhaps a caravan or a tent on a campsite away from the heat and pressures of the city. In some cases the working members of the family simply commute further to work. Whatever, paradise for many is as simple as a *lettino* (sunbed) or *sedia sdraio* (deck-chair) on their allocated patch of a *spiaggia privata* (private beach), soaking up the sun, gossiping with the neighbours. Most Italians take their holiday in the same place year after year, though increasing numbers travel abroad.

Il trikend

Traditionally, Italians have tried whenever possible to *fare il ponte* (to make a bridge) – that is, to take extra days off to link public holidays into a long weekend or a longer break. A recent trend is for Italians to contrive, by whatever means possible, such as flexi-time, to have a three-day weekend whenever possible (hence *trikend*). This seems part and parcel of the growing acceptance that there is more to life than working hard for success and to achieve material prosperity: Italians are becoming more concerned about quality of life.

Everyday routine

Meal times

prima colazione:	breakfast, *caffè latte* with bread, brioche or biscuits
pranzo:	lunch, traditionally the main meal, is usually later than in other countries, from 1.30/2.00 p.m.
cena:	dinner, usually between 7 p.m. and 9 p.m., is increasingly the main meal of the day

Whilst many people used to return home for lunch, nowadays work pressure and traffic congestion make this difficult. Many people work longer, many more women now work, and so fast food is coming to the fore in both towns and cities (see Unit 7) and in the home. In the past, Italian housewives devoted much time to careful cooking of hand-picked ingredients; as in other western countries, most now have less time available and are no longer prepared to spend hours in the kitchen slaving over a hot stove. A growing range of ready-made meals is available to them in shops and supermarkets, and they are heavily advertised on television and in the press.

Customs and folklore

As already mentioned, a high proportion of customs are based in some way on religious observance or superstition. Some of the customs connected with special events are mentioned in the calendar on pp. 108–10, and here are two further anecdotal examples:

San Gennaro v Vesuvius

The unquestioning religious faith of many Italians is such that they address saints in a very different way to invoke their help in times of need. This was once typified in a village on the slopes of Vesuvius. During a minor eruption, the lava flow was threatening to overwhelm the village, so the local priest and the people took the statue of San Gennaro from the church and placed it between the advancing lava and the village, invoking the protection of the saint. Sure enough, the lava flow split and went round the village... and this was in the twentieth century, not in the Middle Ages.

The Friar and the Madonna

On a grander scale, visitors to Pompeii who go to the centre of the modern town will find the foremost among Italy's hundreds of religious shrines, and one which arises out of local folklore. For hundreds of years, the locals were afraid to go to this area, feeling the 'bad vibes' of the Roman city engulfed by lava and dust from Vesuvius. In the nineteenth century, a community of nuns was established there in a missionary effort to exorcize the evil spirits. The nuns needed a focal point for worship in their chapel, and explained their need to a Franciscan friar from Naples. One day this friar, Fra Alberto Radente, walking along a street in Naples, saw a rag-and-bone-man's cart passing by.

On top of a pile of junk was a beautiful painting of the Madonna and Child handing rosaries to two saints. He bought it and duly presented it to the nuns of Pompeii. In due course, a beautiful basilica was built by Bartolo Longo, and to this day its focal point, above the high altar, is the painting discovered by Fra Radente – *La Madonna di Pompeii*.

Ever since, *Pompeii* has been the most important Italian shrine to Our Lady, and among the most visited in Europe. Of course, most of the pilgrims are Italians. Visitors today can admire the Madonna (also seen in virtually every home and every wayside shrine in this region) and can visit the tombs of Alberto Radente, Bartolo Longo and the founding Mother Superior of the convent. They will also see the children of the adjoining orphanage which is supported by the income of the shrine. More curious, though, is the gallery on the north side of the basilica: it is full of crutches and other medical artefacts no longer needed by pilgrims who have prayed to the Madonna and been cured. Even more touchingly bizarre are the photographs and paintings of the most horrendous accidents of road, air and sea which depict the situations survived by devotees of the Madonna, whom she has protected.

Superstitions

- **13**: As in other Mediterranean countries, in Italy the number 13 implies good luck, even on Friday 13th. However, Italians shudder at the thought of 13 people seated at table: to avoid this, they will invite a 14th person, or use two tables. It is the number 17 which is often considered to be unlucky.

- **Corna**: This is a good-luck charm in the shape of a twisted horn, usually red or gold; they are worn on bracelets, necklaces, or chains, or hung in cars, on bikes and anywhere the owner wishes to invoke good luck and ward off evil spirits. By contrast, the expression *fare le corna* describes a gesture in which the hand is held up with the two outer fingers extended, the thumb and two inner fingers folded, the intention being to mimic a devil's horns. The gesture is often made from behind a victim's head, and is rather derogatory, meaning something like the old English 'cuckold', i.e. your partner is being unfaithful to you.

- **Malocchio**: This actually means 'evil-eye', implying that a nasty spell has been cast on you.

Fare le corna

Folklore

Every town and village has its own mythology, legend and folklore, often used as a way of explaining how and why the place came to exist or the exploits of former inhabitants. Some are based on historical fact, others not. The best example is the one concerning the city of Rome.

The founding of Rome

One of the most important bits of folklore involves the founding of Rome. The founder of Rome was Aeneas, a Trojan prince who managed to escape from the destruction of Troy at the hands of the Greeks. Sailing across the Mediterranean with a few followers, after many strange adventures, he landed on the shores of Latium, the area now known as Lazio. (This story is told in *The Aeneid* by the Roman poet Virgil.) Aeneas was accepted by the king of Latium and married his daughter. The alliance of the two peoples would eventually produce the Romans.

According to Roman mythology and legend, the city itself was founded by Romulus and Remus: these twin brothers were abandoned by their mother and reared by a she-wolf. The story goes that when they were building Rome, Romulus challenged Remus to jump over the wall he had just built. Remus succeeded, and Romulus was so incensed that he killed his brother. There is a statue of the baby twins being suckled by the she-wolf on top of a column in the ancient Forum of Rome, and ever since this image has been used as the symbol of Rome. Another symbol of Rome, seen even on manhole covers, is the inscription SPQR: *Senatus Populus Que Romanus* (for the Senate and people of Rome). This acronym has been used to denote public works in Rome since ancient times.

Romulus, Remus and the she-wolf

Traditions

Further to the traditions already described, here are some others.

All roads lead to Rome

A tradition maintained to this day is that the old trunk roads, less used now with the proliferation of *autostrade* (motorways), still bear the names given to them by the Romans who originally built them. Thus the *Via Appia* goes south-east, *Via Flaminia* goes north, the *Via Aurelia* leads north-west along the coast, and so on. From the 1930s to the 1970s, many Lancia cars bore the names of these roads (see Unit 7).

Traditional crafts

Most areas of Italy have their local traditional crafts, usually based on the materials available locally or local needs or conditions. All of the following are appropriate 'good-buy' souvenirs for visitors to the regions mentioned.

- **Marble:** The best Italian marble is the white marble of Carrara on the coast between Genoa and Livorno. Near the area, souvenir shops and stalls in tourist sites like Pisa and Florence offer white marble statuettes. Most are of ground 'reconstituted' marble, of course, moulded rather than sculpted, but the effect of the better-quality examples is pleasing to the eye.

- **Glass:** Most famous for its decorative glass is the island of Murano near Venice. Plentiful supplies of sand, plus the wealth of Venice itself led to the inhabitants of Murano developing this relatively high-value industry. As well as the ornate chandeliers which hang in so many Venetian buildings, multi-coloured glass artefacts and ornaments are exported all over the world.

- **Ceramics**: The best-known Italian porcelain ornaments and statues are those of Capodimonte in Naples. The colours tend to be soft, and the most typical figures are of archetypal Neapolitan characters.

- **Leather**: Florence, and Tuscany in general, is the best area for leather goods of all sorts; most Italian leather goods are of softer leather than is the case in other countries.

- **Lace**: The island of Burano in the lagoon of Venice is known for its lace. It is said that the wives of fishermen took to this slow and painstaking craft to while away the hours when their menfolk were away on fishing trips. Now you can buy lace in every shape and style, though you need to watch out for cheap imported lace sold alongside the genuine local articles.

- **Marquetry**: Sorrento near Naples is known for its marquetry and inlaid wood. In the backstreets there, every little doorway seems to lead into a small workshop, and in the specialist shops you can buy anything from ornaments to chess-boards and furniture in beautifully constructed and lacquered marquetry – but again, watch out for cheap imitations.

- **Cameo**: Sorrento and Naples are also known for their *cameo* products, made from sea-shell carved in such a way that the layers produce reliefs, usually of the bust of a classical woman; the colours of different layers add to the effect of the contours.

GLOSSARIO	GLOSSARY
il mio compleanno è...	my birthday is...
il mio onomastico è...	my saint's day is...
a Natale, mangiamo...	at Christmas, we eat...
a Pasqua, beviamo...	at Easter, we drink...
Buon Compleanno!	Happy Birthday!
Tanti auguri!	Congratulations/Happy Birthday (as in the song)
Buona festa!	Have a happy feast-day (or **Buon onomastico** Happy saint's day, etc.)
augurare a ... tanti auguri	to wish ... a happy birthday

la festa	feast(-day), holiday, party
il festival	festival
il giorno festivo	holiday
festeggiare	to celebrate
mangiare fuori	to go out for a meal
il regalo	present
regalare ... a ...	to give ... as a present
la processione	procession
i fuochi d'artificio	fireworks
la prima colazione	breakfast
fare colazione	to have breakfast
il pranzo	lunch
pranzare	to have lunch
la cena	dinner
cenare	to have dinner

Taking it further

Suggested reading

Eyewitness Travel Guides, published by Dorling Kindersley, contain information of all sorts, including maps and excellent illustrations, available for the following: Italy, Florence and Tuscany, Naples, Rome, Sardinia, Venice and the Veneto.

Italy, Travellers' Handbook contains useful information of all sorts on the whole of Italy. It can be obtained from:

The Italian State Tourist Board,
1 Princes Street,
London W1R 8AY
Email: **enitlond@globalnet.co.uk**
Internet: **www.enit.it**

The Italian State Tourist Board's brochure requesting service will provide specific brochures, for example on a particular area you are interested in; they can also give you the address of the local *Assessorato di Turismo* (where you can obtain guidebooks and free information brochures).

The following books are useful, though in one or two cases they may be out of print; if so an Internet search of bookshops is probably the best way to locate a copy.

Customs and Etiquette in Italy, Hugh Shankland, Global Books Ltd 1996

Italy, Festa, Tim Cooke, Franklin Watts 1997

Celebrating Italy, Carol Field, Harper Perennial 1997

The World of Venice, Harcourt Trade Publishers 1995

Rome, Its People, Life and Customs, Ugo Paoli, Bristol Classical Press 1990

Italy, Festivals of the World, Elizabeth Berg, Gareth Stevens 1997

Places to go

If festivals, customs and traditions are of interest to you, try to arrange your stay in Italy to coincide with the time and place to enjoy some. But be warned that accommodation is fully booked well in advance of local festivals.

Websites

There are websites available on some of the places mentioned in this unit, but of course much of the material covered here is not the sort of thing you will find on the Internet; it is always best to do a search with the appropriate words according to your interest, and using your favourite search engine. Bear in mind that the most probable sources are likely to be Italian websites, and you may need to cope with the Italian.

Try: **www.italyguide.com**

07 modern creativity

In this unit you will learn
- about science and technology in Italy
- about Italy's infrastructure
- about the media, cinema and fashion
- about food and drink

Italy has always been known for creativity and good taste, especially in the fine arts; indeed, in several areas Italy has not only been famed for creativity, but has also created styles, techniques and norms which have then become established around the world (as seen in Units 3–5 on music, art and architecture, and literature). In the last hundred years this trend has continued and spread to other fields of creative activity, often far more than we realize: Italian design and taste has been very influential in technology, food, fashion, cinema, motor manufacturing and many other areas of economic activity.

This broad-based creativeness has a lot to do with qualities possessed by many Italians: resourcefulness and inventiveness, coupled with a love of doing business and striking deals and compromises. Italians are also very industrious and adaptable, as exemplified in the way that those who emigrated in the late nineteenth and early twentieth centuries found so many different ways of making a living in the countries they settled in, adapting to local needs and conditions, and leaving their seal on whatever activity they were involved in. Add to this their obsession with *il design* (they have even made this English word their own!) and you have an appealing recipe for economic and industrial success. This unit cannot cover this vast topic exhaustively, but it should give you a flavour of the most significant aspects of Italian twentieth-century creativity.

Science and technology – the legacy

The Romans were technologically very advanced in their day. Most Roman 'technology' was related to the Empire's war efforts: the defensive 'tortoise' formed by suitably shaped shields, the huge battering rams and catapults, not to mention architectural features of Roman fortifications. More humdrum, everyday artefacts reflecting Roman inventiveness can be seen in the museums of Rome, Naples and Pompeii.

The technology which evolved centuries after the Romans in city-states such as Venice was also to a large extent devoted to war effort. In this era of prosperity founded on trade, maritime power was vitally important to Venice. A visit to the *Museo Marittimo* – a few hundred metres along from St Mark's Square – offers examples of sheer ingenuity such as the gondola, whose twisted shape was developed to allow it to be rowed by a single *gondoliere* rowing on one side. Among the most fascinating exhibits are the models of incredible wooden floating-docks. These were made in two halves, each the mirror image of one half of the hull, enabling them to be secured against the hull of Venetian fighting galleons, and then pumped full of air. Thus cradled, the galleon could be floated into the shallow lagoon to be repaired in safety, and perhaps careened – tilted onto one side using another amazing machine – allowing work to be done on the under-side of the hull.

Among the great Italian scientists of the past, **Leonardo da Vinci** (1452–1519), in addition to being a great artist, anatomist, geologist and meteorologist, was a professional engineer, and designed many devices which became reality in modern times, including the helicopter. The physicist and mathematician **Galileo Galilei** (1564–1642), who more than others proved that the Earth moves around the Sun, was in every sense the father of modern astronomy, and invented the telescope. Other Italian astronomers discovered various comets, and the *canali* (canals) on Mars; it was a Vatican priest who developed the technique for using light spectroscopy to the point where he was able to determine the chemical composition of the Sun, stars and planets. This heritage of inventiveness and problem-solving ability has spawned modern-day Italian technological creativity.

Industry

Italian technological creativity in the last hundred years cannot be fully appreciated without looking at Italian industry from the point of view of the originality and inventiveness which have afforded a number of Italian companies and their products notable success. It is not generally known that Italy's economy is very strong in terms of industrial output and that, whilst Italy has not had great economic and political stability in recent times, economic growth has flourished – perhaps in spite of the politicians! Although the industrial revolution arrived relatively late in Italy, before the Second World War Italy began to make major strides. The war itself was a very major setback, but after it Italy benefited from much-needed new investment; Italian industry had been virtually destroyed, but having to make a fresh start was a great advantage, and the Italian virtues already referred to helped to create an economic miracle. Apart from a few hiccups, this is sustained to this day to the extent that most Italians enjoy a high standard of living, and parts of northern Italy are among the wealthiest in Europe in terms of per capita income.

The motor industry

The Italian industrial products best known abroad are those of the various branches of the motor industry and other consumer industries based on engineering of different types. It is appropriate to mention how important engineering is to Italians: the title *Ing.* (*Ingegnere* – Engineer) is as valued and respected in Italy as *Dott.* (*Dottore*) or *Prof.* (*Professore*). Here we shall consider some of the better-known companies and their products from the point of view of creativity.

The original Fiat 500 – *Cinquecento*

Italians on the move

Every Italian values his or her freedom to move around, yet for most their vehicle means more than just transportation, which may be why Italian cars are known throughout the world as being more than mere vehicles. Most have an added ingredient typified by the frequent description of them as 'drivers' cars'.

The largest manufacturer in Italy, and one of the world's largest, is Fiat (see Unit 10). This company, founded in 1899 by a former cavalry officer, Giovanni Agnelli, and owned by various generations of the wealthy Agnelli family, is a veritable giant on the world stage, as well as being Italy's greatest and most influential industrial company. In fact it is impossible to consider the Italian industrial and commercial scene without mentioning this company.

Fiat is best known for the sort of nippy, practical small cars favoured by Italians needing to zip around city streets or up and down twisty, mountainous roads, yet capable of being loaded up with *mamma* and kids, or – in bygone days – to carry produce to market. Among the generations of fun-to-drive, trend-setting cars with innovative engineering and design, many of which in recent years have won the 'European Car of the Year Award', are:

- 1936 *Topolino* (little mouse), a chic but practical small car
- 1955 *Seicento*, rear-engined, immensely popular
- 1955 *Multipla*, six-seater version of the *Seicento*, arguably the very first 'people carrier'
- 1957 *Cinquecento*, smaller and cuter than the *Seicento*, now a 'cult car'
- 1966 *124*, with several sporting versions
- 1969 *128*, popularized front-wheel drive in Europe
- 1970 *127*, set standards for packaging front-wheel drive; Ford based the Fiesta design on it
- 1980 The small but practical and rugged *Panda*, its four-wheel-drive version being the cheapest 4WD on the market
- 1983 *Uno*, stylish, tough 'supermini', one of the most successful European cars (7.5 million built)
- 1988 The roomy but compact *Tipo*, one of the models built at Cassino, taking industry to the south of Italy
- 1990s *Punto*, another huge European favourite; *Cinquecento*, a favourite small city car, and its larger offspring the *Seicento*; also the *Bravo*, *Brava* and *Marea*
- 1998 *Multipla*, controversially styled but brilliantly packaged six-seater small MPV
- 2001 The *Stilo* and in 2003 the new *Panda*, which yet again won for Fiat the 'European Car of the Year' award.

Some of these and other models have also appeared in high-performance versions prepared by Abarth, Fiat's own motor-sport specialist company.

The great Italian marques

Many great Italian motoring marques were founded by Italian racing-drivers: given the Italians' love of driving, a natural aspiration for former racing-drivers was to make cars which are good to drive. Vincenzo Lancia established his company to build elegant, fast but practical cars, high in engineering sophistication thanks largely to the engineer Vittorio Jano. Lancia pioneered unitary construction (in place of a heavy chassis), independent suspension, the V engine and front-wheel drive. The *Lambda* (1920s), the *Aprilia* (1930s), the *Aurelia* (1950s), the *Fulvia* (1970s) and the *Stratos*, *Beta* and *Delta* (1980s), were all innovative, trend-setting models; many reflected Vincenzo Lancia's racing origins by being the most successful motor-rallying cars of their era, especially in the 1980s. Many engineering solutions pioneered in Lancias have become the norm in all modern cars.

Ing. Enzo Ferrari, a racing driver, set out to build exclusive sports cars with technology developed on the race-track. In recent decades Ferrari has produced the most coveted cars in the world, cars with an enviable cachet never equalled by the best of British, German or Japanese technology. What schoolboy or motoring enthusiast has not thrilled to the blood-red cars with names like *GTO, Daytona, Dino, BB (Berlinetta Boxer), Testarossa, F40, 360 Modena, 550 Maranello* and the *2003 Ferrari Enzo*? The reason is Ferrari's ability to blend engineering quality with style, and the unique 'music' made by Ferrari engines, tried and tested in Ferrari's consistently competitive and successful Grand Prix Formula One racing cars, the vehicles for Michael Schumacher's many F1 World Championships in recent years.

Dino 246 GTS

Fiat money rescued Lancia and Ferrari from financial uncertainty in the 1970s, then in the 1980s did the same for Alfa Romeo, for a while a nationalized company. This company (ALFA = *Anonima Lombarda per la Fabbricazione di Automobili*) built a reputation founded on romance and glamour almost to the same degree as Ferrari, though it has always produced popular cars as well as more expensive models. Among its evocative model names are *Giulia* and *Alfetta*. In more recent years, after some indifferent models, Alfa has regained its name for exciting cars with models like the various *Spiders, Alfasud,* the *GTV, 164, 156, 166, GTA* and *147...* and who will ever forget the '*barchetta*' or 'boat-tailed' Alfa *Duetto*, immortalized by the film *The Graduate*?

Among other great names are Maserati, now revitalized by Ferrari, De Tomaso and Lamborghini: the latter (now owned by

Volkswagen) has a rather curious story behind it which is known by few people, but which is a typical example of the Italian qualities of inventiveness and adaptability. Ferruccio Lamborghini, a tractor manufacturer, used to drive Ferraris: the story goes that one day he had the idea of tuning one of his tractor engines and building a supercar around it. He 'poached' a couple of designers and engineers from Ferrari, and the Lamborghini *350 GTV* was born. The later *Miura* was named after the best breed of Spanish fighting bull. The Lamborghini bull logo is a reminder of the marque's agricultural origins; ironically, most people are unaware that in the UK, for example, there are many Lamborghini tractors, vastly outstripping the number of Lamborghini cars. The tractors are instantly recognizable by their cream colour, with a blue stripe – and of course the Lamborghini name and the bull logo!

The stylists

Italian coachbuilders and stylists have been very influential abroad. Pininfarina designed many Morris, Austin and more recently Peugeot models; the Ghia design studio was actually bought by Ford; Giugiaro styled the original Volkswagen *Golf* as well as the best-selling Fiat *Uno*. Among others active abroad have been ItalDesign and Bertone, and many of the most 'British' cars were actually styled by Italians: even that most British of marques with its James Bond associations, Aston Martin, produced the *Superleggera* with bodywork by the Italian company Touring, which specialized in 'superlight' coachwork. Zagato, among others, produced re-bodied versions of Lancias and Alfas, and other minor coachbuilders used to make their own versions of many popular small Fiats.

Building for the world

Fiat has always sold production techniques and machine tools abroad to companies building Fiat models under licence. The Spanish car industry was effectively established by Fiat (SEAT was part-owned by Fiat and most models were shared with the Italian company until VW took over). They even sold their second-hand machine tools abroad, so that old Fiat models were built in Communist countries in the 1970s and 1980s: Poland (Polski Fiat), the USSR (Lada), Yugo in former Yugoslavia. Even more curiously, some 1950s Fiat models are still going strong in India, kept going with locally re-manufactured spares! Many products associated with motoring, such as Fiat's COMAU car-building robots, have also sold well abroad, and Fiat-manufactured parts are fitted to most European marques. Fiat have also designed and built 'world cars' to rival the VW *Beetle*:

the *178* or *Palio* is built in Argentina, Brazil, Morocco, Poland, Turkey and Venezuela.

Model cars – small is beautiful

Burago, one of the best-known makes of model cars among youngsters today, has gained enormous success since the 1970s, and not just because of the quality and detail of its models. The popularity of Burago models in many countries, including the UK, is probably largely due to the quality of the models it used to concentrate on – those painted bright red – Ferraris!

Italians on two wheels

Scooters offered many Italians much-needed mobility in the post-war period, most important in that era of urgent economic regeneration. Vespas and their rival Lambrettas were first made after the Second World War in former aircraft factories using skills and resources previously used to build aircraft for Mussolini's war effort. These two marques flourished in the 1950s and 1960s, and Lambrettas or Vespas became essential equipment for the British 'Mods' of the late 1960s, every bit as vital a fashion accessory as their sharp Italian suits!

A Lambretta

Lambrettas have all but disappeared, but Piaggio (Vespa) is still going strong and now many 'newer' marques such as Malaguti, Benelli and Aprilia make stylish, modern scooters. These are very popular with Italian youngsters even today, as a practical means of transport which allows them to go out elegantly dressed in high fashion without needing to don leathers; they are cheap to run and easy to park, yet still endowed with the style and chic sought by every self-respecting Italian.

There have always, of course, been powerful Italian motorbikes, characterized more often than not by original and elegant engineering – lighter and more agile than traditional British bikes, and still holding their own in terms of quality and performance in the face of competition from Japanese marques. Such great names as MV Augusta, Moto Guzzi, Laverda, Aprilia, Benelli, Morini and Ducati are all well-known to true 'bikers', the last being regarded as the 'Ferrari' of motorbikes. Many of these have been made famous by racing success in the hands of Italian aces such as Giacomo Agostini, and in more recent times Max Biaggi and the spectacular and characterful Valentino Rossi – the youngest ever world champion (125cc). The rising star in Grand Prix motorcycling is the young Italian Loris Capirossi.

Commercial vehicles

Several major marques of Italian lorry have trundled goods around the roads, not only of Italy but of all of Europe, e.g. OM, Fiat. Even Lancia used to make very individual lorries until the 1960s; indeed, many British bus companies used Lancia charabancs in the early years, and the British Army used Lancia ambulances in the First World War. Now, with rationalization of production and mergers of major companies, IVECO, controlled by Fiat, has brought together the Fiat truck-making division, many other minor Italian and European makes, and Ford commercial vehicles.

Cycles and cycling

One of the most popular sports in Italy is cycling: the *Giro d'Italia* is one of the most important cycle races in the world, and Italian riders and teams have often dominated international cycling events. It is not surprising, then, that Italian bicycles and associated equipment have often been considered among the best available. In the 1960s, many British youngsters aspired to have 'Campag' (*Campagnolo*) gears on their bikes; in the 1990s, many bikes sold in Britain are equipped with Italian-made saddles, brakes, handlebars or Italian *Vuelta* wheels and tyres.

Agricultural engineering

In addition to Lamborghini's continuing success as a tractor manufacturer, mentioned on p. 127, FIATAGRI is prominent throughout Europe as a maker of tractors, combine harvesters and other agricultural machinery, all recognizable by their red/brown colour. Owning New Holland and Case, Fiat ranks as equal number one manufacturer of agricultural machinery in the world.

Into space...

Fiat has many other industrial interests, for example in chemicals, nuclear power generation, and in the space industry.

It builds the booster and separation engines for the Ariane rocket launcher in the European Space Programme, and even owns the launch site in French Guyana!

The aero industry

Several Italian motor manufacturers have also earned a reputation for building aircraft. The Fiat G91 jet fighter of the 1950s was used by other Nato countries as well as by the Italian Air Force. More recently, Italy was one of the partners in the design and building of the successful Tornado fighter-bomber, and Typhoon Eurofighter: this fighter for the new millennium is being built by four countries, but Alenia of Italy owns the development company. The engines are being built by Eurojet, which is owned by four companies, including Rolls Royce and Fiat Aviazione. Fiat produces parts for every western airline and aeroplane manufacturer.

Another company, Agusta which, like Piaggio, continues to make aircraft as well as scooters, has developed into a major international maker of helicopters, forming with Westland the consortium building the new EH101 Merlin helicopter, now in service with the Royal Navy and Italian Navy. Agusta also makes small helicopters with the American Bell Corporation and is working with other European companies to build a new helicopter for use on board naval frigates, the NH90.

Italians afloat

Italy has an excellent reputation for boat and shipbuilding thanks to its superb marine engines. Italians and their boats have for many years been most successful competitors in international powerboat racing. On the canals of Venice, it is no surprise to see that the *vaporetto* in which you are travelling along the Canal Grande is powered by Fiat or Alfa-Romeo engines.

Italian luxury 'powered yachts' such as those built by RIVA are popular on the French and Italian Riviera, and bought by millionaires and royalty. Many Italians are keen sailors, and Italian sailing yachts also have a fine reputation, Italy being one of the seven countries which compete in the Americas Cup. In 2000, the Italian yacht *Luna Rossa*, sponsored by the fashion company Prada, defeated the USA entry for the right to challenge the holder, New Zealand: the first time the USA did not compete in the final. On Lake Garda and in the Bay of Naples, hydrofoils (once considered high-tech) have been providing rapid ferry services for over forty years; they are now rivalled in speed by conventionally hulled and catamaran 'fast ferries'.

An Italian boat powered by Lancia engines – the *Destriero* – won the prestigious Blue Riband award in 1992, beating the world speed record for a non-stop transatlantic crossing. Many of the new generation of super-luxury cruise liners have been built in Italian shipyards, such as the oldest, Fincantieri: this shipyard built *Carnival Destiny* and *Grand Princess*, among the world's largest cruise liners, successfully blending Italian elegance and artistry with technologically advanced computer-controlled construction methods.

Infrastructure

Italians on the rails

Italian trains have a reputation for punctuality; Benito Mussolini ordered that they should run on time – and they still do! If you have travelled by rail in Italy, you may know the Stazione Termini in Rome, built in the late 1950s in an architectural style which was bold and spectacular for its day. On the railways, Fiat, a well-established European manufacturer of locomotives and rolling stock, has in the last three decades had great success with its high-speed, tilting *Pendolino* trains. Fiat Ferroviaria have played a major part in building a new generation of these trains for Richard Branson's Virgin Trains in the UK. (By the time you read this, if you are travelling on a train it could well be a Pendolino!) Public transport infrastructure within cities is somewhat less well developed, but at the time of writing, ASM (*Azienda Servizi per la Mobilità*) is planning, for 2001, an elegant space-age metro which will skim above the canals of Venice to provide a one-kilometre link between Tronchetto and Piazzale Roma, two key points used by visitors and commuters arriving in or leaving the city.

Italians off the rails

The original Italian motorways were built in Mussolini's time, and were the first in Europe. What characterizes many of them is the fact that they are such great feats of civil engineering. Drive to Italy through the Mont Blanc tunnel; Italian and French engineers tunnelled with such precision that they met under Mont Blanc with their drill tips within centimetres of each other. Now travel along one of the newest motorways, with more tunnels than open road. Carry on down to Genoa over spectacularly high viaducts which swoop down towards the Mediterranean. Then follow the coastal *autostrada* towards Pisa, again passing through hundreds of tunnels, with brief open stretches affording fleeting glimpses far below of the pretty towns and beaches of the Ligurian Riviera... These examples of civil engineering indicate how confident the Italians have always been of their building and engineering skills.

White goods

Turning to more mundane products of Italian creativity, it is interesting to note that Olivetti typewriters have won awards for design, in addition to being well-built and efficient. Olivetti are now well-established in all areas of IT, adding computers to their range of products. Italian 'white goods' – refrigerators, washing machines and dishwashers bearing names like Indesit, Candy and Zanussi ('the appliance of science!') are familiar to us all and have a very major slice of the European market in household appliances. Among other significant 'lifestyle' products are the ubiquitous coffee machines made by Gaggia and Lavazza. One of the latest models of coffee machine made by Lavazza was styled by none other than car stylist Pininfarina! The point is that, for an Italian, a good product cannot just be good value and efficient: it must also be good to look at. It is no surprise, then, that in the fields of jewellery, glassware, kitchenware and furniture, Italian products have always stood out for their elegance and style.

The media

Even in the field of the mass media, Italy has given the world an instantly recognizable word, *paparazzi*, now used universally to describe ruthless photographers and journalists who will apparently stop at nothing to get their photograph or their story! At least two Italian media tycoons have been well-known abroad in recent times: it used to be said of the Agnelli family, who own *La Stampa*, one of Italy's most popular newspapers, that they used the paper to manipulate public opinion when strikes threatened Fiat production. Silvio Berlusconi went even further, using his money and the influence of his television companies to get himself elected as Prime Minister!

Many Italians don't actually buy their own newspaper, preferring instead to read those provided in their favourite bar. There are, of course, many press publications, and they vary greatly in quality and credibility; they tend to be much better than many British papers at reporting news from around the world, and not just from Italy. There is no Italian equivalent of the British 'tabloid press'. Here are some of the most useful publications:

National daily newspaper:	Corriere della Sera	Milan
	Il Mattino	Naples
	La Stampa	Turin
	La Repubblica	various editions
Current affairs magazine:	Panorama	
	L'Espresso	
Women's magazine:	Grazia	
Young women's magazine:	Donna Moderna	
Gossip/ society magazines:	Oggi	
	Ecco!	
Cookery magazine:	Rosanna Lambertucci	
House and furniture:	Arredare	
Computing and IT:	PC Open	
Motor magazine:	Quattroruote	

The children's press?

The Italians always seem to have enjoyed comics – *fumetti* – since the American GIs brought them to Italy in the Second World War. Ever since, Italy has had its own range of comics, including what amount to illustrated soap operas in print for adults; and other 'adult' comics abound too!

TV

Italy has many privately owned radio and TV stations and new ones are opening all the time, it seems! *Il Sole 24 Ore*, for example, is a TV station opened on 1 January 2000 which is owned and run by the daily of the same name, and provides three channels largely aimed at their readers. Silvio Berlusconi owns *Canale 5*. Arguably, however, still the most significant Italian TV and radio broadcaster is the original, government-controlled company, RAI (Italian Radio). RAI is known abroad for its involvement in joint ventures with foreign companies; its logo appears often in the credits of programmes shown in other European countries. RAI was partially privatized some years ago, but the Italian State still retains control through its majority shareholding.

Many other channels are available to Italian viewers, including local ones and many which are foreign-owned. The quality of material broadcast – which includes a profusion of glamorous game shows and an excess of dubbed American films – is neither particularly good nor consistent, but Italians at least have plenty of choice. Here are some of the main TV channels available, including some local stations:

Italian TV channels

Raiuno	
Raidue	
Raitre	
Rete 4	
Italia 1	
Canale 5	
Canale 10	
Odeon Teleoggi	
Telemontecarlo	
Crt 34	
Canale 21	
Telelibera 63	
Teleluna	
Videomusic	
Italia 7 Canale 8	
Antenna Vesuvio	*Naples area*
Televomero	*Naples area*
Telecapri	*Naples area*

Radio

There are, of course, private radio stations in every area or town of any size. Here are a few of the national stations, the first three being those of the State Radio and TV company: *Radiouno, Radiodue, Radiotre, Rete 105, Radiomontecarlo.*

Telecommunications

Italians adhere to the philosophy that 'it's good to talk'. The telephone has for many years offered a popular pastime, and now the advent of the mobile phone – *il cellulare* – has brought a new one: to spot the mobile being used in the most unlikely circumstances. Italians seem determined to provide plenty of examples...! Many major telecommunications companies operate in Italy, and there is fierce competition; Tim and Omnitel competed to be the first to offer Internet access via mobile telephones, such is the thirst for this type of technology among Italians.

Sport

In a country as colourful as Italy, it is hardly surprising that two sporting colours are the factors which unify Italians most effectively. Far more than the green/white/red of the *bandiera tricolore*, the three-coloured national flag, Italians are united in support of the emblematic blue shirts of the Italian soccer team (popularly known as *gli azzurri*, 'the blues') and by the red flags bearing the black prancing horse on a yellow shield, waved at Formula One races by tens of thousands of Ferrari fans. Here again, Italy has given the world an evocative word: *tifosi* (fans), which conjures up images of fanatical Ferrari followers.

Cinema

Italy has produced many film directors, actors and actresses, among them several 'big names'. *Cinecittà* (Cinema City) in Rome, while no rival to Hollywood in terms of box-office successes, was nonetheless one of the most influential film studios in the world, especially in the sense of European 'art' films. Ironically it was the 'spaghetti westerns' which gained most financial success. After the Second World War, Italian films began to gain a good reputation, especially via the so-called 'Neorealists' such as Rossellini, De Sica and Visconti. Here are some directors and their best-known films:

- **Roberto Rossellini**: *Roma, città aperta/Rome, Open City* (1945), about the Italian Resistance in the Second World War
- **Vittorio de Sica**: *Ladri di biciclette/Bicycle Thieves* (1948), a father looks for work to support his family... but his bike is stolen
- **Federico Fellini**: *La dolce vita* (1960), about the new rich of Rome; *8¹/₂* (1963), a film-maker, his wife and his mistress; *Satyricon* (1969), a dreamy vision of antiquity

- **Sergio Leone:** *Fistful of Dollars* (1964); *The Good, the Bad and the Ugly* (1971) – both well-known in English ('spaghetti westerns')
- **Pier-Paolo Pasolini:** *Oedipus Rex* (1967), based on the classic story of a son who unknowingly falls in love with his mother
- **Luchino Visconti:** *Death in Venice* (1971), based on Thomas Mann's story of the death of a composer
- **Bernardo Bertolucci:** *L'ultimo tango a Parigi/Last Tango in Paris* (1972), notoriously erotic for its time
- **Francesco Rosi:** *Lucky Luciano* (1973), a US gangster retired in Italy; *Cristo si è fermato a Eboli/Christ Stopped at Eboli* (1979), from Carlo Levi's anti-Fascist novel about southern poverty
- **Franco Zeffirelli:** *The Taming of the Shrew* (1967); *Romeo and Juliet* (1968); *Brother Sun, Sister Moon* (1973); *Tea with Mussolini* (1999), a group of British and American women tend a young boy in Italy during the war
- **Luigi Comencini:** *Traffic Jam* (1979), an enormous traffic jam brings people together
- **Giuseppe Tornatore:** *Cinema Paradiso* (1989), Oscar-winning tale of a small boy fascinated by cinema
- **Gabriele Salvatores:** *Mediterraneo* (1991), Italian soldiers capture a Greek island paradise and fall in love...
- **Ricky Tognazzi:** *La Scorta /The Escort* (1993), a violent story of the men who protect anti-Mafia judges
- **Nanni Moretti:** *Caro diario/Dear Diary* (1994), a hilarious autobiographical tale of the director's life over 18 months; *Aprile* (1998), Moretti's diary from March to August 1994
- **Roberto Benigni:** *Johnny Stecchino* (1991), a frenetic comedy of mistaken identity; *La vita è bella/Life is Beautiful* (1998), Oscar-winning story of a Jewish family in wartime Italy; with his wife Nicoletta Braschi, Roberto Benigni stars in both, and his performance at the Oscar ceremony will always be remembered

Another memorable recent Italian film was actually directed by Michael Radford, though in every other respect it was Italian. Starring the Neapolitan comedian Massimo Troisi and the 'new Sophia Loren' Maria Grazia Cucinotta, *Il Postino/The Postman* (1994) was the most popular foreign imported film ever in the USA. Quite apart from the touching story of a simple postman finding friendship in Pablo Neruda, a Chilean poet living in exile on his island, and using poetry to win the heart of the beautiful Beatrice, there was an unusual and added element of poignancy: while he was filming, Massimo Troisi was actually dying of a congenital heart defect, and he died before the film was finished.

Actors/actresses

- **Anna Magnani** (1908–1973) Trained at the Academy of Dramatic Art in Rome, first major film *La Cieca di Sorrento* (1934). Acted for de Sica and also for Rossellini in *Roma, città aperta* (1945). Won an Academy Award for best actress in an American film, *The Rose Tattoo* (1955); portrayed herself in Fellini's *Roma* (1972).

- **Rossano Brazzi** (1916–1984) A professional footballer and boxer before becoming an actor and director. Best known as the star of such American films as *Summertime* (1955) and *South Pacific* (1958). Yet, this first 'Italian stallion' was incredibly popular in Italy for ten years before going to the USA in 1939; he appeared in films as diverse as *Three Coins in the Fountain* (1954) and *The Italian Job* (1964).

- **Marcello Mastroianni** (1923–1996) Internationally known Italian film actor, started as an extra in the late 1940s then acted under Luchino Visconti. Most notable films: *La Dolce Vita* (1960), *La Notte* (1961), *8½* (1963). He starred with Loren in the comedy *Divorce Italian Style* (1962).

- **Gina Lollobrigida** (born 1927 in Subiaco) Often known as *La Lollo*, she personified the ideal, beautiful but strong-willed Italian woman of the 1950s. At the age of 3, she was elected 'most beautiful infant in Italy'. Among her best-known films: *Les Belles de nuit* (1952) and, in the role of Esmeralda, *Notre Dame de Paris* (1957) – better known as *The Hunchback of Notre Dame*.

- **Antonio de Curtis** (known as Totò) (1898–1967) An extremely popular and well-loved Neapolitan actor, best known for his comedy and humorous films such as *Totò al giro d'Italia* (1948), *Totò nella luna* (1958), *Totò, Eva e il pennello proibito* (1959), *Totò e Cleopatra* (1963) and *Totò d' Arabia* (1965). He also wrote Neapolitan poetry such as the collection *A Livella* – difficult reading, unless you know Neapolitan!

- **Sophia Loren** Born 1934 in Pozzuoli, Naples, discovered at the age of 15 by producer Carlo Ponti, later her husband. After winning a beauty contest she progressed from international sex symbol to Academy Award-winning actress. As well as Hollywood, she worked in Italy on several Vittorio de Sica films, notably *Two Women* (1961) and a series of earthy Italian comedies often with Marcello Mastroianni, notably *Marriage Italian Style* (1964). Other films include the epic *El Cid* (1961), *A Countess from Hong Kong* (1967), and *A Special Day* (1977).

- **Alberto Sordi** (1919–2003) A multi-talented actor who has appeared in dozens of films as diverse as *Those Magnificent Men in Their Flying Machines* (1965), Fellini's *Roma* (1972), *Viva Italia* (1977), *Vacanze di Natale 91* (1992), *Romanzo di un giovane povero* (1995).

- **Isabella Rossellini** Born in Rome in 1952, daughter of Roberto Rossellini and Ingrid Bergman, started as a model, then became a film star; acted in the film *Blue Velvet*, in the TV series *Friends* and as Merlin's wife in the recent film of this name. Married for a time to Martin Scorsese, she was the inspiration for fashion designers Dolce and Gabbana, for whom she used to model (see p. 140).

- **Massimo Troisi** (1953–1994) Started off as a Neapolitan comedian and personality; his tragically short film career was cut short during the filming of *Il Postino* (see p. 137).

- **Roberto Benigni** Actor/director, born near Arezzo in 1952, known as 'the clown prince of Italian film'. Featured in *Son of the Pink Panther*, then later acted and directed his own films such as *Johnny Stecchino* (1991) and *La vita è bella*, which won three Oscars (see p. 137).

- **Nicoletta Braschi** Actress and wife of Roberto Benigni, often stars opposite him in his films such as *Johnny Stecchino* (1991) and *La Vita è bella* (1998).

- **Maria Grazia Cucinotta** Born in Sicily, she has qualities which may make her the next Sophia Loren. She started working as a model in Milan, later went into television, and then starred as the beautiful Beatrice of *Il Postino* (see p. 137); also in *I Laureati*, *Italiani*, *Padre Papà*, *Il Sindaco* and her first American film, *Brooklyn State of Mind*.

Fashion

Italy has probably been influential in fashion since the days of the Roman toga! Style has always been important to Italians when choosing what to wear, and twentieth-century Italy has been one of the world's foremost centres for fashion, providing some of the most famous names of the last few decades. Milan is Italy's answer to Paris, but has not always been the centre of

Italian fashion: previously, the industry was based in Florence. In 1951, Giovan Battista Giorgini realized that Italy had enough fashion talent to be at least as good as Paris. He organized the first major Italian fashion show and it was a roaring success. The result was that the industry moved to Milan, where there was more money and better industrial and transport infrastructure available; besides, Milan is nearer to the markets of Europe. Still the birthplace of Italian elegance and style, Florence remains the centre for footwear and accessories. Among the many great names in Italian fashion are:

- **Armani**, founded by Giorgio Armani in 1973, characterized by relaxed tailoring with a typically southern European laid-back look; his designs were worn by Richard Gere in the film *American Gigolo* in 1980.

A Dolce and Gabbana outfit

- **Dolce and Gabbana** (Domenico Dolce and Stefano Gabbana), known for sexy classic outfits, floral designs, corsetry, romance. Domenico was brought up in post-war Sicily, stitching clothes from an early age, whilst Stefano was a Milanese fashion student. Together they found their identity and developed their style, inspired by the romantic image of the Madonna, the typical Italian woman, and the widows dressed in black of southern Italy!
- **Gucci**: founded by Guccio Gucci in the 1930s, this company specializes in handbags and shoes bearing the double GG logo of the founder. Such is their reputation for quality that among many educated British youngsters the term *Gucci* itself has come to be used to describe any object of good quality.

- **Miuccia Prada,** since the 1990s, has made a range of bags and accessories as well as clothes, characterized by simplicity and bold shapes, completely revamping the leather luggage business she inherited from her grandfather in the 1970s.
- **Versace,** founded by Gianni Versace, is famed for flamboyance and eccentricity, always being over the top. His creations have been worn by great celebrities, such as Madonna, Elton John and Princess Diana; others helped to make the wearer famous, such as the controversial 'safety-pin' dress worn by Liz Hurley at an Oscar ceremony. Even in death Gianni was 'larger than life', being assassinated outside his villa in the USA. Now his sister Donatella continues the family business.

In addition, of course, several up-to-the minute popular high-street brands originate from Italy, among them *Miss Sixty, Diesel* and *Sisley*. Best known of course is *United Colors of Benetton*: this extremely successful company has become notorious in recent years as a result of its controversial advertising campaigns, in which it has used ever more shocking imagery. It was founded by Luciano Benetton, who sold his accordion to buy a knitting machine for his sister. The brightly coloured sweaters they sold were just the start of this company's phenomenal success.

Food and drink

A wide range of Italian produce is available abroad as a result of the boom in the international popularity of Italian cuisine. In fact the Parma area is the most prosperous in Europe in per capita income as a result of the successful marketing of high-value agricultural products such as Lambrusco wines, Parma ham and parmesan cheese (in addition to the auto engineering of the area and production of tiles and ceramics). Many Italian culinary products now figure in the larders and refrigerators of homes all over Europe: *pasta* (= paste/pastry), *pomodori* (tomatoes), olive oil, garlic, ham, cheese, and even chocolate.

La cucina italiana – healthy eating

Italian cuisine has to be among the best known in the world. Its popularity abroad is probably due to two factors: firstly, mass emigration in the latter half of the nineteenth century and the first half of the twentieth took Italian eating habits and cuisine to many parts of the globe, including North and South America and the United Kingdom. Secondly, the Second World War brought many thousands of Allied servicemen to Italy: many developed a taste for Italian cooking – and Italian women – and many took 'war brides' home with them!

Interestingly, some of the best-known ingredients of Italian cooking which used to be derided have now actually proved to be major contributory factors to Italians having a better life expectancy than almost any other nation in the world:

- *pasta*, one of the most versatile 'base' dishes in the world, is an excellent staple: cheap, nutritious, and interesting to eat accompanied by endless varieties of sauces (for types, see p. 144).
- *garlic*, often despised by more conservative foreigners, has properties which contribute to healthy circulation... It is with good reason that vampires fear it!
- *olive oil*, an ingredient of so many dishes and the means of frying others, has really come into its own with the realization of how harmful animal fats are to the human body; best is *extra vergine*.
- *tomatoes*, or at least the Italian varieties, have recently been shown to be a very useful ingredient of healthy eating owing to their high potassium content; Italian plum tomatoes and tomato purée have been popular abroad for years, and *passata* (liquidized tomatoes) and sun-dried tomatoes became fashionable in the late 1990s.
- *pesto* (basil sauce), originally *pesto genovese*, from Genoa, but now readily available in jars from most British supermarkets makes a tasty starter or main meal served on pasta (*linguine* – little tongues – are the proper pasta for this), or can be used as a sauce with fish or meat, or even to enhance soups or stews.
- *balsamic vinegar*, much praised by TV cooks such as Antonio Carluccio.
- *red wine*, so often the best accompaniment to good Italian food, also has properties when drunk in moderation which help prevent coronary disease and promote healthy blood, as well as being a pleasurable drink, with so many excellent Italian varieties available.

Some of these ingredients were appreciated by the Romans; others are examples of how good the Italians are at adapting things to their own tastes, through their creativity, flair and originality. *Pasta* was introduced from China by the Italian explorer Marco Polo; tomatoes were brought to Europe from Latin America by Spanish explorers, but Italy made the tomato its own, even inventing its own word (*pomodoro* = golden apple) rather than adopt a form of the Nahuatl (Mexican Indian) word *tomatl*, as other nations did. However, to assume that these ingredients are the essence of all Italian cooking is to ignore many other elements of the Italian diet: the enormous variety and quality of fruit, vegetables and fish; and the methods of preparation, often surprising in their simplicity, and so sympathetic to the ingredients – as compared to the habit in some countries of boiling vegetables to a tasteless, nondescript pulp. Besides, Italians always insist on using the best ingredients, and to accompany one on a shopping trip to the market is a real education!

Piatti tipici

Here is a brief description of a small selection of traditional dishes which don't conform with preconceived notions of Italian cookery; some are not well-known outside Italy, yet they are very easy to cook and enjoyable to eat. Bear in mind that the details for any recipe vary from region to region, and even according to personal taste! These are given as examples only. For more details and more dishes, a good Italian cookbook is essential (two are recommended at the end of this unit).

- **bistecca alla pizzaiola**: very thin cuts of steak fried with tomato, garlic and oregano
- **gnocchi**: little potato and flour dumplings, usually served with *salsa al pomodoro* (traditional tomato sauce) or *pesto*
- **minestrone**: chunky vegetable soup, usually with beans, diced potato, cabbage, celery and tomato; you can include ham or other ingredients according to availability and preference
- **minestrone genovese**: minestrone strongly flavoured with fresh *pesto* sauce
- **parmigiana**: vegetable and cheese baked in a gratin dish, usually aubergines (*melanzane*)
- **pasta e fagioli**: pasta, usually macaroni, and *cannellini* beans cooked together
- **pasta e lenticchie**: pasta (usually small, short cut tubes) with lentils
- **peperoni ripieni**: peppers stuffed with e.g. tomatoes, anchovies, olives or courgettes (*zucchini*)

- **pesciolini fritti**: best ordered in a fishing area like Venice – a variety of fried small fish, can be enjoyed with *polenta*
- **polenta**: made with *polenta* (maize) flour; rather like thick semolina, or served even as set *polenta*, flavoured in various ways, and usually served with meat or fish
- **polpette**: meatballs or, if flattened, burgers, made with beef and pork mince with parmesan cheese, breadcrumbs, and chopped garlic
- **risotto**: rice dish (with fish, meat or other ingredients), but the rice is fried with oil, onions or garlic before water or stock are added
- **spaghetti alle vongole**: spaghetti served with a sauce made with clams
- **tiramisù**: chilled layered dessert with cream, *mascarpone* cheese and other ingredients, typically coffee- or chocolate-flavoured

Pasta

This major element of Italian cooking comes in such an enormous variety of shapes and sizes that it deserves a section all on its own! Most types of pasta are made from durum wheat, and there are many famous Italian brands available in Britain, but many Italians still prefer to make it fresh if possible. Pasta, which should always be cooked until soft, but still slightly chewy (*al dente* – on the tooth) can be served with almost anything according to what is available. Each type is favoured by Italians for serving with a particular sauce, the shapes often lending themselves to the sauce in a particular way, as can be seen in some of the examples below. Their names sound very exotic, but in fact most have very mundane meanings, and many offer an interesting insight into some of the features of the Italian language as related to other Latin-based languages. Some examples will give you the idea:

cannelloni	this means 'large tubes', which is exactly what they are; served stuffed usually with meat sauce, baked in the oven; according to local tradition, invented by a dubious priest in Sorrento who owned a restaurant (still there, and well worth a visit)
capellini	very fine strands – little hairs
conchiglie	pasta shells, as their name suggests

farfalle	little butterfly shapes, hence the name
fusilli	spiral short-cut pasta, good for soaking up very liquid sauces
lasagne	sheets of pasta baked in an oven dish with alternate layers of meat and tomato *sugo* (sauce) and cheese sauce
linguine	with a flattened oval cross-section the name means 'little tongues': ideal with *pesto*
maccheroni	cylindrical, short-cut tubes of pasta, i.e. macaroni
orecchiette	little pasta 'ears'
penne	pasta quills, usually served with plain tomato 'sugo'
ravioli	envelopes of pasta filled usually with meat paste
spaghetti	the best-known pasta: thin strands – the word derives from *spago* (string) and in this diminutive form means 'little strings'!
tagliatelle	*tagliare* means 'to cut' (as in tailor, tally) and these are flat strips of pasta, originally cut from a sheet
tortellini/tortelloni	curled sachets containing meat or cheese paste, small (*tortellini*) or large (*tortelloni*)
vermicelli	like spaghetti but thinner; its name means 'little worms'

Pizza

Anything goes on this yeasty pastry base… We are all familiar with fast-food pizza places but it all started in Naples, where they even have Olympian *pizzaiolo* competitions in which the contestants practise the technique of whirling the pizza around to stretch the pastry into a flat plate-like shape. The original pizzas date back to before the time when tomatoes were introduced into Europe. Like any great dish, many types of pizza owe their names to particular people or events: King Umberto I took his wife to Naples for her first visit in 1889. She was quite taken with the pizza she was served, topped with red tomatoes and white mozzarella cheese and sprinkled with chopped green basil: the story goes that she realized that here were the colours of the Italian flag! Since then, this style of pizza has borne her name: *Margherita*.

Drinking habits

With or without wine, most Italians drink mineral water with meals; as well as local mineral water and national brands such as San Pellegrino, there are several brands of 'mineral water' which come as sachets added to a bottle of tap water, such as *Idrolitina* and *Cristallina*. One of the high spots of a stay in Italy is the quality of the *caffè*, whether taken as straight *caffè nero*, *espresso*, *caffè latte*, or *cappuccino*... Tea, when drunk, is almost always taken as *tè al limone* (tea with lemon).

Fast food

- slabs of different types of pizza are generally on sale to take away and nibble on the move
- *focaccia* is a similar sort of tasty flavoured bread often eaten in the same way
- *arancini di riso*, rice balls often with cheese and eggs or a meat filling
- *panzarotti*, potato croquettes
- *pollo allo spiedo*, spit-roasted chicken, often bought to take home or for a picnic
- *panini*, filled bread rolls – the Italian answer to sandwiches; to order just one, ask for a *panino*
- American-style fast-food outlets now abound in large cities

Cooked/cold meats

Italy has a range of cooked and cold meats, often served as *antipasti* (starters). The best known and most widely available are:

- *salame*, a spicy sausage made predominantly from pork
- *mortadella*, a sort of pork meat-loaf or large sausage, not so spicy but often containing peppercorns
- *prosciutto cotto*, cooked ham, sliced very thinly
- *prosciutto crudo*, cured ham, the best being Parma ham

Cheeses

Though not known particularly for cheeses, Italy actually has a wide variety, among them:

- *Bel Paese*, a soft, subtly flavoured cream cheese usually sold in small foil-wrapped discs
- *dolcelatte*, a blue-veined full cream cheese

- *fior di latte*, a softish cheese rather like mozzarella
- *gorgonzola*, a blue/green veined cheese, sweeter and slightly less pungent than other blue cheeses
- *mascarpone*, almost too sweet to be a cheese; used in sweet or savoury dishes, usually sold in a tub
- *mozzarella*, nowadays sealed in plastic, but traditionally sold as lumps floating in its milky liquid; made from buffalo milk
- *parmigiano*, parmesan – usually a hard cheese for grating; freshly grated parmesan is infinitely tastier than the pre-grated/pre-packed variety from supermarkets
- *provola*, soft, mellow-tasting cheese, usually in globe shapes or sausage shapes
- *provolone*, like *provola*, but more *piccante* (sharper-tasting)
- *ricotta*, soft cheese often used in sweet dishes as well as savoury ones, usually sold in a tub

Sweets and cakes

Again, Italy has a surprising variety of sweets and cakes; here are some of the main ones, with their traditional uses:

- *amaretti*, bitter almond crunchy biscuits popular at Christmas time and with after-dinner coffee – readily available in 'classy' grocers and delicatessens in the UK
- *confetti*, literally 'confections' – the original *confetti*, sugared almonds traditionally thrown at Italian brides, packets of which are given to family and friends to mark weddings and christenings, often accompanied by a nice ornamental piece of china or glass (a *bomboniera*, sometimes available in the UK in Italian delicatessens)
- *panforte*, a sort of hard, chewy slab cake made with fruit, nuts and honey; popular at Christmas
- *panettone*, sponge cake, in various sizes and flavours, often taken as a present when visiting at Christmas
- *piccola pasticceria*, when visiting, it is traditional to buy a tray of these novelty little fancy cakes to present to one's hostess

Of course one should not forget ice-cream – *gelato/gelati* – another product which Italians have made their own.

Il vino

Italy is one of the world's greatest wine producers. Few people will not have heard of at least a couple of these better-known Italian wines:

- *Asti spumante*, a sparkling champagne-type wine from the Piemonte region of the north
- *Barolo*, a full-bodied red from the Piemonte region
- *Chianti*, the classic full-bodied red from Tuscany, often in traditional straw-covered bottles
- *Frascati*, fresh-tasting white wines from Lazio, south of Rome
- *Lambrusco*, from the Emilia Romagna region of south-central northern Italy, slightly sparkling, available as red or white
- *Marsala*, from Sicily, often considered a liqueur wine, especially *Marsala all'uovo* (with egg!)
- *Merlot del Veneto*, fruity red wines from the Veneto, the region around Venice
- *Montepulciano d'Abruzzo*, a dry, full red wine from the Abruzzo region south-east of Rome
- *Orvieto*, from the hilltop city of this name north-west of Rome
- *Soave*, refreshing but subtle white wines from Verona in north-eastern Italy
- *Trebbiano*, mostly dry whites from the Abruzzo region
- *Valpolicella*, the famous red wines from Lake Garda in the north

Among stronger drinks and spirits, we are all familiar with fortified wines like *Martini* and *Cinzano*, and *Prosecco*, a sparkling champagne-type wine. Italy also has an enormous variety of liqueurs: among them the bright-yellow *Strega* ('witch'!); the dark-brown *Amaretto* (often *di Saronno*), a bitter-sweet digestif (for after dinner) made with almonds and herbs; *anice*, aniseed liqueur often taken with or in strong, black coffee; *crema di cacao* and *crema di caffè*, which are as their names suggest; *limoncello* or *limoncino*, a refreshing but not too powerful lemon liqueur generally from the south, e.g. the region around Naples.

Recipes

Here are four lesser-known dishes which you might like to try; the recipes have been simplified a bit, and like any others, they vary from region to region and family to family.

Parmigiana

Delicious baked aubergines or courgettes, quantity as needed.

1. Slice the aubergines/courgettes thinly, fry in olive oil, drain and dry.
2. Make a plain tomato sauce as for pasta, but without meat.
3 Place aubergine/courgette slices in layers in an oven dish, alternating with sauce and sprinkled parmesan or slices of mozzarella.
4. Top with more sauce and sprinkled parmesan, and bake for 20 minutes at medium heat.

Pasta e lenticchie

Subtly tasty lentil and pasta stew. Once cooked, can easily be kept and reheated until all used.

250 grams of brown lentils (do not need soaking)
500 grams of *tubettini* (short-cut pasta tubes) or *pasta mischiata* (mixed broken pasta)

1. Boil lentils for 10 minutes, drain water, and replace with more hot water.
2. Add a teaspoon per person of olive oil, a little chopped garlic and parsley.
3. Simmer for about 15 minutes.
4. Cook pasta separately.
5. Drain pasta and add to lentils.
6. Add a little chilli pepper to taste if desired.

Gnocchi

Tiny potato dumplings in sauce of your choice; a pleasant alternative to usual pasta.

1 kilogram of floury potatoes
Flour as necessary

1. Boil and mash the potatoes.
2. Add flour into mashed potato in sufficient amount to get right consistency and texture…
3. Mould mix into little shell-shaped dumplings.
4. Boil like pasta straight away or after leaving for an hour or two.
5. Serve with tomato sauce or *pesto*.

Minestrone genovese

A tasty Genoese vegetable stew. Cook quantity desired and use whatever ingredients you have, e.g. green vegetables such as cabbage, courgettes, borlotti beans (kidney beans will do, tinned, or soak if necessary), potatoes, celery, all finely diced.

Just put all ingredients into a pot and simmer for an hour or two; best eaten tepid.

When cooked, you can add pasta if desired.

Promoting Italy abroad: the Italian image

As well as producing goods, Italian companies excel at promoting and marketing them. Benetton have raced their own Formula One cars, whilst their controversial advertising campaign has made them a fashion name known to teenagers everywhere. Fiat sponsorship of the Tour de France cycle race is such that Fiat and Lancia vehicles are used as course cars and to transport press and officials, ensuring that all the television coverage also exhibits their latest models to the world!

To sum up this unit: the inventiveness and artistry of Italians has given their country one of the world's most distinctive and 'familiar' images.

GLOSSARIO	GLOSSARY
la tecnologia	technology
l'industria	industry
la ditta	company, firm, business
l'auto(mobile), la macchina	car
guidare	to drive
(non) so guidare	I can (cannot) drive
la patente	driving licence
la strada	road
l'autostrada	motorway
la moto	motorbike
lo scooter	scooter
il treno	train
la stazione	station

viaggiare in treno	*to travel by train*
andare in/col treno	*to go by train*
l'aereo	*aeroplane*
la barca/la nave	*boat/ship*
il giornale	*newspaper*
la rivista	*magazine*
la radio	*radio*
la televisione/la tivù	*television/TV*
il programma	*programme*
il canale	*channel*
il cinema	*cinema*
il film	*film*
il regista	*film director*
l'attore/l'attrice	*actor/actress*
la moda	*fashion*
essere di/alla moda	*to be fashionable*
essere fuori moda	*to be out of fashion*
cucinare	*to cook*
mangiare	*to eat*
bere	*to drink*
il sapore	*flavour*
la ricetta	*recipe*
il piatto	*plate, dish (including in culinary sense)*

Taking it further

Suggested reading

Cinema

Italian Films, Robin Buss, Batsford 1989
All of the films mentioned are well worth seeing, even on video.

Italian fashion

The Who's Who of Italian Fashion, A. Mulassano and A. Castraldi, G. Spinelli 1979

There are lots of books on modern fashion designers – take your pick! – e.g. *10 Years of Dolce and Gabbana*, Isabella Rossellini, Abbeville Press Publishers 1996

The Italian motor industry

Ferrari, The World's Most Exotic Sportscar, Bill Reynolds, Magna 1993

Great Marques of Italy, Jonathan Wood, Viscount 1987/1989

Lancia Beta, Brian Long, Motor Racing Publications 1991

Italian industry and business

Business Italy, Kenna and Lacy, National Textbook Company 1990

Italian food

Aldo's Italian Food for Friends, Aldo Zilli, Metro Books 1998

Music and Menus from Italy (Great Italian Arias and Classic Italian Recipes), Antonio Carluccio, Pavilion Books 1996

Websites

There are so many websites available on virtually all of the subjects covered in this unit that it is not appropriate to recommend any in particular; instead simply make sure that when you do a web search you base it on a minimal number of words or names according to your interest. Try various search engines, and specify websites if you can cope with the Italian; if looking for film stars or directors, look out for the word *filmografia* (list of films made); however, American sites in particular offer mountains of information on 'international' Italian stars. For example, on any of the great names in fashion or films, you will find 'fan-club'-type pages with potted personal information, details of career, etc. Most of the companies mentioned in this unit also have British websites, e.g: **www.alfaromeo.co.uk**

Try: **www.italyguide.com**

08

present-day political structures and institutions

In this unit you will learn
- about political structures and institutions
- about the wide range of political parties
- about events that led to the demise of some major political parties

From monarchy to Republic

After unification in 1870 Italy was a monarchy with a king as head of state and Prime Minister as leader of the government. This system continued until June 1946 when, in a referendum, the Italian people had to choose between the retention of the status quo or the formation of a Republic. The majority chose the latter option, with 12.7 million in favour and 10.7 against.

The reasons for this radical change were perfectly understandable. Italy had just emerged from the Second World War morally dejected, and was faced with widespread destruction of homes, roads and industries. The people had endured twenty years of Fascist dictatorship that had been supported by the monarchy, and these facts were fresh in the minds of the voters.

Defeat for the monarchy was quickly followed by the expulsion from Italy of King Umberto and the royal family. A fresh chapter in the country's history was about to start. A new constitution was drawn up which clearly established the system and basis on which the Republic would evolve. This took effect from 1 January 1948 and the basic framework is the main substance of this unit.

The President

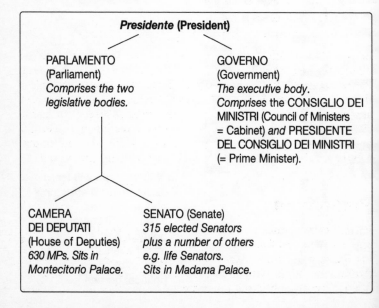

***Presidente* (President)**

PARLAMENTO
(Parliament)
*Comprises the two
legislative bodies.*

GOVERNO
(Government)
*The executive body.
Comprises* the CONSIGLIO DEI
MINISTRI (Council of Ministers
= Cabinet) *and* PRESIDENTE
DEL CONSIGLIO DEI MINISTRI
(= Prime Minister).

CAMERA
DEI DEPUTATI
(House of Deputies)
*630 MPs. Sits in
Montecitorio Palace.*

SENATO (Senate)
*315 elected Senators
plus a number of others
e.g. life Senators.
Sits in Madama Palace.*

The President is usually an experienced politician and is elected by the two Houses of Parliament and three elected delegates of each Regional Council (see p. 165) in a joint assembly. He or she must obtain a two-thirds majority. The current holder of this post is Carlo Azeglio Ciampi, now in his eighties, and he won 70 per cent of the vote in the first ballot in the May 1999 elections to become the tenth President of the Republic. Normally presidential elections go to more than one ballot. Ciampi was governor of the Bank of Italy for fourteen years until 1993 and acted as a caretaker Prime Minister during a political crisis in the early 1990s.

The President remains in office for seven years and can be re-elected for a further period. The nominees for this position must be at least 50 years of age. The President, as head of state, represents national unity but cannot directly influence government policy. Official duties and responsibilities include:

- ratification of international treaties
- declaration of a state of war once this question has been deliberated by the two Houses
- appointment of the Prime Minister and his Cabinet once these have been nominated and approved
- acceptance of the Prime Minister's resignation
- dissolution of the two Houses of Parliament or one of them, e.g. before general elections
- conferring titles on those nominated
- commuting prison sentences and granting pardons

Before taking office the President has to swear an oath of allegiance to the Republic and its Constitution before Parliament. The President enjoys parliamentary immunity unless there is a violation of the Constitution or an act of treason against the State. This simply means that, whereas 'ordinary citizens' could end up behind bars if they have infringed certain laws, the President escapes prosecution while still in office. Maybe serving as President is considered punishment enough!

Parliament

Parliament operates *un sistema bicamerale* (two House system) and is situated in Rome, the capital city. The Prime Minister and his government ministers sit in the House of Deputies. Parliament fulfils two main functions, one legislative and the other executive. It is the government of the day that is chiefly responsible for devising laws that are discussed separately by the two Houses. Once laws are approved and ratified the government has the executive power to implement them.

Another important function of Parliament is to give a vote of confidence to the government. A no-confidence vote usually means crisis time. The Prodi government fell in October 1998 precisely over a vote of confidence regarding the *Finanziaria* (Budget). Prime Minister Prodi failed by the narrowest of margins to gain Parliamentary approval and was left with no option but to resign. This highlighted an inherent problem of Italian coalition governments, where a minor party can play a major part in bringing a government down.

Election to the Houses of Parliament

The House of Deputies

Each House has its own distinct election rules. Election to the House of Deputies is by a very mixed system. A fairly recent electoral reform has meant that 75 per cent of its MPs win their seats via *un sistema maggioritario* (first-past-the-post majority system), while the remaining 25 per cent of the seats are allocated through *un sistema proporzionale* (proportional representation), which had always been the one used prior to the reform. Two ballots are held on the same day: one for the first past the post and the other for proportional representation.

The reform has created more problems than it has solved, as the system is now more fragmented, confusing and ambiguous than ever before. It means that the losers in the 'majority' race get a second chance when the votes are cast for the 'proportional' race and their survival is ensured despite their very small percentage of the vote.

For voting purposes Italy is divided up into a number of *collegi elettorali* (constituencies) and the number of seats allocated to each constituency is in proportion to its population. MPs must be at least 25 years of age and the voting age is 18. Up to around 1993 most Italians exercised their right to vote, with the average turnout in excess of 90 per cent. Since the electoral reform the number of voters has declined and in recent elections the turnout was as low as 65 per cent.

The Senate

Elections to the Senate are on a regional basis. Each region is entitled to one senator for every 200,000 inhabitants. No region can have fewer than seven senators, with the exception of Molise (two) and Valle d'Aosta (one), which are the two smallest regions. To stand for the Senate the minimum age is 40 and the voting age is 25. Former Presidents of the Republic become *senatori a vita* (life Senators). The President of the Republic can nominate a number more, the criteria for selection being that the nominees have distinguished themselves and brought credit to the State through their artistic, literary or scientific achievements.

The representatives of both Houses have a legislative duration of five years but their general elections are not held concurrently and not necessarily even in the same year. Each House functions independently. For instance, *un disegno di legge* (a bill) drawn up by the government is first discussed by the House of Deputies. After a majority vote here it then passes to the Senate for further examination and debate. This House may disapprove of certain parts of the bill and refer it back whence it came for possible amendments and yet more debate and discussion. The bill becomes a kind of political football, and the eventual passing of it depends on the staying power of the Italian government, which in most cases is not that long (more about this later).

Like the President, members of both Houses enjoy parliamentary immunity while still in office.

The government

The government operates on two fronts. It promotes and co-ordinates the internal affairs of the State but its role also extends to international matters. The composition of the government is set out in the Constitution. It must consist of *il Presidente del Consiglio,* i.e. the Prime Minister and the various ministers that hold Cabinet posts, for example the Minister for Education. Italian governments have nearly always been coalitions, which means that bargaining and compromise are essential ingredients for their survival. The Prime Minister is normally chosen from the majority party within the coalition and the other partners are kept happy by receiving their fair allocation of Cabinet posts.

When there is *una crisi di governo* (a government crisis), such as the one referred to earlier with the Prodi government, the President of the Republic has to initiate discussions and consultation with the leading politicians to try and solve it. There are two possible solutions: the President asks the same Prime Minister to try to form a new government or, should this offer be rejected, approaches someone else to assume the mantle. The Prime Minister's first task is to submit the list of ministers who will form the Cabinet. The President then proceeds with the formal acceptance of the resignation of the previous government and the nomination and swearing in of the new one. Within ten days the Prime Minister appears before a joint assembly of the two Houses to outline the government programme and ask for a vote of confidence.

The Prime Minister

The role of Prime Minister is never easy but within the Italian system the leader is constantly involved in a juggling act and needs to be well trained in this art to survive long. The Prime Minister is responsible for the overall policy and direction of the government and oversees the work of Cabinet Ministers. Italian governments since 1948 have often consisted of four or five different parties, each with its own strategies and ideological differences. The system inevitably provokes scepticism from the voters and the facts speak for themselves. There have been 59 governments – it could well be 60 before this sentence is complete! – in fewer than 60 years.

This does not smack of a stable political situation. Italian politics could be likened to a game of musical chairs, with one significant difference: nobody is eliminated from the game when the music stops. The participants just occupy different chairs. This was particularly true in the 1980s. Governments came and went in rapid succession yet the coalitions remained very much unchanged. The leading player was always the Christian Democrat Party which joined forces at varying stages along the route with the Social Democrats, the Liberals, the Republicans and the Socialist Party. The country therefore had a number of Centre or Centre-Left governments depending on their exact composition.

The average life span of an Italian government since the war is about ten months. However, a fall of government does not necessarily lead to *elezioni anticipate* (early general elections). The duration of a Parliament is five years and within this period the President of the Republic has the right to re-form a government without resorting to general elections. Many Italians are unhappy about this because they feel that democracy is being undermined as changes are implemented without their consent through the ballot box. Were the system otherwise, however, the politicians would spend most of their time campaigning and the inhabitants voting! Some of the shortest governments – in duration, not stature – have lasted as little as two weeks. Consequently there is no Appendix listing their achievements during their time in office; they probably didn't have time to *find* their office!

Political parties

The Christian Democrats (DC)

Political parties were forced underground during the Fascist period and they re-surfaced once democracy was restored at the end of the Second World War. The party that gained the widest support was the *Democrazia Cristiana* (Christian Democrat Party), originally named *Partito Popolare* and founded by a

Catholic priest, Don Luigi Sturzo. In the 1948 general election the party emerged with sufficient majority to form a government on its own – *un governo monocolore* – but it preferred to join in a coalition with other parties referred to earlier. This became the general pattern for the next 40 years or so.

As the name suggests, the DC has always had close links with the Church and it gained much of its support from its religious followers, particularly in the south, and from the middle classes. It was also the party to benefit most when women were enfranchised in 1946. Over the years much of its support was retained through a system of *clientelismo* (political patronage). As the leading and most influential party it greatly increased the number of jobs in the public sector. However, it was jobs in return for votes, a system that helped the party keep its opponents at bay.

The Communist Party (PCI)

The strongest opposition to the DC was provided by the *Partito Comunista Italiano* (Italian Communist Party), founded in January 1921 following a break with the Socialist Party. In the aftermath of the Second World War the Communists were strongly supported by the working classes, the poorer sections of society and also many leading 'intellectuals'. The party was part of the government for a short time during this period. However, it soon joined the ranks of the opposition.

The party after the war had very close ties with the Soviet Union and this represented a threat to Western democracy. Italy joined Nato and the Council of Europe in 1949 and the United Nations in 1955, yet the PCI supported the 'other side', i.e. the Eastern Bloc countries. The Communists were subsequently kept out of power by the fact that the DC was able to gain the support of minority groups to form successive governments.

Under the leadership of Enrico Berlinguer, a most respected figure in Italian politics, the Communists greatly increased their percentage of the vote and they became the biggest Communist Party in western Europe. The party gradually distanced itself from the Soviet Union. Events such as the Russian invasion of Hungary in 1956 displeased many party activists and started off the process of Italian alienation from Soviet ideology.

The Socialist Party (PSI)

The *Partito Socialista Italiano* (Italian Socialist Party) was the third party of great significance in post-war Italy. It was founded in 1893 and in the course of its development groups split away and formed other parties, e.g. the Social Democrat Party in 1947 led by Giuseppe Saragat. The PSI was very successful in the elections to the Constituent Assembly in 1946, winning 20.7 per cent of the vote. Thereafter there were peaks and troughs but the summit of the party's achievement was Bettino Craxi's appointment as Prime Minister in 1983 and the party's 11.4 per cent share of the vote in the general election, confirming it as the third party behind the DC and the PCI.

The *Lega Nord*

This right-wing party led by Umberto Bossi was formed in 1989 from the joint forces of northern regional parties in Veneto, Liguria, Piemonte and Lombardia. The aspirations of the party are to create an independent northern Italy. The Lega Nord consider the south a burden to the rich and prosperous north; they do not want to see hard-earned money fall into the hands of unscrupulous, corrupt individuals who, according to them, occupy the southern half of the country. The 1992 general election saw the party make considerable gains, obtaining 55 seats in the House of Deputies and 25 in the Senate. It obviously reaped the benefit of the political scandals that beset the country at the time, and became the fourth most important party. However, its stronghold is in the north and the party's beliefs, policies and somewhat racist tendencies are unlikely to win them much support in central and southern Italy.

Social turmoil and its political consequences

The PCI started to increase its share of the vote from the 1963 general elections onwards. Prices were rising, there was a shortage of housing and public services were inadequate. The rise in popularity was also due to the efficient way in which communist administrations ran the regions and local authorities in central Italy – Emilia-Romagna, Tuscany and Umbria, the so-called 'red belt' area.

161
present-day political
structures and institutions
08

The year 1968 was significant for *le contestazioni studentesche* (student protests). The students found allies in the workers and a period of great social unrest ensued. The autumn of 1969 became known as *autunno caldo* (hot autumn), as the country became the hotbed of wildcat strikes. Workers wanted an improved wage structure and better working conditions. The country on occasions was almost brought to its knees. This period of turmoil resulted in further substantial gains for the PCI – 26.9 per cent of the vote.

The neo-Fascist party *il Movimento Sociale Italiano* (MSI), which had hitherto been very much on the periphery, also made considerable gains. It was during this period that terrorism reared its ugly head and 14 people were killed following the bombing of a Milan bank. Bombs planted by either extreme Fascist or Communist groups exploded in stations and squares. It was the time of the petrol crisis and car use was restricted. The 1970s became known as the *anni di piombo* (literally, 'years of lead' but meaning 'era of terrorist outrages'). The worst tragedy took place at Bologna railway station on 2 August 1980, when a bomb killed 80 people.

During this critical period the leader of the PCI, Enrico Berlinguer, put forward a proposal that marked a shift in the ideological position of his party. It was 1973 and his idea was *un compromesso storico* (an historic compromise), which would require all the democratic parties to join forces as a symbol of national unity to resolve the country's social, economic and civil crises. A leading figure in the DC, Aldo Moro, a left-winger in the rather conservative party, was attracted by this idea.

The Communists benefited enormously as a result of this proposal and their percentage of the vote reached the giddy heights of 34.4 in the 1976 general election, just short of the DC's 38.7 per cent. However, in 1978 a tragic event brought an end to this remarkable, if brief, period in Italian politics – the kidnapping (18 March) and eventual murder (two months later) of Aldo Moro by *le Brigate rosse* (Red Brigades), an extreme left-wing terrorist organization. Obviously some people didn't take kindly to the idea of a 'merger' of the PCI with the DC.

Thus in 1979 the PCI decided to withdraw its support from the government and another general election duly followed. Many Communist supporters had become disenchanted by the historic compromise and this was reflected in a drop in the party's share of the vote to 30.4 per cent, its first decline in more than 30 years. The Communists moreover lost credibility after the Soviet invasion of Afghanistan, even though Berlinguer had already started the process of distancing the party from Moscow and he strongly supported the Solidarity movement in Poland.

Economic revival

In the 1980s Italy risked being excluded from European monetary union because of its fragile, unstable democracy and because the public debt was spiralling. Italy was one of the founder members of the European Community, established in 1957, and looked to Europe to provide a stabilizing influence. The criteria to be part of monetary union were low inflation and a healthy balance of payments. Italy fell way short of these criteria but a period of austerity and the emergence of entrepreneurs in the fashion industry and private television sparked an economic revival.

Significant events that sparked off radical political changes

1989 was the year the Berlin Wall finally came down. It signalled not only the end of the Cold War but also of the PCI in Italy, which changed its name to the Democratic Party of the Left.

1992 heralded the start of a major judicial inquiry called *Mani pulite* (literally, 'clean hands'). Its aim was to investigate bribery and corruption within the political system, especially in the PSI and DC. Italians had always known that corruption was rife in the system. The parties in question, however, were the main

opposition to the PCI. An earlier investigation could have opened the door to the Communists and there was still a fear inside and outside Italy that a Communist government would affect the European balance. The fall of the Berlin Wall ended this threat.

The *Mani pulite* affair revolved around contracts for State public works. It is alleged that many politicians involved in assigning the contracts had their palms greased to the tune of 5 to 10 per cent of the stake. The first discoveries were made in Milan, which became widely known as *Tangentopoli* or Bribesville. A pertinent reference in *The New Italians* by Charles Richards explains that because so many politicians were seen in Milan jail the term VIP assumed a whole new meaning; *visto in prigione* (seen in prison).

Italians were outraged and became deeply disillusioned with politics and this affair brought the most radical changes to the Italian political system. The DC and the PSI came to the end of their political life. Yet another period of instability followed as makeshift governments (1992/1993) and the President, Oscar Luigi Scalfaro, endeavoured to keep the country moving.

In 1994 Silvio Berlusconi burst on the scene as leader and financier of yet another new party called *Forza Italia*, a football slogan meaning 'Go/Come on Italy'. He became Prime Minister of a government that lacked the necessary experience in the political arena but he did survive about eight months.

Devolution of power

Although the Government and Parliament have overall control of the nation's affairs, power is devolved down through the 20 regions, 105 provinces and 8,100 local boroughs. The Constitution provided for this devolution of power but only Sicily, Sardinia, Valle d'Aosta, and Trentino-Alto Adige were granted immediate independence on 26 February 1948 through *uno statuto speciale* (a special statute). Friuli-Venezia Giulia had to wait until January 1963 for similar status after the settlement of the territorial claim to Trieste. These regions were accorded special status because in Sicily and Sardinia there were separatist tendencies and, in the other three, linguistic minorities. The remaining regions had to wait until 7 June 1970 for their autonomy under *uno statuto ordinario* (an ordinary statute).

Regional feelings have always been very strong in Italy. Most of the present regions had been independent states pre-unification. After unification, therefore, it was understandable that the government wanted to maintain a highly centralized structure. This attitude prevailed after the end of the Second World War because separatist movements threatened to create internal divisions. The majority party, the DC, wanted to hold on to its power. The granting of autonomy to all regions would almost inevitably have led to the PCI, which was in the ascendancy in the 1960s, gaining control over several regions. The DC also argued that the regions would create another level of bureaucracy and feared they would be constantly at odds with the central government. However, in the 1960s the power of the DC started to wane and it needed the support of the Church and the PSI to keep the Communists at bay. The PSI offered its support on condition that the remaining fifteen regions were established. Compromise yet again!

Organization of the regions, provinces and local boroughs

Each *regione* (region) has a president, a regional council that has the legislative power and the *Giunta*, which is the executive body. The regions take responsibility for:

- legislation and planning – within central government guidelines
- overseeing the economic activities of the agricultural, craft and tourism sectors
- building roads and hospitals

The *provincia* (province) has a president as its head and two governing bodies: the provincial council, which has deliberative functions, and the *Giunta*, with executive powers. Areas of control include public works, health, social care, education and training.

A province is distinguished by its postcode and (until recently) by its car number plates. New cars no longer indicate the province of origin.

The *comune* (local borough) has a mayor who is now elected directly by the people and not by the council, as in the past. The council is the deliberative body and there is also the *Giunta*, which consists of the *assessori*, who are in charge of the various departments in the town hall. The council's responsibilities cover the police, local transport, nursery education, public health, social assistance, refuse collection, environment, tourism, registry of births and deaths.

The *comune* is the basic unit of local government and therefore much closer to the local inhabitants. It recognizes the basic needs of the community and does its best to accommodate them. Central government is often seen as a remote body.

Church and State

The 1929 Lateran Pacts (see also Unit 1) guaranteed the Catholic Church its independent Vatican State and recognized its sovereignty. The 1948 Constitution reaffirmed this position. The Church worked in close liaison with the DC until the 1960s, when the links became more tenuous. Pope Pius XII considered it to be the party of the Catholics and many party members came from Catholic Associations. It proved difficult for successive Popes not to become embroiled in certain 'political' developments. When, for example, the PCI looked like becoming the leading political force in the 1970s, Pope Paul VI was quick to point out the inherent dangers of Communism and urged people not to vote for them.

Obviously the Church did not favour the laws on divorce and abortion, as they ran counter to doctrine (see pp. 225–6). There was a referendum on both these laws in 1974 and 1981 respectively but the majority vote was in favour of their retention. This was a clear indication of both a loss of support for the Church and a change of mood and direction in society.

The DC's stance over these issues was political rather than religious, illustrating that the Church and its 'former party' had gone their separate ways.

The State has reacted to changes in society by revising parts of the Lateran Pacts. The revision process started in 1966 but 18 years elapsed before everything was finalized and signed by the socialist Prime Minister Craxi. One significant change was that Catholicism was no longer regarded as the sole religion of the State. The State realized that it had to recognize and respect the religions of other ethnic minorities living in Italy. Consequently, parents now have the right to choose whether their children do religious studies at school, a subject that previously was compulsory and taught by a Catholic priest.

What's in a name?

> Parties come
> Parties go
> There have always been many
> Now there are more!

Since the end of the 1980s events such as the fall of the Berlin Wall and *Mani pulite* (p. 163) have resulted in the biggest transformation of party names and proliferation of other 'factions' in the history of Italian politics. For details refer to 'Taking it further', p. 171.

Italy has always had this tradition of warring factions within a party splitting off and forming other parties. The *Verdi* (Green Party) is yet another case in point. They came on the scene in 1985, gained in popularity after the Chernobyl nuclear reactor incident in 1987 but then split into two groups, the *Verdi del sole* and *Verdi arcobaleno* (*arcobaleno* = rainbow). Obviously this group didn't find its pot of gold because the two factions reunited in 1991.

Such an occurrence does not normally send the electorate into paroxysms of uncontrolled rage, as Italians are used to political instability. Discord within any party is normal and to a certain degree healthy. However, discord that breeds more parties is not going to solve the nation's problems. Ask the ordinary citizen to explain the differences between the various socialist parties that now exist and they would be hard put to provide an answer. This tendency towards division is perhaps a reflection of the

Italian character: very parochial with no strong feelings for the State as such. In a 1998 survey only about 10 per cent of the population favoured a system that had such a proliferation of political parties.

D'Alema to Berlusconi

Massimo D'Alema succeeded Prodi as Prime Minister in October 1998. He was the first leader of an ex-communist party to attain this high office. His Cabinet consisted of Ministers representing ten different parties, an illustration of how complicated the system had become. He appointed six women to his Cabinet, a record number to hold such high office. A lot of skill and 'wheeling and dealing' would be required to prevent further immediate government crises which, over the years, have meant essential reforms being delayed or shelved, as new governments often have different priorities. A radical reform to the education system had been on the political agenda for approximately thirty years and as D'Alema retained the same Education Minister from the preceding government there seemed every chance that this essential reform would finally go ahead. Another priority on D'Alema's agenda was further electoral reform so that the system became 100 per cent *maggioritario*. Such a reform would certainly not meet with the approval of the 'fringe' parties as it could lead to their demise, but it was probably the only solution to continuing political instability.

D'Alema's reign came to an end in April 2000 when he resigned after his centre-right opponents made significant gains in local elections. Giuliano D'Amato acted as 'caretaker' Prime Minister until the general election on 13 May 2001, the outcome of which saw the return to power of Silvio Berlusconi, who had gained a rather brief experience of the post in 1994. Berlusconi is not only Italy's wealthiest man but also one of the richest in the world. He is the head of Italy's biggest media empire – he owns and controls the three largest private television channels, *Italia 1*, *Rete 4* and *Canale 5* – so it is fair to say that he was not lacking in support in the run-up to the elections. He also has a number of other business interests that include the ownership of one of Italy's leading football clubs, AC Milan. This conflict of interest remains, as a government majority in Parliament allowed him to keep his company empire but he cannot personally lead it. Instead he has to employ managers, who will undoubtedly remain close supporters.

A big contributor to Berlusconi's election victory was Sicily, which returned all 61 seats to Berlusconi's own right-wing party *Forza Italia*, which subsequently joined forces with the neo-Fascist *Alleanza Nazionale* 'National Alliance' and the separatist *Lega Nord*, to form the biggest right-wing Italian government since the end of the Second World War. Berlusconi, rather unusually, even held two posts concurrently at one stage – those of Prime Minister and Foreign Minister. He later relinquished the latter post.

Berlusconi's honeymoon period did not last long. Political promises of tax cuts, pension reforms and the creation of one million jobs are easier to make than fulfil. It was not long before we witnessed strong opposition to his ultra-conservative policies. At the end of March 2002, a leading trade union movement organized one of the biggest demonstrations in the history of post-war Italy, attended by over two million people. The same trade union called a general strike for 18 October to protest against Berlusconi's economic policies and labour reform.

Berlusconi faced another threat: the attempt to try him on corruption charges. However, he seems to have a certain contempt for those aspects of Italian law that he regards as obstacles to his drive for economic and political power, and he proceeded to introduce legislation that would scupper any attempts to try him on corruption charges. On 16 September 2002 around 200,000 demonstrated in Rome against such legal reforms. Nanni Moretti, the well-known Italian film director, is reported to have said, 'The Italians who voted for Berlusconi were following a dream – and they woke up in a nightmare.'

GLOSSARIO	GLOSSARY
la monarchia	monarchy
il governo	government
lo Stato	State
il sistema politico	political system
la Repubblica	Republic
i partiti politici	political parties
i partiti di destra	right-wing parties
i partiti di sinistra	left-wing parties
gli elettori	voters
andare alle urne	to go to the polls
votare	to vote

il voto	vote
il voto di fiducia	vote of confidence
il voto di sfiducia	vote of no confidence
la Costituzione	Constitution
il Parlamento	Parliament
il ministro	Minister
il primo ministro	Prime Minister
il presidente	President
il deputato	MP
la Camera dei Deputati	House of Deputies
il Senato	Senate
la Magistratura	Magistracy
il seggio	(parliamentary) seat
la prima votazione	the first ballot
il potere legislativo	legislative power
il potere esecutivo	executive power
dimettersi	to resign
la coalizione	coalition
indire le elezioni	to hold elections
le elezioni generali	general election
la percentuale	percentage
l'immunità parlamentare	parliamentary immunity
il compromesso	compromise
la democrazia	democracy
la chiesa cattolica	the Catholic Church
la scissione	splitting up (of a political party)
la caduta del muro di Berlino	the fall of the Berlin Wall
la provincia	province
il comune	local borough
i patti lateranensi	Lateran Pacts
l'inchiesta	investigation, inquiry
la tangente	bribe
la regione	region

Taking it futher

Suggested reading

Italy, Russell King, Harper and Row Publishers 1987

Italian Labyrinth, John Haycraft, Penguin 1987

The New Italians, Charles Richards, Martin Joseph 1994

Modern Italy 1871–1995 (Second Edition), Martin Clark, Longman 1984

Modern Italy: Representation and Reform, Paul Furlong, Routledge 1994

Contemporary Italy (Second Edition), Donald Sassoon, Addison Wesley 1997

A History of Contemporary Italy, Paul Ginsborg, Penguin 1990

L'Italia del tempo presente, Paul Ginsborg, Einaudi 1998

I partiti italiani, Piero Ignazi, il Mulino, Bologna 1997

Websites

www.initaly.com (for information on regions plus other aspects)

www.partiti.net/ (for some useful information on Italian politics)
www.parlamento.it

Political parties

List of old traditional parties that have changed their name since 1990

The **MSI** has been replaced by **Alleanza Nazionale** (AN) (National Alliance).

The **PCI** has split into three groups: **Democratici della sinistra** (DS) (Democratic party of the left), **Comunisti italiani** (CI) (Italian communists) and **Rifondazione comunista** (RC) (equivalent to 'hard left' Communist party).

The **DC** has split into various factions – **Partito popolare italiano** (PPI) (Italian popular party), **Centro cristiano democratico** (CCD) (Centre Christian democrat party), **Cristiani democratici uniti** (CDU) (United Christian democrats), **Unione per la difesa della Repubblica** (UDR) (Union for the defence of the Republic).

The historic **PSI** has split into more segments than a standard orange: **Progressisti**, **Laburisti**, **Rinascita socialista**, **Federazione liberalsocialista**, to name but a few!

Berlusconi's party **Forza Italia** is a right-wing party that together with the **Alleanza Nazionale** and **Lega Nord** formed the government after the elections in May 2001. These parties are often referred to as **il Polo** in the media and the term used for the opposition parties is **l'Ulivo**.

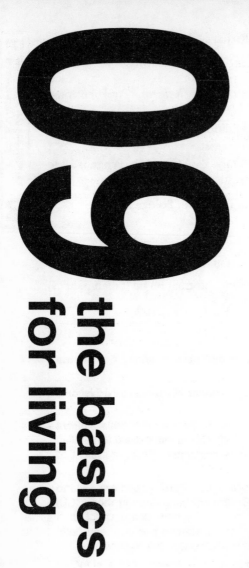

09 the basics for living

In this unit you will learn
- about recent developments in education and proposals for further reform
- about the restructuring of the health service
- about various modes of transport

Education

The Italian education system is about to undergo its most radical reform for over 80 years. The reform was proposed under D'Alema's government but was shelved when Berlusconi came to power. It has since been resurrected and revamped by Letizia Moratti, the Education Minister, and was approved by the Senate (see p. 157) in March 2003. A major overhaul of the system has long been overdue given that most of the present structure dates back to 1923, when Giovanni Gentile was Minister for Education. Since that time apparently there have been 34 attempts at major reform! Below is an outline summary of the system largely in operation up to the end of the 2003 school year and what it will be like once all the proposed changes are implemented, which could be some light years away yet, given the lack of financial resources!

System up to 2002/3	New system
SCUOLA MATERNA Nursery school, from 3 to 6. Attendance not obligatory	**SCUOLA D'INFANZIA** Nursery school, from $2^{1}/_{2}$–3 to 5–6. Attendance will become obligatory between $5^{1}/_{2}$ and 6
SCUOLA ELEMENTARE Elementary school, from 6 to 11.	**PRIMO CICLO** – 8 years, from $5^{1}/_{2}$–6 to $13^{1}/_{2}$–14. Incorporates former **Scuola elementare** and **Scuola media inferiore** and will now be called **Scuola primaria** and **Scuola secondaria di primo grado**
SCUOLA MEDIA INFERIORE Lower secondary school, from 11 to 14.	
SCUOLA SUPERIORE from $13^{1}/_{2}$–14 to $17^{1}/_{2}$–18. Upper secondary school, from 14 to 19.	**SECONDO CICLO** – 4 years, split into two distinct sections: 1. **Liceo** 2. **Istruzione professionale**

Until fairly recently obligatory schooling was for eight years, up to the end of the lower secondary school. However, a law passed in January 1999 raised the school leaving age to 15 and this came into force in September 1999. This was done to bring Italy more into line with what happens in other European countries. The vast majority of Italian schools are public, i.e. State-run. Let's briefly look at the system prior to the proposed Moratti reform.

Elementary school (6–11) *scuola elementare*

Compulsory education starts here at the age of six. The aims of primary education are to provide a basic grounding in maths, reading, writing, history, geography, science, etc. and inculcate the essential skills of social interaction and integration. A foreign language, usually English or French, is introduced from age eight or nine.

Since 1990 three teachers have been allocated to every one class, each with a responsibility for a particular module, e.g. maths and science. Prior to that the same teacher taught a whole range of subjects within a given class.

Many elementary schools operate two different timetables. Parents can choose between the traditional model of approximately five hours a day, 8 a.m. to 1 p.m. Monday to Saturday, or the *tempo prolungato* (extended/full-time model), about 40 hours per week, from 8 a.m. to 1 p.m. and 2 p.m. to 5 p.m. (starting and finishing times can vary slightly between schools). The latter option suits those families where both parents have full-time jobs.

Pupils' progress is carefully monitored and parents are kept informed via written reports. The exam at the end of the five-year cycle, *licenza elementare*, consists of written tests in maths and Italian and oral tests in the remaining subjects. Assessment of performance is based on a written comment that ranges from *non sufficiente* (fail) to *ottimo* (very good/excellent). Elementary schools generally provide children with a good basic education.

Lower secondary school (11–14) *scuola media inferiore*

Completion of this three-year cycle marks the end of *la scuola dell'obbligo* (compulsory education). However, the vast majority of students carry on, as the *licenza media* (school leaving certificate) is not considered an adequate qualification for immediate employment.

At the *scuola media* all subjects are studied in more depth but are assessed in the same way as in the primary sector – written comments on a *scheda personale* (personal record-card). A law passed in August 1977 abolished the system of allocating marks out of ten. Another law passed in February 1979 stipulated that there must be a specialist teacher for each subject. The same law also underlined the need for closer co-operation between individual teachers to provide interdisciplinary activities as a way of preparing pupils for life and careers.

The passport to the next tier of education is the *licenza media diploma*, which consists of three written tests in maths, Italian and a foreign language and a multidisciplinary oral test. Assessment is based on comments as for the *licenza elementare*.

The Ministry of Education in Rome determines the content of the primary and secondary school curriculum. Some variations to the programme are permitted in the autonomous regions that have special status, e.g. Friuli-Venezia Giulia.

Non-compulsory education

This could start as early as a few months old at the *asilo nido* (crèche) and continue from age three to six at the *scuola materna* (nursery school). The popularity of these schools has grown as the number of working mothers has increased. At this early stage activities include sleep, games and sing-songs, not necessarily in that order.

The *scuole superiori* (upper secondary schools) come into the non-compulsory category although this changed to a limited extent once the school leaving age was raised to 15 in 1999. The range of schools is enormous and the problem for parents and students is making the right choice. The teachers in the *scuola media* do offer some guidance but very often children follow in the footsteps of their parents. Once a course has been chosen it is difficult to change in midstream as the various schools have their own particular study programmes ranging from three to five years in duration. The main schools are:

- *Istituti professionali* (vocational schools) – three to five years
- *Istituto magistrale* (trains primary-school teachers) – four years. There is also the *scuola magistrale* (for nursery-school teachers) – three years

- *Istituti commerciali/tecnici* (business/technical schools)
- *licei* (comparable to 'grammar schools'), of which there are four types: *classico/scientifico/linguistico/artistico* – five years

The *istituti professionali* prepare students for employment in the sector relevant to their course of study, e.g. Hotel and Catering. The five-year courses tend to be very academic and consequently students usually go on to university provided they attain the required pass mark (minimum of 60 out of 100) in the *esame di Stato* (final examination). Those on three- or four-year courses can only qualify for university admission if they undertake *un corso integrativo* (a top-up course) to complete the five-year programme.

The school timetable can be anything from 35 hours or more per week, mainly mornings from Monday to Saturday. Students are kept on their toes with regular *interrogazioni* (oral tests) in their chosen subjects. Up until 1995 there were *esami di riparazione* (resits) in September in the failed subjects – failure meaning a mark of less than 6 out of 10 – but these have been abolished in favour of *corsi di recupero* (remedial classes). Students are given a year to recover the lost ground. If they don't, they could end up with a new set of classmates the following year.

The *esame di Stato*

This is the State exam taken after five years study in the *scuola superiore*. A recent change to this exam came into effect at the start of the 1998 school year and it now means that students have three written tests and one oral (previously there were two written and two oral tests). One of the written tests is an essay in Italian that all students have to do irrespective of the secondary school they attend. The other written exams will depend on the area of study. The oral starts with a discussion of a subject chosen by the student and then moves on to a discussion of other subjects studied in the final year. The oral examiners are now chosen from within the school whereas in the past there was an external panel of examiners. Out of the maximum total of 100, 45 marks are allocated to the written tests, 35 to the oral and the remaining 20 per cent is for *credito formativo* (continuous assessment), based on the final three years' work.

The Moratti reform

The table on p. 173 gives only a brief outline of the 'new' school system. The following details will put a bit more flesh on these bare bones:

- parents will have the option to send their children to the *scuola primaria* at $5^1/_2$ but the obligatory starting age remains unchanged at 6 years of age
- the first *esame di Stato* (State exam) will be at the end of the *primo ciclo* and not at the end of the the *scuola elementare* as in the past
- all students will be expected to study two foreign languages, the first of which will be introduced at the start of the *primo ciclo*. Children will also get their first taste of IT at the outset of the *scuola primaria*; a second foreign language will be introduced in the *scuola secondaria di primo grado*
- the *secondo ciclo* will comprise two parallel tracks: the more traditional *liceo* (there will be a choice of eight different types) and the more practical work-oriented *istruzione e formazione professionale*; as the new system has been designed to be more flexible it should not be a problem if students decide to switch tracks at some stage
- the *secondo ciclo* will last four years but those who wish to go on to university will do a further year of preparation and specialization before taking the *esame di Stato*
- the *primo ciclo* and *secondo ciclo* will consist mainly of *bienni* (periods of two years); at the end of a *biennio*, if a student's progress is unsatisfactory, then that student can be asked to repeat the year
- anyone wishing to enter the teaching profession will have to have a university degree and be teacher-trained

Universities

In December 2002 the Chancellors of Italy's 77 universities took the unprecedented step of resigning en masse to protest against cuts in the 2003 budget. The response from the treasury was immediate. Levels of funding were restored to those in the 2002 budget and the resignations were withdrawn. The Chancellors' reaction was understandable given that most institutions are grossly overcrowded and very expensive to run. Since job opportunities are scarce many students who meet the entry requirements use the university as a temporary parking-place.

The fact that only a third of enrolled students complete their course is a clear indication that there is something radically amiss. Overcrowding means that students are not able to attend all lectures even if they want to and personal contact with many lecturers is almost impossible. One of Rome's universities, La Sapienza, had more than 170,000 students enrolled in 1997. Some universities now impose *il numero chiuso* (limit) on enrolments to certain faculties, e.g. Faculty of Medicine.

University grants are a rarity and students rely heavily on their family for financial support. In fact most students commute between home and the nearest university as a way of reducing costs. The standard four-year degree course – five for Engineering and six for Medicine – has frequently been extended by up to four years by those students who postponed or repeated exams. In fact only about 9 per cent of students complete their course 'on time'. On average Italians are 28 when they graduate, four years later compared with the rest of Europe. A reform of the university system was first approved by the Italian government in 2000 and Moratti's more recent reform is no different. The four-year degree will be abolished and replaced by a three-year one, after which it will be possible to do a further two-year specialization course. One of the aims of the reform is to reduce the drop-out rate. Another is to make the degree more suitable for the world of work. Students who followed the *istruzione e formazione professionale* track at school can go on to university and do a more advanced two-year training course.

The teaching profession

Italian teachers are generally poorly paid and often do a second job to achieve a reasonable standard of living. A teacher of Design, for example, might have his or her own private studio. Directors of Education recognize and accept this situation which, in their opinion, provides a link between the school and the outside world.

The majority of Italian teachers, except for those in the nursery and primary sector, have received no specific training for the profession. Secondary-school teachers, after graduating from university, sat a *concorso* (competitive exam) which was a test of knowledge not of aptitude to teach. This exam was offered rather infrequently in the 1990s because of the surplus of teachers due to falling rolls. Consequently, many prospective candidates, who often paid out of their own pocket to attend courses, were denied the opportunity of a permanent teaching post and had to resign themselves to *fare il/la supplente* (doing supply teaching).

Private education

Private education is more prevalent at nursery level than in elementary and secondary schools. According to government statistics for 1995/96, 67 per cent of children attended a State-run nursery school and 33 per cent a private one. The main advantage of the private nursery schools is that they offer a more flexible system. They have an extended school day and remain open more days a year.

At the upper secondary-school level the *liceo linguistico* is usually privately run, although now it is also possible to attend a State-run *liceo linguistico*, but the Ministry of Education controls the curriculum, as in all private schools. Students choose the *liceo linguistico* because there is more choice and a greater concentration on languages than in State schools.

Other reasons why parents opt for the private sector: most schools are Catholic; students get more individual attention; and they provide a better chance for those who struggle in the State school system and need to recover lost ground.

GLOSSARIO GLOSSARY	
il sistema scolastico	*school system*
la riforma	*reform*
il Ministro della Pubblica Istruzione	*Minister for Education*
la materia	*(school) subject*
il/la maestro/a	*primary-school teacher*
il/la professore/ssa	*secondary-school teacher*
insegnare	*to teach*
l'orario	*timetable*
l'alunno	*pupil*
lo studente	*student*
la prova scritta/orale	*written/oral test*
il programma (di studi)	*curriculum*
l'aula	*classroom*
frequentare	*to attend*
la lezione	*lesson*

la lezione universitaria	lecture
il tema	essay
protestare	to protest
iscriversi all'università	to enrol at university
dare un esame	to sit an exam
passare/superare un esame	to pass an exam

Health

Diagnosis of the problems

On 20 July 1996 an Italian national newspaper, *Corriere della Sera*, reported some of the comments made in a reputable English journal (*The Lancet*) about the state of the Italian health system. These were some of the findings:

- insufficient money for research and in some cases the money was used badly
- the system was very expensive
- the service was better in the north than in the south
- too many doctors, many of whom were often out of touch with developments in their field (at the time there were 70,000 unemployed graduates in Medicine)

Italy once held the record in Europe for the number of doctors per capita of the population. Some years ago most university graduates wanted to become either doctors or lawyers. This matter was addressed in 1986, when a limit on admissions to medical faculties was imposed.

In the 1970s and 1980s the health system was being run as if money were no object. The country was not lacking in well-equipped hospitals, it was mainly a question of managing the resources efficiently and ensuring that public money was not being squandered. There was a need for greater accountability. The time was ripe for the Ministry responsible, *il Ministero della Sanità*, to re-examine the patient in its care. This it proceeded to do.

System undergoes major surgery

The process of reorganization and restructuring of the Health Service started with the 1992 reform. Perhaps one of the most important aspects of this reform was that the 300 *Unità*

Sanitarie Locali (Local Health Authorities) were to be given more autonomy, business status and their managers greater responsibility for running them cost-effectively. Thus, all operations and treatments had to be properly costed. The effects of this 'new' approach are already being seen. The huge deficit that had accumulated in the preceding years is now beginning to fall. There was a drop in the number of family doctors by 10.5 per cent between 1991 and 1996. The thrust of the remainder of the reform was as follows:

- the need to consider alternative ways of treating the sick other than admission to hospital
- develop and strengthen other medical structures such as home help and care for the elderly and handicapped, thereby reducing the pressure on hospital beds
- National and Private Health Systems should operate alongside each other
- people continue to contribute to the National Health System but also, where possible, take out private health insurance
- increase the number of day hospitals and provide them with more facilities

More investment in home help and care in the community will be essential in the long term. As in other countries, Italy has an ageing population. In 2020 it is predicted that one quarter of the population will be *anziani* (elderly). At present life expectancy is approaching 77 for men and 83 for women. It is inevitable that the health system will be put under increasing strain. According to government statistics, 2,600,000 inhabitants have some form of disability and more than 75 per cent of these people are over 60 years of age. Almost a million are practically confined to their own home. There are *ospizi* (homes for the elderly) but not

as many as in some European countries. Italian families are generally close-knit and prefer to look after their elderly relatives at home if possible.

In recent years there has been a considerable increase in *volontariato* (voluntary help). Those who assist on hospital wards have to do some basic first-aid training and are only allowed to do menial tasks. However, their contribution is invaluable. A lot of the work to help drug addicts, for example, is done by voluntary organizations.

How is the national health system financed?

All public employees pay approximately 10 per cent of their earnings into INPS (*Istituto Nazionale Previdenza Sociale*, or Social Security system). The same applies to the self-employed but many also pay into a private health scheme as well. The national health contributions provide free medical care. The charge for *il ticket* (fixed charge for prescribed medicines) was abolished by the Health Minister in 2000 but it has since been re-introduced. In fact Lombardy became the eleventh region to re-introduce it in December 2002. Senior citizens and the long-term handicapped are required to pay a nominal charge. If all regions re-introduced these prescription charges it would save the public coffers 2.1 billion euro a year. The budget for medicines now amounts to approximately 13 per cent of the total health budget.

Future prognosis

Despite the lack of funding for medical research, what is available is being put to good use. A lot of high-quality and widely acclaimed research has been done on Aids. The following are also highly regarded: the National Institute for Cancer Research in Milan, the Centre for Rare Diseases in Bergamo, the European Oncology Institute in Milan and the Institute for Scientific Research in Pisa, which is developing the artificial heart.

The medical advances in Italy and elsewhere and the discovery of new and better drugs will undoubtedly increase the overall cost of health care. Italy, however, has taken some positive steps to restructure its Health System and even if the initial diagnosis was not good the prognosis seems much better.

GLOSSARIO	GLOSSARY
il Servizio Sanitario Nazionale	National Health Service
la ricerca	research
il medico	doctor
il medico della mutua	National Health Service doctor
il laureato	graduate
disoccupato	unemployed
l'ospedale	hospital
ristrutturare	to restructure
l'autonomia	autonomy
un calo	a drop
curare	to treat
la cura	treatment
i malati	the sick
gli handicappati	the handicapped
gli invalidi	the disabled
l'assicurazione	insurance
l'invecchiamento	ageing
la speranza (media) di vita	life expectancy
il tossicodipendente	drug addict
la percentuale	percentage
finanziare	to finance

Housing

Home ownership

At present about 75 per cent of Italians own their own home. This is about 10 per cent more than in 1984. The percentage of home ownership is higher outside the major cities, cost being the determining factor. For most Italian families a home is for life, which means that they seldom move to a bigger or more expensive property. They prefer to spend money on improving, modernizing or restoring their existing one. Some families living in flats invest their money in *una seconda casa* (a second home) by the sea, in the mountains or countryside.

Palazzi (apartment blocks) in historic centres and 'old' cities can look quite run-down from the outside but inside the flats are often beautifully modern. Many apartment blocks have a system of *condominio* (joint ownership) and the *inquilini* (tenants) contribute to the general running costs of the building – cleaning, maintenance, etc. The heating is usually centrally controlled and a regulation stipulates that it cannot be switched on until 1 November, although this may vary according to geographical area. This regulation also applies, incidentally, to private homes, even if it is not always strictly observed.

Ville (detached houses) are to be found predominantly in the suburbs, small towns and rural and more isolated areas. In cities and in the more sought-after locations detached properties are usually owned by the wealthier members of society. The iron railings around the perimeter, the *cancello automatico* (automatic gate), the Alsatian dog patrolling the garden all give some indication of the property's value and status.

Purchasing a house or flat

Property is generally very expensive and those who buy a house or flat arrange a *mutuo* (mortgage) through a bank. The amount of the loan will depend on earnings and/or other assets and most people have a fixed term for repayment of about ten years. There are no building societies in Italy as there are in Great Britain, for example. Because of the high price of property, especially in the cities, many young married couples prefer to invest in a smaller but cheaper house in one of the outlying districts. In fact it is now becoming commonplace to move back to the countryside, where in some areas it is still possible to buy an abandoned, derelict house, restore it on the outside to its original design and modernize the inside, all at a reasonable price. Of course there is some land for a garden and vegetable plot as well, a rare commodity in a city. Unmarried men and women tend to remain with their parents rather than buy or rent a property of their own. It's cheaper.

Council houses

The poorer members of society and immigrants live in *case popolari* (council houses). The rent is not high but the general quality of the accommodation is not good either. The council houses in towns and villages are generally much nicer than those in cities. Some local councils and charity organizations like *Caritas* help immigrants by providing simple dormitory accommodation.

Some characteristics of Italian houses and flats

- the balconies and/or terraces
- the *persiane* (shutters), which provide security and keep the inside of the house cool when it is scorching hot outside
- marble/tiled floors that are cool under foot
- the *citofono* (intercom) outside to announce oneself and gain access to the building
- the locks – most Italians are very security conscious and like a series of locks and bolts on the solid doors

GLOSSARIO	*GLOSSARY*
l'edificio	building
una casa di due piani	a two-storey house
il cortile	courtyard
il proprietario	owner
il padrone (di casa)	landlord
il tetto	roof
il legno	wood
la pietra	stone
costruire	to build
il balcone	balcony
la terrazza	terrace
l'appartamento	flat
comprare	to buy
affittare	to rent
l'affitto	rent
il riscaldamento centrale	central heating
la speculazione edilizia	building speculation
il contadino	peasant, farm worker
il pavimento di marmo	marble floor
la serratura	lock
il portiere	porter
vivere in periferia/in campagna	to live in the suburbs/ countryside

Transport

Travel by rail

Some basic facts:

- the State railway network (FS, or *Ferrovie dello Stato*) is one of Italy's oldest nationalized industries although it has now been partially privatized
- there are 19,437 kilometres of track, more than half of which is electrified
- rail fares are subsidized by the State and are amongst the cheapest in Europe
- ticket prices are calculated on the length of the journey, indicated on the ticket

Quality and variety

The quality and speed of service is normally determined by the choice of train. Trains that bear the name of *interregionale* or *regionale* tend to stop at anything that resembles a station. The *espresso*, despite its name, might not get to its destination any quicker. However, a *rapido* or *Intercity* (IC), for which the traveller requires a *supplemento* (supplement) in addition to the 'standard' ticket, is always quicker. There are no extra charges for the *Eurocity* (EC) as the *prezzo globale* (global price) covers everything.

Travel on most main-line routes, Milan to Rome for example, is comfortable and very rapid, especially on the new high-speed *pendolino* (tilting train). Booking, even if not always obligatory, is advisable on the busiest routes. Trains are very full at peak times and in the height of summer, when Italy's population is swelled by millions of tourists, standing in the narrow corridor while passengers laden with luggage zigzag past you is not a pleasant option. There are pull-down seats along the corridors of the older trains but they have not been designed for long-term comfort.

Some coastal routes are very slow but wonderfully scenic, such as the one that winds along the Ligurian coast from Ventimiglia to Genoa, darting in and out of *gallerie* (tunnels) as it does so. A lot of the track is single line so trains are carefully timetabled to pass at stations. The cost of improving this line would be prohibitive, given the geography of the area.

Attenzione! (Careful!)

Travellers must *convalidare* (stamp) their tickets and purchase their *supplemento*, if required, before boarding the train. Failure to perform either of these tasks will increase the cost of the journey. Once the *controllore* (ticket inspector) tracks a culprit down and discovers an infringement of the regulations, *la multa* (fine) is usually the inevitable outcome. The penalty is occasionally waived for the first misdemeanour and replaced by a more subtle form of punishment. This involves the passenger partaking in a quick descent at the next station and a frantic search for the yellow machine to stamp the ticket before re-boarding the train. Sometimes it's easier to pay the fine.

Future investment

A lot of future investment is going to be needed to replace many carriages and trains that are more than 30 years old. Every day 40 trains are out for repair; there is a shortage of spare parts as well as maintenance specialists. Eurostar and Intercity services have absorbed much of the budget these past 15 years or so and consequently investment in regional and inter-regional lines has been drastically reduced; for example, the launch of the *TAF* (*treno ad alta frequenza* – frequent train service) for commuters in Tuscany had to be deferred to September 1999. Among Prime Minister Berlusconi's major projects is the proposed Turin–Lyon link. This involves boring a 53-kilometre tunnel through the Alps to take high-speed trains as well as vehicles on a six-lane motorway from Italy into France.

Travel by road

The Italian peninsula is long and narrow and the Apennines, which run through its centre, represent a barrier to rapid movement from the western coast to the Adriatic and vice versa. Those who travel by car through the mountainous areas have to contend with narrow, winding roads, hairpin bends and a succession of ascents and descents but their efforts are rewarded with picturesque scenery. Anyone in a hurry chooses the less direct but more rapid communication link, i.e. one of the three *autostrade* (motorways) that connect Florence to Bologna, Rome to Pescara or Naples to Bari.

Italy has a good *rete autostradale* (motorway network) but the volume of traffic has increased to such an extent that accidents, and repairs to overused stretches of motorway, sometimes cause massive traffic jams. The main motorway, *autostrada del sole* (motorway of the sun), which runs from the north to Calabria on the toe of the peninsula, was originally constructed to carry six to seven thousand vehicles a day. No one could have envisaged the enormous amount of traffic it would be carrying today. The problem is exacerbated by the fact that 80 per cent of goods are transported by road.

Motorway travel is very expensive as a result of the cost of constructing innumerable viaducts and tunnels on many stretches of motorway. Motorists pay a *pedaggio* (toll) at the various toll stations en route. A day's travel can end up being quite costly. Petrol is comparatively expensive too.

The increase in traffic in cities, especially Milan, Rome, Naples and Turin, where many families own two cars, is a major problem. (In 1981 Italy had almost 25 million registered vehicles and in 2000 almost 44 million.) There have been attempts to reduce the volume of traffic, some successful, others not. In Florence, for example, a scheme was tried whereby car owners were allowed access to the city on alternate days depending on whether their car had an odd or even number plate. Italians, however, have a penchant for ingenuity, initiative and circumventing regulations. In this instance, families with two cars tried to ensure that one had an even number plate and the other an odd one. Visitors who travel by coach or car to Siena have to park outside the city. At least here one can roam around in comfort and drink in the beauty of this medieval city. The creation of *isole pedonali* (pedestrian precincts) in many towns and cities has been a positive step. Another solution might be the introduction of a congestion charge. Genoa was the first Italian city to introduce it on a trial basis but Milan is seriously considering adopting this measure and charging 3 euro to go into the centre.

Traffic congestion might possibly be reduced if more major cities had a *metropolitana* (underground system). There is one in Rome, Naples and Milan but it is only Milan's that can be considered adequate for the size of the city. The total length of Italy's underground system is 122 kilometres (compared to 330 in Great Britain, 531 in France and 717 in Germany).

Historic Venice at least is car-free. The most common modes of transport are walking and the canal 'bus' service, *vaporetto*. Those who wish to indulge themselves take the gondola with on-board entertainment from the gondolier displaying his dexterity with the paddle while singing an aria from an Italian opera! It's like travelling in a surrealistic world where the police, firemen, ambulance-men, refuse collectors (or ecological operators as they are now called) skilfully manoeuvre their craft along the myriad of canals. The *vaporetto* is reasonably priced but 'long-stay' visitors of a week or more would do well to invest in a weekly or monthly ticket – a passport to unlimited travel.

Italian car drivers

Many visitors to the country get the impression that Italians:

- drive fast
- take hairpin bends on two wheels
- park on the pavement
- proceed with caution through a red traffic light
- hoot the horn if another driver dares to hesitate for a split second when a red light changes to green
- consider the white rectangular shapes on the road to be purely decorative and consequently swerve around pedestrians who mistake them for a pedestrian crossing

Such things do happen but it would be grossly unfair to stereotype all Italian drivers in this way. However, it must be pointed out that Italy has one of Europe's worst records for accidents and is second in the European table after France for road deaths – 6,682 in 2001, an increase of 2.7 per cent on the previous year.

Road tax and breathalyser laws

The *bollo stradale* (road tax) is no longer calculated according to the engine capacity of the vehicle. Drivers currently pay 2.58 euro per kilowatt. It still means that those who want more power and speed pay the price.

As in other countries, Italy does have a breathalyser law and drivers caught drinking and driving can face heavy fines and lose their licence. Most Italians have a tradition of consuming wine at meal times but those who drive for a living remain abstinent during working hours while others are now more wary than they were previously. However, this law is not as yet strictly enforced, although young people who drive to the disco for the Saturday night rave are likely to be stopped, particularly as they will be returning home late at night. As in all countries, drivers who drink and cause accidents are the ones who face the heaviest punishment.

Travel by bus

It's difficult to understand why so many city dwellers prefer the car when the bus is so cheap, especially as finding a legitimate parking space is often a nightmare. Tickets are not purchased on the bus but from the *tabaccheria* (tobacconist's), *edicola* (newspaper kiosk) or *capolinea* (bus terminal). A single ticket is normally valid for about seventy minutes and entitles the passenger to use more than one bus, break a journey, etc., providing that the time limit is not exceeded. The ticket must be stamped in the machine on the bus at the start of the journey. Passengers not in possession of a valid ticket will be fined if caught by a ticket inspector. It is slightly cheaper to purchase *un blocchetto* (a block of tickets). Children less than one metre tall travel free. It's payment according to height not age.

Local buses have a seating capacity of about twenty whereas standing capacity seems unlimited. As a general rule he who

hesitates at a congested bus stop waits for the next bus. *Fare la coda* (to queue) is not a concept that comes readily to most Italians. There are a few cities that have trams, such as Milan, Turin and Rome. Florence has a small fleet of electric buses that operate in the town centre.

Despite the advantages of the bus service Italians still complain that it is slow and infrequent and therefore prefer the convenience of the car. The situation is not helped when the *corsie preferenziali* (bus lanes) are sometimes blocked by some nonchalant car driver who has kindly switched on the emergency flashing lights before nipping into an adjacent bar for a quick *cappuccino*, *pasta* (cake) and a glance at the daily paper. Often it is quickest to walk. A panacea may be the Vespa, which is making a comeback, and these motorists at least are not hindered by traffic jams. They swerve in and out of the traffic as if they are taking part in trials for the Olympic slalom event.

Air and sea transport

Rome (Ciampino and Fiumicino) and Milan (Linate and Malpensa) are by far Italy's busiest airports and they handle the vast majority of international flights. Malpensa recently opened a new terminal to enable it to cope with an increased volume of traffic. The national airline is *Alitalia* but there are a number of private companies that mainly operate the *voli interni* (internal flights). Italy has many regional airports, which, particularly during the summer season, handle a considerable number of charter flights bringing tourists to their holiday destinations. There are rapid links between some airports and city centres. Step outside the Marco Polo airport in Venice and there is the *vaporetto* service to various parts of the lagoon. A rail service links Pisa airport to Florence.

Genoa still remains one of Italy's major seaports. Passengers bound for America or on Mediterranean cruises can depart from here. There is also a passenger- and car-ferry service to the islands of Elba, Sardinia and Sicily. Its main importance now lies in the export and import of commercial and industrial products. For example, tankers bring in vast quantities of crude oil that is refined in Genoa's refineries. Other major ports are Naples and Venice.

GLOSSARIO	GLOSSARY
sovvenzionare	to subsidize
la distanza	distance
il viaggio	journey
viaggiare in macchina/treno/ autobus/aereo	to travel by car/train/ bus/plane
un biglietto di andata e ritorno	a return ticket
un biglietto di sola andata	a single ticket
la prenotazione	booking, reservation
la stazione	station
l'aeroporto	airport
comodo	comfortable
il casello	toll station (motorway)
la benzina	petrol
la patente (di guida)	(driving) licence
l'ora di punta	rush hour
gli ingorghi stradali	traffic jams
parcheggiare	to park
il camion	lorry
guidare	to drive
il semaforo	traffic lights
la multa	fine
il traghetto	car ferry

Taking it further

Suggested reading

Live and Work in Italy, Victoria Pybus, Vacation Work 1998. This book provides information on a wide range of topic areas.

Italian Labyrinth, John Haycraft, Penguin 1987

La scuola in Italia, Marcello Dei, Il Mulino, Bologna 1998

Those interested in travel and tourism will find a good selection of books on Italy in any well-stocked library. There are books on individual cities, e.g. Rome, Venice, Florence, or on the separate regions. Guide books of course will also supply you with a variety of information.

The Italian State Tourist Board is another obvious source of useful information (see p. 120).

Websites

For train timetables and other information:

www.trenitalia.it

For towns, cities, regions to visit and facts for the traveller, the following websites should be most useful:

www.sil.org/ethnologue/countries/ital.html

www.lonelyplanet.com/dest/eur/ita.htm#facts

www.discoveritalia.it

For education:

www.istruzione.it

www.ilsegnalibro.com/educatio.html

10

Italians at work and play

In this unit you will learn
- about Italy's leading industries
- about a range of issues that affect employment
- about common interests and leisure pursuits

Agriculture

The majority of the fertile arable land is in the vast northern plain, the *Pianura Padana*. The reasons for this were explained in Unit 1. By contrast, agriculture in the south has had to contend with a history of mismanagement and neglect, as well as a mountainous terrain and unfavourable climate. The 1950 agrarian reform eventually led to the breaking up of the *latifondi* (large agricultural estates) and the creation of smaller holdings. However, there was no clear cohesive policy and the farmers lacked the technical know-how and real will to make positive progress. Thus the underdevelopment in the south at that stage was attributable both to natural conditions and human inadequacy.

Before the advent of mechanization agricultural produce was for self-consumption. The farm workers either received a small salary or shared the produce in lieu of monetary payment. Farming was seen as a very hard way to earn a living, hence the exodus from the countryside to the cities when industrialization took off in the late 1950s.

From self-consumption to mass production

In Italy, as throughout the world, agriculture has been transformed into a big, mass-production business. It uses more machinery, more advanced technology and an increasing number of fertilizers to boost production, a transformation that has meant fewer workers. The best results have been in areas where farmers have formed co-operatives.

Increasingly, there has been a greater emphasis on the export market, which sparked off a big expansion in food-processing industries. The enormous potential for development has attracted both internal and foreign investment.

Italy, however, is by no means self-sufficient. When standards of living started to improve in the 1960s people's dietary habits changed. Pasta and bread remained part of the staple diet but meat consumption rose dramatically. This demand was met by importing meat and additional livestock, a policy that resulted in a considerable balance of payments deficit. Even today the balance sheet for this sector is negative.

Main agricultural products

Italy's geography and climate help us understand why some areas are more conducive to certain kinds of farming than others. The north has the vast open fertile plain, the centre and south a high percentage of hills and woods, and the island of Sardinia meadows and pasture land. Below is a general 'agricultural overview'.

	Animals	Crops	Products
North	cattle and pig farming (more than two-thirds of country's livestock)	maize, wheat, sugar beet, rice, vines, fruit trees	meat, butter, milk, cheese, animal feed, rice, sugar, wine, apples, peaches
Centre	buffalo, pigs, sheep	wheat, barley, vines, olive groves, fruit trees	olive oil, wine, fruit, sugar, ham, cheese, pasta, tinned tomatoes, jams
South		hard-grain wheat, olive groves, fruit trees, vegetables	olive oil, lemons, oranges, mandarins, peaches, cherries, figs, apricots, potatoes, beans, tomatoes
Sicily		vines, olive groves, fruit trees	citrus fruits
Sardinia	sheep, goats	vines, olive groves, wheat, fruit trees	wine, milk, wool, goat's cheese, citrus fruits, almonds, vegetables (especially artichokes), animal feed

The export market

About 65 per cent of agricultural exports are to Europe, with France and Germany being the main recipients. The Eastern European market is an expanding area. Further afield the United States is a major importer. Some of the main exports are wine, grapes, fruit, fresh vegetables, pasta, rice, olives, olive oil and flowers. The main flower-growing industry is on the Ligurian coast – aptly named the *Riviera dei fiori* – from Ventimiglia as far as Albenga. All along this stretch the hillsides are an endless sea of greenhouses.

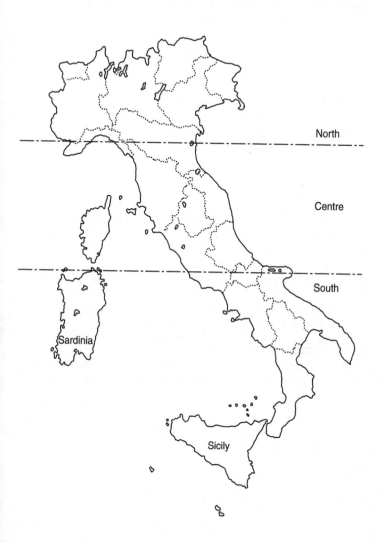

North

Centre

South

Sardinia

Sicily

Map illustrating agricultural divisions

The Common Agricultural Policy

Vast sums of European money have gone into animal farming. As in many other member states, money has been made available:

- to develop and improve efficiency in the more disadvantaged regions, e.g. the south
- to encourage existing farmers to remain on the land, as concern mounts for the protection of the countryside and natural environment
- to provide subsidies to farmers to reduce output, e.g. fruit, milk, so that it doesn't exceed market demand

Wine

Bacchus, the god of wine, certainly smiled on Italy, now the biggest wine producer and exporter in the world. Wine is produced in vast quantities throughout the country. Modernization and a government law passed in February 1992 gave the industry a tremendous boost. The label must now indicate the wine's geographical origin and production quality. The label DOCG (*Denominazione di origine controllata e garantita*) guarantees both the origin and quality, whereas the DOC label (*Denominazione di origine*) means you can rest assured that your Chianti wine does originate from Chianti land in Tuscany and not elsewhere. Chianti wines are well-known, as are the sparkling Asti wines produced in Piedmont. However, many excellent wines are produced in all parts of the country.

A similar law has been passed to guarantee the origin and quality of olive oil. Good quality olive oil bears the label *vergine* and the best *extravergine*. Taste the difference between *olio di semi* (vegetable oil) and *olio di oliva extravergine*. The next time you season your salad, spoil yourself.

GLOSSARIO	*GLOSSARY*
l'agricoltura	agriculture
agricolo	agricultural
la siccità	drought
sottosviluppato	underdeveloped
la meccanizzazione	mechanization
trasformare	to transform

i prodotti	products
la mano d'opera	workforce
i fertilizzanti	fertilizers
esportare	to export
importare	to import
produrre	to produce
auto-sufficiente	self-sufficient
la carne	meat
la pastorizia	sheep farming
l'allevamento di bestiame/	cattle/pig rearing/breeding/
suini	farming
il frumento	wheat
il granoturco	maize
l'orzo	barley
la barbaietola da zucchero	sugar beet
gli alberi da frutto	fruit trees
la viticoltura	wine-growing
il vigneto	vineyard
l'olivo	olive tree
gli agrumi	citrus fruits
gli ortaggi	vegetables

Industries

The north

The north and north-east – mainly the regions of Piedmont and Lombardy – have the highest concentration of big, medium and small enterprises. In Lombardy can be found:

- engineering, chemical, pharmaceutical, textile and electronic industries
- steel works and oil refineries
- the tyre industries (Pirelli)
- factories that produce cars (Alfa Romeo, Maserati, Innocenti), agricultural machinery, motorbikes, domestic appliances (Ignis), footwear and furniture
- the publishing companies Mondadori and Rizzoli

Piedmont is best known for Fiat (*Fabbrica Italiana Automobili Torino*), the privately run car industry based in Turin and Italy's biggest industrial employer. It took over control of Alfa Romeo in 1986 and has plants in other parts of Italy (e.g. Pomigliano near Naples) and abroad. Fiat also makes trucks at its Iveco plant in Turin and has factories that produce accessories for the car industry. Apart from Fiat there are the prestigious, very expensive Ferrari and Maserati cars made at factories in Emilia Romagna.

In the regions of Friuli-Venezia Giulia and Veneto the main products are domestic appliances (fridges, washing machines, dishwashers), clothes, furniture, ceramics. The industrial picture further south, however, becomes much more fragmented. Why is this the case?

- The north has several European neighbours on its doorstep.
- The communications network is good.
- Historically, everything has favoured the north. Once the industrial triangle – Genoa, Turin, Milan – developed in the 1950s and 1960s there was a ready supply of cheap labour provided by the influx of people from the surrounding countryside and the underdeveloped regions in the south.

Poles apart

Italian governments post-unification tended to ignore the South until the setting up in 1950 of the *Cassa per il Mezzogiorno*, 'the Fund for the South' (to include the islands of Sicily and Sardinia). Most of the initial investment went to improve the infrastructure – land reclamation, irrigation projects, transport network, etc. The government also gave financial incentives, e.g. easy repayment terms, to encourage investment from Italian and foreign entrepreneurs.

Later, attention was switched to industry and the government plan was to create *poli di sviluppo* (areas of development). Thus in Campania a car plant was built in Pomigliano and a huge steelworks in Bagnoli near Naples. In Puglia the biggest Italian steelworks was built in Taranto, a petrochemical plant in Brindisi and an engineering industry in Bari. These designated areas of development have often been referred to as *cattedrali nel deserto* (cathedrals in the desert), because they were constructed in isolated areas that lacked the necessary support of smaller and medium-sized industries.

The idea that these industries would solve the unemployment problem was a vain hope, as they did not require masses of workers to operate them. The overall plan therefore was rather disjointed. The south historically started off at a disadvantage (see Unit 1) and has been trying to catch up with the north ever since.

One of the main products in the south is footwear produced at factories in Abruzzo, Puglia and Campania. Italian shoes are well-known and figure highly on the list of exports. Other products include ceramics, textiles and furniture.

The boom years

The often-referred-to *miracolo economico* (economic miracle) occurred between 1958 and 1963. Labour was cheap and in plentiful supply and production costs were low, making prices competitive on international markets. Internal demand for electrical and household appliances – televisions, radios, fridges, washing machines – and cars rose sharply. The following companies figured prominently:

- *Olivetti* – office machinery such as typewriters and calculators. Today the company is more involved in information technology
- *Fiat*, *Innocenti* – cars (Innocenti produced the Mini)
- *Indesit*, *Ignis*, *Zoppa*s, *Zanussi* – fridges and washing machines
- *Pirelli* – tyres

Economic ups and downs

All economies experience peaks and troughs. Since the end of the 1960s Italy has had its fair share. A major drawback has always been the country's lack of raw materials and natural resources. Oil fields were discovered in Gela and Ragusa (Sicily) but the quality of the product is not that good. The sulphur mines in Sicily are not very productive either. On the positive front there are plentiful supplies of hydroelectric power in the north – Piedmont, Lombardy, Trentino-Alto Adige, Valle d'Aosta – and Agip has plans to extract *il metano* (methane gas) for the next 25 years from 15 platforms off the coast of the northern Adriatic.

Italy, therefore, has had to rely heavily on imports of essential raw materials, especially oil. The oil crisis in 1973 – Italy at the time imported 78.6 per cent of her oil from the Middle East –

meant that the price of imports rocketed. Production costs inevitably rose. At the same time unions were demanding higher wages and improved working conditions. Inflation started to spiral and Italian products became uncompetitive on world markets. Furthermore, the many nationalized industries were over-manned, inefficient and no longer economically viable. Italy started to develop nuclear power as a way of supplying essential energy resources but abandoned its programme in 1987 following the Chernobyl incident. Things had to change, and they did.

Automation and privatization

At the start of the 1980s automation and more advanced technology were introduced into many factories. It relieved the boredom from tedious production-line jobs but it relieved a lot of workers of their jobs too. Robots took over. Production was increased as the same targets were achieved with only half the manpower. The Fiat car factory was one of the first to go down this road. Unemployment rose sharply but industries became more competitive again. In fact, in 1986 Italy was ranked fifth among the world's top industrial nations. Today it is still in the top seven.

Privatization didn't get under way until the start of the 1990s, later than elsewhere in Europe. Apart from long-established companies like Fiat and Olivetti, most industries were previously under State control. Privatization has noticeably arrived in the fashion industry, and designer clothes (Armani, Versace, Valentino, Moschino) are big business both at home and abroad.

The change of economic climate has brought a lot more foreign investment. A fairly recent trend has been for smaller, privately-owned firms to open factories outside the chief cities but along the main arteries of communication. There is more space and the costs are lower. Many of these factories produce furniture, leather bags (another famous Italian product), ceramics, musical instruments, shoes and clothes.

GLOSSARIO	GLOSSARY
l'industria metalmeccanica/ tessile/chimica	engineering/textile/chemical industry
l'impresa	enterprise
l'imprenditore	entrepreneur
assumere	to take on, employ
licenziare	to sack, dismiss
investire	to invest
sviluppare	to develop
modernizzare	to modernize
l'azienda	firm, business
piccolo	small
medio	medium
l'acciaieria	steelworks
gli elettrodomestici	domestic appliances
i mobili	furniture
la calzatura	footwear
la ceramica	ceramics
il triangolo industriale	industrial triangle
l'infrastruttura	infrastructure
le materie prime	raw materials
la mancanza	lack
la moda	fashion
lo/la stilista	fashion designer
l'automazione	automation

Tourism

Tourism is one of Italy's main industries (more than 30 million visitors a year) and in 1999 was ranked fourth in the international tourism table. In 2001 the number of tourists dropped by 5 per cent on the previous year, almost certainly due to the impact of the tragic events of 11 September. Italy depends greatly on the influx of tourists from the USA along with those from Japan and central Europe. The sector has since picked up and the prediction is for continued growth. The next section underlines why there should always be reason for optimism as far as the tourist sector is concerned.

Map illustrating tourist attractions

A whistle-stop tour of Italy

Italy can cater for most tastes. Entire books have been written about Italy's tourist attractions but here are a few nuggets.

- For those whose preference is the sea there is the beautiful *Costa Smeralda* (Emerald Coast) in Sardinia, Taormina in Sicily, and the resorts along the toe of Italy in Calabria or the Amalfi Coast in Campania. The south has beautiful beaches, clean sea and many areas remain as yet unspoilt. For mass tourism the highly developed areas are those along the Ligurian Coast and the ones on the Adriatic between Ravenna in Emilia Romagna and Civitanova in the Marche.
- There are the northern lakes – Como, Maggiore, Garda and Lugano (on the Italian side of course).
- The variety of cities is endless: Venice, Rome, Florence, Siena, Perugia, Bologna, Ferrara, Ravenna. Each has its own historical, archaeological and cultural heritage. A trip around central Italy alone makes the traveller realize the inestimable treasures that lie around almost every corner – the beautiful hillside towns of Volterra, Urbino, San Gimignano, for instance. Then there is Gubbio, Spoleto, Orvieto, or Assisi (subjected to a very serious earthquake in 1997) and the independent state of San Marino.
- If you are wanting to explore the islands then, apart from Sicily and Sardinia, you have Elba (off the coast of Tuscany), Capri and Ischia (fairly adjacent to Naples) and the Aeolian islands north of Sicily.
- For a relaxing, healthy holiday or for relief or cure for medical ailments, there is a vast choice of thermal spas, such as Salsomaggiore (Emilia Romagna), Montecatini and Chianciano (Tuscany), and Fiuggi (Lazio).
- Archaeological enthusiasts need look no further than Pompeii (Campania), buried by an eruption of Vesuvius in AD 79. This is one of the most important archaeological sites in the world. For Greek temples and theatres visit Agrigento, Syracuse and Taormina on the island of Sicily.
- If it's farm holidays you are looking for then the most developed region is Tuscany.
- For the energetic holidaymakers who love walking, climbing, fresh air and spectacular scenery the Alps and the Apennines beckon.

Most people go on the above holidays during the summer season, from June to September. The *alta stagione* (peak season) is July and August, the period favoured by most visitors and Italians themselves. Italy, however, has such a good climate that anyone taking a holiday in May or October can be blessed with good weather, bearable temperatures and fewer tourists.

The winter season

Italy has taken advantage of its high mountain ranges to develop a number of *stazioni sciistiche* (ski resorts), the best known of which are in the Alps: Sestriere and Limone (Piedmont), Cervinia (Valle d'Aosta) and Cortina d'Ampezzo in the Dolomites (Veneto). The latter is perhaps the only one to have become a recognized tourist centre. The skiing season normally operates from the beginning of December until the end of March.

Seasonal employment

Tourism is an important source of seasonal employment. For some it means work for three to four months but for others who alternate between the summer and winter resorts, seven to eight months. Just imagine the extra staff taken on in hotels, restaurants, and shops. Most hotels by the sea have their own private beach and employ staff to keep it tidy, act as bathing attendants, man the bars, etc. Public beaches are less common so the majority of visitors and local residents prefer to pay for the amenities: *ombrellone* (parasol), *sdraio* (deck chair), *lettino* (sun bed), *cabina* (changing cabin) and *doccia* (shower).

Like anywhere else, there is no dearth of tourist shops during the summer season, selling souvenirs and local craft products. Landscape artists, portrait painters and buskers display their array of talents in the popular tourist haunts. Tourist guides are everywhere revealing their linguistic competence and cultural knowledge. Even the birdseed sellers in St Mark's Square in Venice boost their sales in the summer season. Despite the thousands of tourists that gather in this square in the height of summer, they seem to be outnumbered by the pigeons who drop in to be fed and have their photo taken with delighted groups of tourists.

Environmental issues

Tourism has its down side too. Here are some of the problems it brings:

- overdevelopment of some seaside resorts, e.g. excessive construction of hotels and blocks of flats. In some ski resorts, as well as the hotels, restaurants, bars, flats, etc., the carrying capacity of ski-lifts and cable cars has been increased – total capacity for the whole of Italy has now reached the two million mark. There are so many skiers on a Sunday that the ski-runs look like motorways. To solve overcrowding wider ski-runs are created. The result, of course, is more environmental damage to the mountainsides.
- increase in the volume of traffic
- increase in noise level, bringing scores of complaints from local inhabitants (see also Unit 11)

GLOSSARIO	*GLOSSARY*
il turismo (di massa)	*(mass) tourism*
le vacanze	*holidays*
la stagione estiva/invernale	*summer/winter season*
la bassa stagione	*low/off-peak season*
il turista	*tourist*
l'influsso	*influx*
il centro/la stazione balneare	*seaside resort*
il bagnino	*bathing attendant*
il mare pulito	*clean sea*
la spiaggia privata/pubblica	*private/public beach*
i laghi	*the lakes*
le isole	*the islands*
le terme	*spas*
l'agriturismo	*farm holidays*
l'ambiente	*environment*
il rumore	*noise*
l'inquinamento	*pollution*

Working practices

Working practices in Italy are much the same as elsewhere in Europe. The standard working week is around 40 hours although the Italian government has been discussing for some time the introduction of a 35-hour week. Factories usually keep the production lines running 24 hours a day and employees do seven-to eight-hour *turni* (shifts). Office workers may have the option to work flexitime.

The *liberi professionisti* (self-employed) or families that have small private businesses normally work much longer hours, e.g. tobacconists and small shops remain open 12 hours or more a day and bars as much as 18 hours a day. A nice bonus for full-time employees is the *tredicesima* (13th) and the *quattordicesima* (14th), and the majority of people receive both. These are two extra months' pay, one in the summer and the other at Christmas, just right for the two most expensive holiday periods of the year.

Unemployment

In 2002, despite the creation of 1.8 million jobs in the previous six years, unemployment in Italy stood at 9.6 per cent compared with the European average of 7.4 per cent. In the overall unemployment picture southern Italy has always been the poor relation. Some facts and figures produced by the government agency Istat in 1997, when unemployment reached 12.3 per cent, illustrate this point.

• The regions with the highest unemployment figures were Calabria, Campania and Sicily.

• At its peak, unemployment in Calabria was 25 per cent of the workforce, and 35 per cent of the unemployed were women. In Campania the figure was almost one million, with over half a million in and around Naples. In 1995, 40 per cent of the 5,520 businesses that closed through bankruptcy were in Campania. Between 1992 and 1996 more than 200,000 people lost their jobs in Sicily.

• Unemployment was highest amongst the 15–29 age bracket (33.5 per cent of the potential labour market).

• 8.3 per cent of the total was made up of long-term unemployed.

• Unemployment was almost twice as high among the female job seekers.

Statistics, as we know, do not always paint the real picture. The following unemployed would not be included in the figures:

• Students who are enrolled at university simply because they cannot find a job. Admittedly many find seasonal or part-time work to pay for their studies and/or rely heavily on their parents for financial support.

- The *cassintegrati* (workers laid off by companies in times of crisis). However, the State pays a good proportion of the salary during unemployment and the workers are recalled when production picks up. Those under this scheme are not supposed to do other paid work but some moonlight. In the first eleven months of 2002 INPS, the State Social Security System, discovered 111,169 moonlighters, a figure that included pensioners, sick people, minors, foreigners and *cassintegrati*.

Moonlighting in Italy is rife – 3.5 million workers according to one official source. It is illegal because both workers and employers avoid paying taxes. This illicit workforce will contain, among others, registered unemployed in addition to those in employment but doing a 'second' job. Survival for many in Italy revolves around *l'arte dell'arrangiarsi* (the art of getting by) and in areas of high unemployment moonlighting is well established. The government is aware of the situation but often prefers to turn a blind eye.

The causes of unemployment

These have been referred to in earlier sections: mechanization, automation, restructuring of public and private companies, economic recession, balance of payment deficits and lack of competitiveness in both European and international markets. In the period between 1971 and 1997 the percentage of workers employed in agriculture and industry fell from 20.1 per cent to 6.8 per cent and 39.5 per cent to 32.1 per cent respectively.

Unemployment benefits

Employees made redundant receive *la liquidazione* (lump sum) based on level of pay and years of service. They are entitled to sign on the dole and receive *il sussidio di disoccupazione* (unemployment benefit). Young first-time job seekers receive nothing whatsoever, hence the reason for remaining with the family. Those on temporary contracts must work a minimum of four months a year to qualify for dole payments.

One door closes, another opens

Whereas the workforce has shrunk in the primary and secondary sectors, i.e. agriculture and industry, there has been rapid expansion in the tertiary or service sector, from 40.4 per cent in 1971 to 61.1 per cent in 1997. This sector includes some of the following categories: office workers, travel agents, insurance brokers, accountants, social workers, solicitors.

World economy experts are predicting that the majority of jobs in future will be in the service sector and leisure industry. The younger generation will probably be required to accept more flexible working arrangements and lower their initial expectations in terms of salary and choice of profession, even if they are well qualified. Initially, many may be obliged to accept part-time or temporary work, which is on the increase. With unemployment around 10 per cent it is an employer's market.

GLOSSARIO	GLOSSARY
la settimana lavorativa	*working week*
i dipendenti	*employees*
il datore di lavoro	*employer*
fare i turni	*to work shifts*
l'orario flessibile	*flexitime*
il tasso di disoccupazione	*rate of unemployment*
essere disoccupato	*to be unemployed*
fare il lavoro nero	*to moonlight*
il lavoro stagionale/part-time/	*seasonal/part-time/*
provvisorio	*temporary work*
il settore terziario	*tertiary sector*
l'industria del tempo libero	*leisure industry*
essere costretto a	*to be obliged to*
predire	*to predict*
accettare	*to accept*

Trade unions

Trade union movements started towards the end of the nineteenth century but it was not until 1944 that they became a more unified force with the founding of CGIL, the *Confederazione Generale Italiana del Lavoro* (Confederation of Trade Unions). General accord soon led to discord and, like political parties, dissident groups broke away and formed other unions (1950), namely CISL (*Confederazione Italiana dei Sindacati dei Lavoratori*) and UIL (*Unione Italiana del Lavoro*). These three main unions split up along political lines. CGIL, the biggest of the three, was mainly Communist; CISL, Christian Democrat; and UIL, Socialist and Republican. Over the years a number of *sindacati autonomi* (independent trade unions) have sprung up and they represent the interests of particular categories, e.g. train drivers, airline pilots, post-office workers.

The three big unions, CGIL, CISL and UIL went their separate ways until the end of the 1960s. The year 1969 was the start of a period of great social and political unrest and the unions realized that they had to work together to achieve common goals – fair wages and good working conditions for their members. As time went on, unions were not just concerned with salary increases. They campaigned, for example, against social injustice, the increasing divide between the north and south, and for the right to work. They made some significant gains:

- the introduction of a Workers' Charter in 1970 that made it difficult to sack people
- anti-trade union behaviour by employers became illegal
- a *scala mobile* (wage indexing) agreement was reached in 1975 with *Confindustria* – the Confederation of Industries. This meant that every three months or so wages were increased automatically to counterbalance price rises and inflation

A significant turning point

In 1980, when the privately owned Fiat won its legal battle to make thousands of its employees redundant, the 1970 Workers' Charter became a less meaningful document. Other companies followed Fiat's lead and proceeded to lay off workers. In 1982 *Confindustria* went back on its original agreement of wage indexing. It was the start of the demise of the big industries and the development of small and medium-sized enterprises as well as the expansion of the tertiary sector. The new growth sectors gave the cold shoulder to the three main unions but the 'autonomous' unions mushroomed. This has led to a kind of dichotomy. The big unions continue to consult with government and employers over a number of issues, not just pay, and endeavour to represent the workforce as a whole, whereas the brief of 'autonomous' unions is focused more on the interests of a particular category of workers.

Strikes

With rising unemployment, union demands have generally become more moderate and wage increases, unlike in the past, are now linked to productivity deals. Prolonged strikes are no longer the threat they once were, because with such high unemployment workers fear losing their jobs. Having said this, Italy holds the world record for strikes. Between 1970 and 1996 three times as many days were lost to strikes as in the United States and the average yearly loss during this period was 11.7 million days. In the first eight months of 2002, 25 million hours had been lost to strikes, the highest figure recorded since 1979. Thus strikes are still numerous but the tactics are more subtle, with different categories of workers coming out at varying times. In Rome, in the week beginning 9 November 1998, the taxi drivers ceased to operate from Monday to Thursday. On the Thursday and Friday there were no buses, trams or underground trains. By sheer coincidence, on the Monday of the same week there was a four-hour strike in all Italian airports. No category sacrifices too much but this snowball effect usually causes widespread chaos.

GLOSSARIO	*GLOSSARY*
il sindacato	*trade union*
il membro	*member*
lo sciopero	*strike*
fare sciopero	*to go on strike*
perdere il lavoro	*to lose one's job*
lo stipendio	*pay*
aumentare	*to increase*

Leisure pursuits

What is happening in Italy is probably no different from anywhere else:

- the most common pastime for 97 per cent of the population is watching television, occupying about a third of people for more than three hours a day
- about 42 per cent enjoy going to the cinema regularly
- interest in reading is declining – e.g. only 1 in 8 reads a newspaper – and women read more than men
- video games, surfing the Internet, mobile phones and text messaging are high on the list of priorities of the younger generation in particular
- a small minority of people listen to classical music and go to the theatre
- more than half of those over 27 do not participate in any sporting activities

Sport

At school level sports provision is no more than adequate. Most schools have a *palestra* (gymnasium) but *campi sportivi* (sports fields) are few and far between. The keen activists join a club and pursue their sporting interests in their spare time. There are privately or publicly run *centri sportivi polivalenti* (sports centres) in the big cities, but very few facilities in the less populated areas.

Italy is internationally renowned for its involvement in sports such as basketball, water polo, cycling, athletics, skiing and football, and the national teams have often distinguished themselves on the world stage, e.g. the Olympics. In recent times the country has made great strides in rugby and in 2000 was invited to participate in the tournament that hitherto had been the reserve of the four British nations plus France. Thus far the team has only managed to register two victories, the second of which came in 2003 against Wales, causing great dismay to the author of this unit, whose country of origin remains a closely guarded secret.

L'automobilismo (motor racing)

Motor racing has a big active and passive following in Italy and two of the Formula One Grands Prix are staged there: *il Gran Premio* (Grand Prix) of San Marino, the independent State, which is held in Imola (Emilia Romagna) and the one in Monza (Lombardy). The nation takes great pride in this sport because one of the principal car constructors is Ferrari and this household name in the world of fast cars was top of the constructors' league table in the 1999–2003 seasons. Italy's leading drivers in 2003 were Trulli and Fisichella.

Il calcio (football)

Despite the financial crisis facing many clubs at the start of the 2002 season, football remains the big money sport and the focus of the sporting calendar for much of the year. It is played on a Sunday and only occasionally on a Saturday. Most of the teams in *Serie A* (the first division) have huge, fanatical followings. Italian fans in general are very volatile and, particularly at the start of a game, you would think you were at a fireworks display, with flares and rockets being launched from all parts, giving the impression that a fog has suddenly descended on the ground.

If things are not going well for the home team then a whole series of objects rain down onto the pitch and players – plastic bottles, coins, fruit, etc. Any player who enjoys an orange during the course of a game need not signal to the bench to provide one.

Another favourite missile is *la carta igienica* (toilet paper) and the areas around the goal-mouth are sometimes littered with it. It constitutes a potential danger and this was underlined in a crucial end-of-season match between Perugia and Milan (1999). The *petardi* (firecrackers) ignited the toilet paper causing the start of the second half to be delayed by some 15 minutes or so. It could have been a pure accident, but suspicions are aroused by the fact that the home team was losing and fighting desperately against relegation.

The fans are fenced in, some grounds even have a moat between the pitch and the terraces, and the riot police are in their full battle-charging regalia. In the event of a minute's silence before a game, Italian spectators start clapping; this is their way of showing respect for the deceased person or persons.

The popularity of football can be gauged by the amount of newspaper and media coverage dedicated to it. The most widely read sports papers are the daily *La Gazzetta dello Sport* and *Tuttosport*, with about two-thirds of the content devoted to football. Even national papers have a four- to six-page spread and the occasional article on another sport.

Italian teams have been very successful in European competitions – figuring in at least one of the finals between 1989 and 1999 – then, after what one might consider a rather barren period, three leading clubs, Juventus, AC Milan and Inter-Milan featured in the semi-finals of the European Cup in 2003, with the first two teams contesting the final. The Italian national team has had its fair share of success in the World Cup. The last time Italy won was in 1982, an occasion when the nation united in celebration. Car drivers went around tooting their horns and the streets were awash with flags. Even dogs were seen parading the streets decked in the Italian colours, no doubt barking '*Italia*' in unison with the chants of their irrepressible owners.

Many Italians like to meet up in a bar and follow the match on television, debating excitedly every incident. For anyone learning the language it is an ideal opportunity to observe a whole gamut of gestures and note down a series of more colourful, extremely colloquial expressions.

Lo sci (skiing)

Skiing is a popular activity for people of all ages. A high percentage of the population lives within a one- to two-hour car drive from the nearest resort and on Sundays especially the slopes are crowded. Those who have a second home in the mountains often make a weekend of it. Skiing can be a very expensive hobby, as Italians love to have the latest fashion in clothing and equipment. Italy has churned out its fair share of national and international stars. Perhaps the best known was Alberto Tomba, and more recently Debora Compagnoni. For *la discesa* (downhill) there is now Christian Ghedina.

La passeggiata (the leisurely stroll)

Italians enjoy taking a stroll along the main street/s in the evening or after Mass on a Sunday. They will walk up and down the same street for ages, chatting and maybe stopping off at one of the numerous bars en route for an *aperitivo* (aperitif) or *gelato* (ice-cream). It has become for many a kind of ritual and a way of meeting up with friends and neighbours. Many promenaders, including young children, are immaculately dressed and eyes turn in all directions to observe the latest fashions. It's an ideal opportunity to *fare bella figura* (make a good impression), a typical Italian trait. It's also a good chance for outsiders to observe the formal way that Italians tend to greet each other: '*Buona sera, professore, ingegnere, ragioniere*' (Good evening, teacher, engineer, accountant). They love to use titles.

All Italian cities, towns and villages have a *piazza* (square) and it is a normal leisure activity for groups of people to gather in the square and engage in animated discussions. In smaller towns and villages families will take the children there to ride their bikes and play with their friends.

Andare al mare (going to the seaside)

Many Italians tend to go the seaside for the weekend from about May onwards, in the same way as they go skiing during the winter season. Once again the majority do not have far to go to have a swim in the sea. Tourists who holiday by the sea may well wonder why the Italians are so sun-tanned. Even if many do have naturally swarthy skins, you can bet that they have been developing this tan for a few months and are usually very proud of it.

Mangiare e bere (eating and drinking)

Italians in general enjoy going out for a meal and restaurants are particularly crowded at the weekend. The cuisine is excellent, there is a fantastic selection of wines, and the climate allows them to eat outside for many months of the year. A very popular haunt for people of all ages, especially the younger generation as it's not expensive, is the *pizzeria*, where a good pizza and *una birra alla spina* (a draught beer) are more than adequate.

Traditionally Italy has bars but there are an increasing number of pubs – often called Irish pubs – in towns and cities and they are very popular with the younger generation. These pubs have been created in the British style and they have an atmosphere that is much more appealing to the young than a bar. Italians don't necessarily consume large quantities of alcohol. They can quite happily sit and chat for hours over the one drink.

Il rito del sabato sera (the Saturday night ritual)

A night out clubbing is a common pursuit for most young people. Italians, however, have become accustomed to a Saturday night ritual whereby they are prepared to travel hundreds of kilometres for their weekly rave-up. For example, there will be an exodus from Turin (Piedmont) bound for Rimini (Emilia Romagna) on the Adriatic coast. Buses and trains are organized to transport these *pendolari della discoteca* (discotheque commuters) to their favourite night-spot. The revellers usually book overnight accommodation to which they return in the early hours of the morning bleary-eyed.

The *Dopolavoro*

The *Dopolavoro* (literally 'after work') is a kind of recreational and cultural club. A typical centre has tennis courts, areas for bowls and for children to play, a cinema, bar, TV room, etc. In the past, people of all ages went there, but now it tends to be the domain of the older generation. The men enjoy playing bowls or cards while the women sit and chat and supervise their children or grandchildren. Cards is a recreational activity enjoyed by a good number of the older generation (men mostly). They regularly meet up at the *Dopolavoro* or at their local bars in towns and villages and play for hours.

La caccia (hunting)

Hunting is another popular pastime. In Tuscany alone there are approximately 130,000 *cacciatori* (hunters). A referendum was held in the early 1990s to abolish hunting but it was defeated. Both legalized hunting and indiscriminate shooting of wildlife take place in Italy. Many Italians are prone to shooting any animal that moves or doesn't move quickly enough. The writer Muriel Spark said in a newspaper article that during her 25 years in Tuscany she had 'witnessed the almost total obliteration of wildlife'. Animals such as rabbits, hares, ferrets, songbirds and migrating birds had virtually disappeared.

What has happened in Tuscany is not uncommon in other regions of Italy. To protect certain species of bird and other wild animals from extinction more stringent hunting regulations have been introduced – designated areas, specifically appointed periods – and there are heavier penalties for offenders that are apprehended. The national parks do afford greater security for the animals but, overall, it would be impossible to provide sufficient manpower to monitor the situation adequately.

Raccogliere i funghi (mushroom picking)

Mushroom picking has many enthusiasts who will get up at the crack of dawn and head for the areas where they know they will find rich pickings. It's a fairly active interest as it often necessitates walking far off the beaten track. The rewards are usually worth it but it is not an activity for the inexperienced. A tiny portion of the wrong kind of mushroom can be fatal or at best make you very ill. Some of the mushrooms will be for immediate consumption, others will be pickled and preserved for a later date. Mushrooms such as *porcini* are a real delicacy and expensive to buy. Pigs are very adept at discovering their whereabouts.

There is a lot of money to be made from the picking of highly prized and priced *tartufi* (truffles) and dogs are specifically trained to sniff them out. It has become such big business that rival gangs are reportedly poisoning each other's working dogs.

GLOSSARIO	GLOSSARY
lo sport	sport
il calcio	football
lo sci	skiing
sciare	to ski
fare il bagno	to have a swim
la pallacanestro	basketball
la pallavolo	volleyball
la pallanuoto	water polo
il ciclismo	cycling
il nuoto	swimming
l'atletica	athletics
la squadra	team
l'equitazione	horse riding
ascoltare la musica	to listen to music
guardare la televisione	to watch television
leggere	to read
andare al cinema/a teatro/in discoteca	to go to the cinema/theatre/disco
giocare a tennis/bocce/carte	to play tennis/bowls/cards
abolire	to abolish
la caccia	hunting
la licenza	licence
i funghi	mushrooms

Taking it further

Suggested reading

Italy, Russell King, Harper and Row Publishers 1987

Italian Labyrinth, John Haycraft, Penguin 1987

Contemporary Italy (Second Edition), Donald Sassoon, Addison Wesley 1997

GEO Fare Geografia (Second Edition), Alida Ardemagni, Francesco Mambretti and Giovanni Silvera, Principato 1991

For information and maps plus, on request, lists of hotels and farm holidays for specific areas, contact: The Italian State Tourist Board (see p. 120).

Websites

www.lonelyplanet.com/dest/eur/ita.htm#facts

www.sil.org/ethnologue/countries/ital.html

www.uni.net/spc/istat.htm (young people and work – in Italian)

www.discover.it

On the environment:
www.legambiente.it
www.amicidellaterra.it

On sport:
www.gazzetta.it

The national newspapers always have articles on a variety of topics:
www.correiere.it
www.repubblica.it
www.lastampa.it

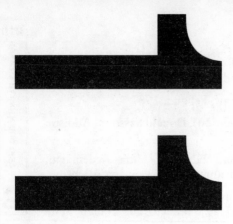

the people

In this unit you will learn
- about the major influences
  on population change
- about changes that have
  had an impact on the role of
  women and family life
- about environmental
  problems

Population

Since the baby boom in the 1960s the birth rate in Italy has declined dramatically, so much so that the country now has the lowest birth rate in the world. In 2001 the average was 1.26 children per couple compared to the European Union average of 1.47. The figure is higher in the south (1.4), whereas in the centre-north it is between 1 and 1.1. The regions with the lowest birth rate are Friuli-Venezia Giulia, Liguria, Emilia-Romagna and Tuscany, and the highest, Campania and Sicily.

Demographers predict that, despite the declining birth rate, the population of just over 57.8 million in 1997 will not have altered much in 2025. This prediction is based on two key points: people are living longer and the immigrant population will continue to have children at the present rate. Italians would need to have two children per family on average to maintain their current level and recent trends clearly suggest that this is unlikely to happen. Italy will become a far more multi-ethnic society than she is at present, with the Italian proportion decreasing.

GLOSSARIO	*GLOSSARY*
la popolazione	*population*
il tasso di natalità	*birth rate*
calare	*to fall*
la media	*average*
basso	*low*
alto	*high*
predire	*to predict*
diventare	*to become*
la società	*society*
multi-etnico	*multi-ethnic*

The family

The family has always been the foundation stone of Italian society and still remains an institution that has stood up well to developments and changes that have had a more detrimental effect on family life in other European countries. In Italy it is not just a question of the immediate family – parents and children – but the extended family: the grandparents, aunts, uncles, cousins, nephews, nieces, etc.

The feeling of closeness and solidarity is reflected wherever you go and nowhere more so than on special occasions – christenings, marriages, a child's first communion – which are all extremely important. The entire family gathers to celebrate such events, which are usually followed by a meal at a restaurant. On happy or sad occasions the family unit rarely conceals its emotions.

The importance of the family and family life is in keeping with the tradition of the Catholic faith. Paradoxically, however, married couples are now having fewer children. One of the reasons for this is the more widespread use of contraception, which is strongly condemned by the Catholic Church.

The failure of the nation to provide certain essential social services in the past has strengthened family bonds. It has fallen on the family to fill this void by caring for sick relatives who in other countries might have been looked after in an institution. This has never been considered a chore but rather a duty.

The family as an economic unit

The financial burden on Italian parents is quite considerable given that many 'children' remain with their parents until the age of 28 or 30, usually until they marry. Those who study at university until their mid-twenties or beyond are almost certainly dependent on the family, whereas those in employment would normally make some contribution to their upkeep. Nearly 60 per cent of Italian males remain at home until they are 30 – the highest percentage in Europe.

This is the norm for most Italian parents and they are perfectly happy about it. The attitude of young people to their parents is very positive because they appreciate the sacrifices made on their behalf. Thus this important family tradition carries on. When their parents get old they feel obliged to look after them as long as possible. The idea of putting parents or grandparents in a home is alien to most Italians.

Italian parents are very protective, rather over-protective at times and this can have negative consequences, particularly for the male, who becomes used to having everything done for him and is at a loss when he has to fend for himself. The mother seems to carry on this tradition by getting the daughter to do the housework and the cooking. Mothers will fret over their 30- or 40-year-old sons who have gone abroad to work. Who will do their laundry? What about the cooking? 'We suffer from *mammismo* [a maternal cult]', says Antonio Gambino in his book *An Italian Journey.*

Are changes inevitable?

If recent developments have any significance then the question arises as to how long it will be before cracks appear in this family foundation stone. Some fissures are already appearing but Italy still has some way to go before it is on a par with what has already happened in many other Western European countries. Here are some facts and figures:

- the low birth rate means that the number of old people is increasing. Italy now has one of the oldest populations in the world. In 1973, 1 in 10 of the population was over 65. This figure rose to 1 in 5 by the end of 2002 and is predicted to become 1 in 3 by 2033
- the days of large families – households of six or more – seem to be over
- the number of single old people is rising, as is the number of older couples without children
- 11 per cent of families are single-parent
- very few families have two children and women are tending to have their first child much later – at 28 in 1995 compared to 25 in 1970. Those who have at least three children number less than 15 per cent
- there is a big increase in married couples without children
- there is a rise in the number of separations and divorces which increased by 37.5 per cent and 39 per cent respectively between 1995 and 2000. One marriage in four ends up in legal separation and one out of nine in divorce
- there are fewer marriages – 260,000 in 2001 compared with 290,000 in 1995 – and living together is preferred by 20 per cent of women. The number of *matrimoni misti* (mixed marriages) has increased – more than 20,000 in 2000.

On the above evidence there are going to be fewer younger people around to look after ageing parents or grandparents. Many young couples only have one child because they realize that bringing up a family has become very expensive. There is also evidence to suggest that the next generation of Italian mothers will be less willing to spend time in the kitchen, bring up children and look after them until late in life. Thus they will no longer be fulfilling the traditional family role.

Although at the moment the sense of the family remains very strong, any combination of these facts could have a detrimental effect on the Italian family some time in the future.

GLOSSARIO	GLOSSARY
la famiglia	family
l'istituzione	institution
la vita familiare	family life
mettere su famiglia	to start a family
un'occasione speciale	a special occasion
il battesimo	christening
il matrimonio	marriage
la tradizione	tradition
badare a	to look after
i parenti	relatives
i genitori	parents
spendere	to spend (money)
educare i figli	to bring up/educate children
rimanere a casa	to stay at home
fino a	up to, until
apprezzare	to appreciate
il sacrificio	sacrifice
le faccende domestiche	the housework
essere abituato a	to be used to
gli anziani	the old/elderly
aumentare	to increase
rispetto a	compared to
la madre	mother
il ruolo	role

The roles of the sexes

The feminist movements

Article 3 of the Italian Constitution states that *'tutti i cittadini sono uguali di fronte alla legge senza distinzione di sesso, razza, di lingua, ecc.'* (all citizens are equal before the law without distinction of sex, race, language, etc.). Article 37 states that men and women should receive *le stesse retribuzioni* (the same pay) for doing the same work. This same article, however, reflects the influence of a strong Catholic tradition as it implies that the woman's first duty is to the home and family life, an attitude still prevalent today in the Catholic Church.

The Fascist regime tried to exclude women from the world of work. Despite the fact that women had served in the partisan movement during the Second World War, obtained *il diritto di voto* (the right to vote) in 1946 and were accorded certain rights in the 1948 Constitution, they remained in a state of inferiority and subordination in a male-dominated society. Once the post-war economic boom came to an end they were the first to lose their jobs.

The seeds of change were sown in the 1960s, when a higher percentage of women than ever before continued their studies in upper secondary schools and then at university. They started to become more aware of their position in society and realized that they had achieved a degree of emancipation without this being adequately reflected in the laws. Feminist groups began to form and in 1968 they protested against the lack of reform. Their cause was supported by the Radical Party.

The road to progress lay in the foundation of Women's Movements that would act as a platform and co-ordinating force for their views. The two most important movements of the time were UDI (*Unione Donne Italiane* – Union of Italian Women) and the MLD (*Movimento di Liberazione della Donna* – Women's Liberation Movement). These associations gave the women a consciousness previously lacking. They became people with rights.

The following are among a number of significant developments in the 1970s:

- **1970** – a divorce law was passed and upheld by the 1974 referendum with 60 per cent in favour. It became possible to divorce after a five-year separation.
- **1971** – the law on the protection of women's jobs. Expectant mothers were entitled to two months' maternity leave before the birth and three months afterwards. The present entitlement is five months leave on full pay and six on 30 per cent, if only the mother or only the father stays at home. If the parents wish to take it in turns to stay at home after the birth, then the *congedi parentali* (parental leave) entitlement extends to ten months rather than six. This leave can be taken over one continuous period or at convenient intervals until the child is three.
- **1975** – the reform of the family law which gave the wife and husband equal rights. Adultery was no longer considered a criminal offence. A married woman had the right to retain

her family name. Children born in and out of wedlock were also accorded equal rights.

- 1977 – the law against sexual discrimination in the workplace. Women were entitled to the same pay as men for doing the same job.
- 1978 – the law on abortion was passed and upheld by the 1981 referendum.
- 1980s – other laws were passed allowing women to enter professions that had been entirely male-dominated, e.g. the police force.

The crime of honour

It was not until 1981, however, that the *delitto d'onore* (crime of honour) became illegal. Before that, a man had the right to kill his wife if she committed adultery, without facing the possibility of imprisonment. Adultery was considered an act of betrayal to the man personally and brought great dishonour to the family name. If a husband indulged in extramarital activities, it was deemed to be a display of his manhood. The daughter of the family also had to conduct herself in the proper manner if she did not want to incur the wrath of her father or brother(s), whose duty it was to seek vengeance either on her personally or on the offending male.

The *delitto d'onore* was more of a custom in southern Italy. A lovely scene in the early *Godfather* film illustrates these attitudes. The Godfather's son, Al Pacino, has been sent in exile to Sicily, where he meets a beautiful young girl. In the scene referred to they are walking through the woods. Suddenly the camera swings back to a whole line of the girl's family walking behind, just to ensure, of course, that family honour is not sullied in any way. It was not uncommon for young girls in all parts of Italy to be chaperoned by their mothers or grandmothers when they went to a dance, for example.

A change of direction!

As elsewhere, Italian women nowadays decide how many children to have, they divorce and/or separate, work, study, etc. They generally have a higher level of education than the male population (see next section). They are more career-minded and consequently tend to get married much later than in the past – the late, as opposed to the early, twenties. Those who find good jobs are reluctant to give them up and are therefore less keen to start a family straightaway, one of the principal reasons for the decrease in the birth rate.

Changing attitudes

Equality of opportunity has meant that you now see women working in sectors that were once entirely male-dominated. There are women ticket inspectors, traffic wardens, pilots, engineers, etc. In the D'Alema government six women held Cabinet posts, an all-time record. Previous to this, the highest office in Italian politics was held by Nilde Iotti when she became President of the House of Deputies in 1979. In general, however, there are few women in Parliament and on administrative councils.

Thus, despite changing attitudes, the following facts do illustrate that the playing field is far from level:

- in 1993 only 16 per cent of managers in industry, agriculture, the retail and service sectors were women; five years later the proportion was nearly 18 per cent
- in 1995 more than half of university graduates were women yet only six out of every hundred were managers of companies
- in 1998 only one in three women had a contract of employment
- women represent a high proportion of the unemployed
- women rarely figure in the top bracket of wage earners because most are doing the lower-paid jobs in the service sector – secretaries, receptionists, nurses, civil servants
- many women are involved in casual and part-time work
- in the health and education sectors, where there is a predominance of women employees, the top managerial positions are held by men

We must not omit from the equation the fact that there are women with families who are happy to accept not being promoted to the higher echelons and earning the top salaries because they prefer to spend more time at home with the children. At least women can retire earlier. Until the end of 1999 the age was 64 for men and 59 for women. From 1 January 2000 it rose to 65 and 60 respectively, as there is no longer enough money in the pension pot to pay those seeking early retirement.

From work to work!

Despite changes in the workplace outside the home, the results of surveys have underlined that habits and attitudes in the home have been much slower to change. (In fairness, this picture is not peculiar to Italy alone.) Many Italian men would need to go on an orienteering course to find the kitchen, let alone know how to operate the gadgets in it – the cooker, for example.

Now the woman has to play her 'traditional' role plus do a hard day's 'career' work. Paradoxical as it may seem, she herself is often to blame. The figure of the *mammone* (mummy's boy) is still a reality. The young girl is trained to follow in the mother's footsteps whereas the young male is mollycoddled and protected from the potential dangers of housework.

However, there is a ray of hope in the younger breed of married couples. Amongst this younger, more emancipated generation there are men who have come to realize that they can push the pram and not just lean on it and who do the household chores while the wife has a night out with her friends. These are positive signs but there is still some way to go. Some Italians are concerned that things may go too far and are marrying girls from the Far East, such as the Philippines, because they are more obedient!

GLOSSARIO	*GLOSSARY*
i movimenti femministi	*feminist movements*
all'inizio (di)	*at the beginning (of)*
la parità	*parity, equality*
il dovere	*duty*
l'atteggiamento	*attitude*
perdere il posto di lavoro	*to lose your job*
riprendere	*to resume*

la casalinga	*housewife*
tre su quattro	*three out of four*
la società patriarcale	*patriarchal society*
un essere umano	*a human being*
la legge	*law*
la riforma	*reform*
separarsi	*to separate*
l'aborto	*abortion*
avere il diritto (di)	*to have the right (to)*
comportarsi	*to behave*
il costume	*custom*
divorziare	*to divorce*
sposarsi	*to get married*
la metà dei laureati	*half the graduates*
il contratto di lavoro	*contract of employment*
interrompere	*to interrupt*
la carriera	*career*
guadagnare	*to earn*
un'indagine	*a survey*
mettere in rilievo	*to highlight*
la colpa	*fault, blame*
coccolare	*to mollycoddle*

Immigration

Italy was once the country of mass emigration (see also Units 1 and 2). She is now experiencing the reverse trend, something which some of her European partners, Britain, France and Germany, have experienced much earlier. The immigrant population in 1992 stood at 700,000. This rose to 1.7 million by 2002, representing about 3.4 per cent of the country's population. Italy proceeded to tighten up on its immigration policy and the Bossi-Fini law approved on 30 July 2002 stipulates that 'foreigners', except for reasons of study or tourism, can only enter Italy if they have *un contratto di lavoro* (a contract of employment). In the first four months of 2003 more than 33,000 immigrants arrived in Italy and more than 19,000 illegal immigrants were expelled. Despite this substantial increase in numbers in recent years Italy still has fewer foreign residents than most other European countries. The table on p. 230 lists the top ten countries of origin.

Country of origin	Immigrant population
Morocco	122,230
Tunisia	41,439
Former Yugoslavia	73,492
Albania	72,551
Romania	28,796
Philippines	57,312
United States	44,652
China	35,310
Germany	32,442
Senegal	32,037

*Statistical information, as at 1 January 1998, provided by
ISTAT Istituto Centrale di Statistica.*

Since 1998 the number of immigrants from Morocco, Albania
and Romania has increased significantly.

Why Italy?

About 40 per cent of the immigrants are from North Africa.
Most are fleeing the poverty and civil wars raging through their
countries. Albanians, Romanians and inhabitants of the former
Yugoslavia seek refuge in Italy from political strife. Other
reasons for choosing Italy are: the proximity, the realization that
she has hitherto adopted a very lax and highly considerate
immigration policy and the fact that Italy figures among the
leading industrial nations in the world.

Those from the Philippines come to the country to work mainly
as *colf* (domestics/home help). Many of the Chinese immigrants
are employed in the smaller factories in central Italy. A number
of Germans have bought homes in Tuscany and acquired Italian
residence in this way. A reasonable percentage of the Americans
work for companies like IBM.

Fairly recently there has been a flood of Albanian refugees, many
of whom have been shipped into the country illegally via Puglia
in the south. Among them are hundreds of unaccompanied
minors, mostly 14- to 16-year olds, who are given every
assistance to try and track down their families. If this proves
unsuccessful they are put up for adoption. Unfortunately, some
of these youngsters escape the clutches of the authorities and fall
prey to unscrupulous racketeers, who get them involved in
criminal organizations. Italy has entered into bilateral
negotiations with Albania to try to resolve the crisis.

Employment

According to a news report on Italian television (1999) immigrants are mainly employed in the following sectors:

- 22 per cent as home helps
- 14 per cent in restaurants
- 14 per cent in the building industry
- 14 per cent as *venditori ambulanti* (pedlars)
- 10 per cent in agriculture
- 6 per cent in factories

Italy needs to take on immigrants to make the economy function and they are most welcome to the employers in the north-east, where there is a shortage of labour. Given the scenario forecast by demographers for the year 2017, when the Italians will be 6 million fewer because of the drop in the birth rate, the role of the immigrant population will become even more economically and culturally significant. During the time of the economic boom in the late 1950s, southern Italians were prepared to move to the north in search of work, especially to the industrial triangle of Genoa, Milan and Turin. Today the most sought-after areas are in the booming north-east, which has become the heartland of the small and medium-sized industries. Italians generally are not keen on moving too far away from their home to seek employment but this remains the only option for many southerners in particular. Immigrants, on the other hand, will go where the work is and are prepared to do the lesser-paid menial tasks and manual work. The cities and regions preferred by the immigrants are Turin (Piedmont), Milan (Lombardy), Rome (Lazio) and Naples (Campania).

The government stance

The immigrant population started to rise sharply in the latter half of the 1990s and the trend has continued ever since. The D'Alema government in 1998 was prepared to accept a further 230,000 immigrants on the waiting list provided that they met certain requirements. To accept this number at the time meant that the total number of legal foreign workers would surpass the million mark, equivalent today to only 2 per cent of the entire population – compared to 7 per cent in Germany and 5 per cent in France. This unprecedented measure, however, will not be repeated since future policy is to impose a yearly limit, taking account of employment prospects and the capacity of the country to provide adequate provision for their stay. It is estimated that there will be an annual increase of 110,000, which would mean that in 2010 they would constitute 4 per cent of the country's population. On the question of illegal immigrants both the Bossi-Fini law mentioned previously (see p. 229) and the Home Office Minister have made the government position quite clear. There are immigration laws and they must be respected. Infringements of these laws will result in expulsion, the fate of 81,936 illegal immigrants in Berlusconi's first year in office, an increase of 31.95 per cent on the previous year.

The Government wants to promote good relationships between Italians and foreigners, and the new immigration law of 6 March 1998 paved the way for a more integrated policy. To achieve this it is always going to be necessary to intervene on different levels: cultural, educational, social, job training and accommodation. One important objective in the integration process is to teach the immigrants Italian. Children of immigrants have already been integrated into the education system. In 1998 there were 63,199 foreign children in Italian State schools and 36,591 were *extracomunitari* (a term usually used to convey 'non-European'). Compare this total figure with the one in 1983, when there were little more than 3,000. The Government also organizes courses for adults. In addition to government aid, voluntary organizations like Caritas and the church parishes do a lot to integrate and welcome the immigrants into their communities.

The 1998 law sees legal immigration as a positive resource and a cultural enrichment from which the whole nation can benefit. The Government's fair and responsible attitude to immigration has the support of the Church, the trade unions and *Confindustria* (the Confederation of Italian Industry). A positive example of good race relations and respect for another culture has been given by certain factories in Emilia Romagna. They allow their Muslim immigrant employees to work on Saturday instead of Friday.

Racism

Italians are on the whole tolerant towards the immigrant population. However, there are the almost inevitable episodes of xenophobia and you see graffiti daubed on walls, e.g. *Non si affitta agli extracomunitari* (We don't let property to non-European residents). There has been a reaction in some quarters to the use of *extracomunitario* as a racist label. One suggestion is that *forestieri* (foreigners) should be used in its place. It has to be remembered that acts of racism are not confined to foreigners.

Southerners who came to work in the industrialized centres of the north in the past were subjected to racial abuse. The most commonly used derogatory term was *terrone* ('inhabitant of the south'; the word derives from *terra* meaning 'earth').

The major preoccupation of most Italians is that with high unemployment the foreigners are further jeopardizing their job opportunities. Those who come from a poorer society will accept wages and conditions that the indigenous population would not. Immigrants are often made the *capri espiatori* (scapegoats), unjustifiably according to statistics, for the rise in crime and social disorder. Right-wing groups such as the *Lega Nord* and *Forza Italia* are inclined to seize on moments like these to highlight the inherent dangers for Italian society. They depict a gloomy picture, which, in their estimation, can only be brightened if more hard-line policies are adopted. The *Lega Nord* wanted a repeal of the 1998 law on immigration and it managed to get 150,000 signatures on a petition in just two days.

GLOSSARIO	*GLOSSARY*
l'immigrazione	immigration
immigrare	to immigrate
il numero	number
la percentuale	percentage
il permesso di lavoro	work permit
il permesso di soggiorno	residence permit
rilasciare	to issue
l'immigrante	immigrant
emigrare	to emigrate
la lista d'attesa	waiting list
i documenti	papers
tenere conto (di qc)	to take (something) into account
le prospettive di lavoro	job prospects
rispettare	to respect
l'arrivo	arrival
i profughi albanesi	Albanian refugees
trattare	to treat
rintracciare	to trace (a missing person)
un fenomeno recente	a recent phenomenon
la lingua	language
imparare	to learn
la firma	signature
clandestino	clandestine
incoraggiare	to encourage

The environment

Pollution

The main causes of pollution in Italy are no different from those in any other major developed nation – industry, agriculture, traffic, tourism, urban and domestic waste, etc. They all contribute in varying degrees to the pollution of the rivers, seas, lakes, air, and also to various health problems. *L'ambiente* (the environment) has paid a heavy price for the economic progress achieved since the early 1960s. Let us consider some of Italy's main concerns.

Drinking water

Water is an essential resource for the whole nation. Yet there are serious distribution problems in some parts of the country, mainly in the south, and the overall quality of drinking water is not good. Most Italians drink *acqua minerale* (mineral water) rather than *acqua del rubinetto* (tap water). The current situation is the result of decades of pollution of the rivers, lakes and underground water channels, industry and agriculture being the principal culprits. Agriculture's dependence on fertilizers can be gauged by the fact that *agricoltura biologica* (organic farming) accounts for only about 5 per cent of its produce.

The sea

The seas most affected by pollution are those off the western and eastern coasts of northern Italy. The north and centre-north are highly industrialized, far more developed agriculturally than elsewhere in Italy and have areas of mass tourism along the coast. The overall picture is one of expansion and economic success but environmental neglect. The large petrochemical complex of Porto Marghera near Venice is a case in point. The development of this site depended greatly on big oil tankers gaining access to the harbour area. To accommodate these ships wider and deeper channels had to be dug at the mouths of the Lido di Malamocco. The city of Venice has been paying the price of this development ever since, because mud banks that served as natural sea defences have been removed. A combination of high tides and strong winds now regularly brings flooding to St Mark's Square and surrounding areas. However, a flood relief system, approved by Berlusconi's government, might just be around the corner. (It has been on the agenda of various governments for more than thirty years!) The project is aptly named Mosè (Moses – and the parting of the Red Sea) and will involve the construction of barriers that can be raised at times of high tide. If it all goes to plan it will be completed by 2010.

The construction of *impianti di depurazione* (purification plants) along the coast has been a positive step towards limiting sea pollution. Voluntary environmental groups like *Legambiente* and *Amici della terra* (Friends of the Earth) help to clean the beaches and the shoreline, which are constantly threatened by the oil tankers heading for Italy's many oil refineries.

Deforestation

Italy has extensive woodlands and forests that are extremely vulnerable during the hot, dry summer months. If you glance at the newspapers during this period it is rare not to read of a forest fire raging somewhere in the hills or mountainous regions. In the first eight months of 2003 – a particularly bad year in Europe generally – the number of fires was almost double the figure recorded over the same period in 2002. These fires are not always started accidentally. The *tagliafuochi* (firebreaks) do help to contain them; nevertheless the environmental cost – loss of trees, animal and plant life – is huge.

A further consequence is that the unprotected soil becomes loose and causes landslides at times of heavy rainfall. In the late 1990s a landslide in the vicinity of Naples brought thousands of tonnes of mud cascading down on a village, destroying everything in its path and resulting in the death of a number of local inhabitants. Landslides occur frequently throughout Italy. Observe the signs along the roadsides and you regularly come across *Pericolo frane* (Danger landslides) or *Caduta massi* (Falling rocks).

In addition to the destruction of forests by fire, whole areas of woodland have been cut down to develop ski resorts and build roads, tunnels and viaducts.

Nature conservation

Construction work for the development of tourism and indiscriminate hunting over many years have led to the disappearance of animal species that were once commonplace in mountain areas – for example, deer, chamois, bears, eagles and peregrine falcons. The creation of more national and regional parks has certainly saved some of these animals from extinction. These reserves have strict regulations in place to protect the fauna and flora – limits are imposed on hunting, fishing and flower-picking, and rangers patrol the parks to ensure that the code of conduct is respected.

Traffic pollution

Much has already been said in Unit 9 about traffic problems. The pollution caused by traffic in most cities reaches dangerous levels at times and the number of people with respiratory complaints is on the increase. In Turin many days can go by without being able to see the surrounding mountains because of the smog hanging over the city. In Rome the traffic reaches nightmare proportions on most days. Air pollution, moreover, attacks and gradually erodes the thousands of outdoor ancient monuments and buildings.

On a more optimistic note a survey in 1999 conducted on behalf of ACI, *Automobile Club d'Italia* (the Automobile Association) found that car use had decreased in Rome, Naples and Milan during 1998 (but had increased in the smaller and medium-sized cities). The reasons given for the decrease were traffic congestion and the difficulty of finding a parking space; many of those interviewed said that they now used the *motorino* (moped), *mezzi pubblici* (public transport) or walked.

The environmental situation is not helped by the lack of parks. The average 'green space' per citizen is very low compared to other European cities. Most of the available space has been taken up by industries, housing, etc. Here are at least some more positive pointers to the future:

• *isole pedonali* (pedestrian precincts) are becoming much more common

- access to some parts of towns and cities is limited to residents only
- visitors and tourists have to park their cars outside some town centres, e.g. Modena and Siena, and use public transport if they so wish. Modena is in Emilia Romagna, a region that has always been a shining example to others when it comes to adopting sensible policies.

Noise

Another serious concern in built-up urban areas is the noise level. It has been reported that the noise level in most Italian cities, during the day and at night, usually reaches levels on the decibel scale well beyond those recommended by the European Union. The constant pounding of the traffic is the main contributory factor. Italians are also inclined to toot their car horns at frequent intervals. Not to be discounted in this cocktail of noise are the animated and normally loud conversations. To an outsider it would seem that a violent quarrel is taking place. To anyone who knows something about the Italian character it is a quiet debate. Add to the equation the millions of tourists who invade Italy every year and you have a recipe for a lot of noise.

Domestic and urban waste

Rubbish is another of the chief causes of environmental pollution. What makes matters worse in Italy is the existence of *discariche abusive* (illegal dumps) – forest rangers counted 4,866 in 2002. Far too little waste is taken to legal sites where by law the rubbish is then sorted. Some is burnt in *inceneratori* (incinerators) but the cost of this operation is much higher and more dangerous for the environment because of the toxic gases released into the atmosphere. Less than 5 per cent is recycled, although there are containers in the streets for paper, glass, cans, and unused medicines. A separate tax is levied by the local authorities for the collection of household rubbish.

Smoking

According to a survey carried out in 2003, 27.6 per cent of the population are smokers and far fewer women (22.5 per cent) smoke than men (33.2 per cent). The general trend is down. A ban on smoking on public transport, in cinemas and theatres has been in force since 1975 but this has since been extended to most public areas.

General attitudes to the environment

Italians, like other nationalities, become more concerned about the environment when tragedies strike. The Seveso (near Milan) incident some years ago was quite devastating. Poisonous gases were released into the atmosphere, causing severe health problems to local inhabitants and making the surrounding land unusable for years afterwards. The Chernobyl nuclear incident served to re-awaken awareness of the dangers of this form of energy and the overall reaction of the Italian people led to an abandonment of the country's nuclear programme.

Elementary school children are involved in projects that are aimed at making them aware of the importance of protecting their environment. Amongst the remainder of the population there are, as everywhere else, the committed environmentalists but the pendulum is still swinging on the side of economic gain, which usually means environmental loss. Pope John Paul II underlined this point in an article in the Italian newspaper *La Repubblica* (13 March 1999) – '*l'egoismo dei ricchi distrugge il globo*' (the selfishness of the rich is destroying the globe).

GLOSSARIO	GLOSSARY
l'acqua potabile	drinking water
la causa	cause
il disboscamento	deforestation
l'inquinamento	pollution
inquinare	to pollute
i rifiuti domestici	domestic waste

la qualità	*quality*
il mare	*sea*
la marea	*tide*
l'inondazione	*flood*
pulire	*to clean*
il bosco	*wood*
la foresta	*forest*
un incendio	*a fire*
abbattere	*to knock down (a tree)*
l'albero	*tree*
costruire	*to build*
la caccia	*hunting*
la scomparsa	*disappearance*
il parco nazionale	*national park*
la pesca	*fishing*
cogliere i fiori	*to pick the flowers*
la mancanza di verde	*lack of green (greenery)*
il parco	*park*
il parcheggio sotterraneo	*underground parking*
il rumore	*noise*
sorpassare	*to exceed*
la mostra	*exhibition*
creare	*to create*
smaltire i rifiuti	*to dispose of the rubbish*
riciclare	*to recycle*
il contenitore	*container*
la carta	*paper*
il vetro	*glass*
la lattina	*can*
la raccolta	*collection*
fumare	*to smoke*
un divieto	*a ban*
proteggere	*to protect*
la marmitta catalitica	*catalytic converter*
il tubo di scappamento	*exhaust*
i bus navetta	*shuttle buses (park and ride)*
le busvie	*bus-lanes*

Religious observance

Italy's population is 98 per cent Catholic but only around 25 per cent regularly attend church. This number is boosted on special occasions such as baptisms, weddings, funerals, Easter Sunday and the Christmas midnight mass. The first communion still remains a popular event. Church weddings have decreased as more couples opt for *il matrimonio civile* (civil wedding) at the *municipio* (town hall). There was a time when Italy was very liberal with its days off to celebrate a whole host of saints. The saints remain but the days off for religious celebrations have been drastically reduced. Two that have remained, which are outside the 'normal' holidays, are *Ognissanti* (All Saints' Day) on 1 November and *l'Immacolata Concezione* (Immaculate Conception) on 8 December (see Unit 6).

The second largest religious community in Italy is Muslim. The majority of the Muslims originate from North Africa. There are 30 Islamic centres in Italy and mosques in most regions.

Mosques in Italy (by region)	
Liguria and Piedmont	18
Lombardy	18
Tuscany	8
Emilia Romagna and Umbria	17
Lazio and Abruzzo	18
Campania, Calabria, Puglia, Sicilia	20

Given that Italy once recognized Catholicism as the sole faith within its territory, a symbol of the changing times was the inauguration of the first mosque in the headquarters of the Catholic Church, Rome, in 1995.

GLOSSARIO	GLOSSARY
il paese cattolico	Catholic country
la religione	religion
la chiesa	church
andare in chiesa	to go to church
il battesimo	baptism
il matrimonio	wedding
sposarsi	to get married
la moschea	mosque
i musulmani	Muslims
ridurre	to reduce

Taking it further

Suggested reading

Contemporary Italy – Politics, Economy and Society since 1945 (Second Edition), Donald Sassoon, Addison Wesley 1997

Modern Italy 1871–1995 (Second Edition), Martin Clark, Longman 1996

A History of Contemporary Italy, Paul Ginsborg, Penguin 1990

Italian Cultural Statistics: An Introduction, ed. David Forgecs and Bob Lumley, OUP 1996

L'Italia del tempo presente, Paul Ginsborg, Einaudi 1998

The most recent **Microsoft Encarta Encyclopedia** on CD ROM.

Websites

www.lonelyplanet.com/dest/eur/ita.htm#facts
www.initaly.com
www.istat.it
www.legambiente.it
www.amicidellaterra.it

12

Italy in the wider world

In this unit you will learn
- about the role and importance of Italy on a European and world-wide scale
- about recent changes and reforms that have been implemented
- about some long-standing problems that remain unresolved

The European dimension

Italy – a founder member of the Common Market, now the European Union – has always seen herself at the heart of Europe and dutifully joined the euro band at the start of the new millennium. She is a long-standing member of Nato and was very prominent in the headlines during the 1999 conflict with Serbia, as most of the aircraft that bombarded targets in Serbia or Kosovo took off from Nato bases in Italy. In the Italian Parliament there were rumblings of discontent regarding Nato policy. Throughout the conflict there was great concern about the refugee problem. Despite the recent immigrant influx into the country (see Unit 11), Italy made a greater aid contribution than most countries to alleviate as much as possible the plight of the refugees.

In the recent Iraq conflict Italy did not send troops to join the American and British forces but Berlusconi's government supported the cause and made its military bases available. Berlusconi is a great ally and supporter of George Bush and this, coupled with the fact that there are a number of American bases in Italy, has meant that the country, along with many other countries it has to be said, remains a potential target for terrorist attacks.

The reason for the Nato and American bases in Italy can be traced back to the end of the Second World War, when the country became a kind of buffer state between the Western democracies and the Communist Eastern bloc. Italy occupied a crucial strategic position in the Mediterranean during the time of the Cold War. In Unit 8 the gradual increase in the political power of the Italian Communist Party was highlighted. The Americans were prepared to pour Marshall Aid into Italy to help the economy and the restructuring process on condition that the Communists were kept out of government. The Americans have had a foothold in Italy ever since.

The European elections

The outcome of the 1999 European elections highlighted once again the need for electoral reform in Italy to go the whole way. The results of these elections meant that leaders of seven different factions between them polled about 11 per cent of the vote. These leaders were aptly referred to as '*i sette nani*' (the seven dwarfs) in the national newspaper *Corriere della Sera*.

In political elections there are very often no winners and no losers and this has made the country virtually ungovernable at times. The ordinary citizens may have become blasé to some extent but they have also become very frustrated. In internal elections there is a general feeling that parties with less than 5 per cent of the vote should not be represented in Parliament. This would probably have the desired effect of reducing the number of political parties to more manageable and more meaningful proportions. D'Alema (see p. 168) had the idea of a 100 per cent majority system of voting high on the agenda. It didn't happen during his term in office and is unlikely to happen for some time yet!

Political scandals

Following the scandals and resignations of ministers of the European Commission in Brussels in 1999, Romano Prodi, a former Italian Prime Minister, was elected President of the Commission. A connection was made in the Italian press between the scandal on the European scale and the *Mani pulite* (see Unit 8) scandal that rocked Italy in 1992. Prodi drew up a list of 'Ten Commandments' in an attempt to root out corruption and ensure that ministers abide by a strict set of rules. The scars left by the *Mani pulite* affair in Italy will take a long time to heal and, like Prodi, present and future ministers have a lot to do to win back and retain the trust of the majority of the electorate.

To continue on the political note, Italy finds herself in a rather curious, paradoxical situation as regards Europe. The country had to make great sacrifices to get its economy on a reasonably even keel before joining the euro, and being part of this monetary system was seen as a route to greater stability. D'Alema hoped that the euro would signal the end of the model of development founded on economic deficit and would lead to a change of direction in Italy's history. However, the strength of the link with Europe will require internal modernization. Italy has already gone some way down that road. Gone are the days of huge public companies. According to very recent figures produced by the government agency ISTAT, 77.8 per cent of businesses employ 1–2 people, 17.5 per cent 3–9 and only 0.2 per cent have more than 100 employees.

Italy finds herself in an anomalous situation as part of a European political system that wishes to present a united front when within Italy there is danger of creating greater divisions. The *Lega Nord* remains strongly in favour of the northern regions breaking away from the rest of Italy, thus creating a kind of federalist State. This is a reminder of the north–south question that has remained unresolved since unification.

What of the future?

Italy now adopts an economic policy that other European nations embraced much earlier, i.e. a greater balance between the private and public sectors. The D'Alema government contributed to this process either by bringing in or proposing changes that at the time seemed almost revolutionary, in some cases at least. For instance:

- It ended the State gas and electricity monopolies, opening the market to private companies.
- A reform of the Health Service that obliged doctors to choose to work either in the public or private sector. They can no longer have a foot in both camps. They also have to attend *corsi di aggiornamento* (refresher courses) to keep abreast of the latest developments in their field. Previously many qualified doctors continued to practise medicine for the remainder of their working lives without ever attending another course.
- *I primari* (chief consultants) in charge of hospital units once had their jobs guaranteed for life and had almost god-like status. The new reform has brought an end to this 'golden' era. They are to be made more accountable, and every five years they will have to go before a medical council to determine whether their contracts will be renewed.
- There has been a great deal of discussion about the pension system and employees are going to have to pay contributions for up to 40 years. (Pension reform remained high on Berlusconi's agenda when he came to power in 2001.) In the past there were people on pensions who were in their early thirties. The question of fraud also needs to be addressed. There have been instances of 'blind' people on a disability pension still driving a car. There was an extreme case of someone who was on a disability pension for being severely handicapped and confined to a wheelchair. The person in question was one day seen being hotly pursued – on foot – by the police after committing a bank robbery.

- The 35-hour working week is still on the agenda. It will be interesting to see if this measure is realized and the possible effect it will have on reducing unemployment.

- On 21 June 1999 a new quick delivery postal service came into operation to ensure that at least 70 per cent of the mail gets to its destination in 24 hours. This innovation has been given the title of *Posta Prioritaria* (Priority Mail). This has brought Italy in line with other European countries where the system is already in operation.

- An attempt has been made to reduce bureaucracy and red tape. No country is without its bureaucratic machine but Italy's at times has been top-heavy. As a result, Italians have a knack of circumventing the system and show a high degree of initiative in this regard! To get something done on an official level, e.g. the extension of a fishing licence, often means acquiring a collection of *carta bollata* (official stamped paper), which is time-consuming and can be very expensive as it incurs a charge every time.

- Parts of the education reform have been introduced, e.g. the *esame di Stato* (see p. 176) and the raising of the school leaving age to 15. Before these initial changes were finally implemented there was the inevitable reaction and protest from both teachers and students that culminated in marches and the occupation of school buildings. Before all the more recent Moratti proposals (p. 177) see the light of day, in ten or so years' time, the academic road ahead will no doubt be a little bumpy – understandable, perhaps, given that it is the biggest educational shake-up since 1923.

- The question of immigration is constantly under review (see Unit 11).

The current government under Silvio Berlusconi's leadership will almost certainly want to encourage private enterprise and initiatives. Given some of the hugely expensive projects in the pipeline it would be difficult to see how they could be financed just from the public purse. Reference has already been made to some of these projects in earlier units. One which hasn't been mentioned – save the best until last! – is the construction of a 5-kilometre bridge across the Straits of Messina, which would link Sicily to mainland Italy. It would indeed be a tremendous feat given that this area is prone to considerable seismic activity. Should it go ahead the projected completion date is 2015.

Two issues that governments over the years have addressed but failed to resolve are tax evasion and criminal organizations.

Tax evasion

Italians complain about the burden of direct and indirect taxation. Italy is no different from any other country in that the government of the day has to raise revenue from taxation to fund public services. The problem for decades has been that too many belonging to the ranks of the highly paid have, according to their tax declaration forms, been earning less than a manual worker. The second home by the sea, the yacht, the high lifestyle are obviously all thanks to some Charitable Institution. Attempts have been made to cut down on the tax dodgers but newspaper stories today are no different from those you would have read 30 or so years ago.

Criminal organizations

Italy has three long-established criminal organizations, the *Mafia*, the *Camorra* and the *'ndrangheta*. The former's home base was Palermo in Sicily but it has developed its business quite extensively over the years. The last big trial, which brought some 400 *mafiosi* to justice, was when Buscetta *il pentito* (supergrass) decided to break the *omertà* (vow of silence) and spill the beans. Such a courageous act normally involves a subsequent change of name, a change of face, quite literally, and a lifetime of looking over your shoulder.

The *Mafia* had been kept in harness during Mussolini's regime but resurfaced when its help was enlisted at the time of the American landings in Sicily during the Second World War. It has generally flourished ever since, spreading its tentacles far and wide. Following the mass trial of the *mafiosi* there were concerted efforts to pursue others involved in the organization. There were the inevitable tragic losses along the way, one of the most notable being the assassination of Judge Falcone. These past years have brought some arrests but generally a certain amount of momentum has been lost. *Mafia* activities include drug trafficking, money laundering, extortion, and illegal building contracts. (In 2002 over 30,000 illegal homes were built in Italy, a 9 per cent increase on the previous year.)

The *Camorra* is based in Naples and mainly controls organized crime in this area. *Camorra* derives from the Spanish word *gamurra*, meaning 'extortion money', and this 'secret society' dates back to the mid-nineteenth century. Like the *Mafia*, the *Camorra* gets its income from building projects, dealing in drugs and contraband cigarettes and extortion. After the 1980 earthquake in the Naples area, the region received the equivalent of billions and billions of lire to help the reconstruction process. Much of this money ended up in the *Camorra* coffers, which helped them develop and diversify their business.

The *'ndrangheta* has its home in Calabria and the word originates from a Greek dialect, meaning 'bravery/courage'. The activities of this organization are similar to those of the *Mafia* and *Camorra*, although kidnapping is one of its specialities. One of the most notorious kidnappings was of the 16-year-old oil heir John Paul Getty III back in the 1970s. One of the boy's ears was severed before his final release.

What is interesting about these particular organizations is that they have their origins in the south and in areas of poverty and high unemployment. There are bound to be inextricable links between crime and social deprivation. That is why the present and future governments of Italy need to address the economic imbalance that still prevails between the richer regions of the north and the poorer areas of the south. (Twelve per cent of Italian families live below the poverty threshold, mainly in the south, where 24 out of 100 families fall into this category compared to 5 out of 100 in the north.) To achieve some success in providing employment would be a step in the right direction and this, in turn, might bring success in the fight against crime.

The present government has ambitious plans that are intended to provide the solid base for the country's long-term future. Italy will need longer periods of sustained political stability if all the proposed plans are to see daylight and come to fruition.

Past and present glories revisited

Italy, like any country, has had its fair share of economic and political setbacks, yet there is something about the general character of the people that always pulls them through. This *arte dell'arrangiarsi* (art of survival) always comes to the fore. We have seen throughout the centuries that Italians are endowed with a certain flair, imagination and creativity that has not only enriched the history and culture of Italy herself but has also touched in some way other countries throughout the world. Here is a quick reminder of some of these contributions:

- **design** – clothes and shoes, cars, the home, buildings
- **art and architecture** – the golden age of the Renaissance will always be a time of unparalleled creativity which produced a host of immensely talented artists. We should never forget the legacy left by the Romans and while the monumental arches, the temples and amphitheatres remain we will have a constant visual reminder
- **literature** – the twentieth century produced numerous writers that have acquired a world-wide reputation
- **the cinema** – the post-war era was extremely productive, churning out excellent films by directors such as De Sica, Rossellini, Fellini, Pasolini, Visconti and Bertolucci. A lean period followed, but now *La vita è bella* (*Life is Beautiful*) judging by the success of Benigni's Oscar-winning production!

- **the language** – Italian was the first language of opera. Italian is a beautiful, musical language that inspires enthusiasm. Despite the fact that Italian territory has shrunk since the time of her colonies in North Africa and the occupied area along the Dalmatian coast in the former Yugoslavia, the Italian influence remains in those areas and elsewhere through the language. Many of the inhabitants are bilingual and Italian is still widely taught in the schools. Let us not forget the Italian emigrants in the United States, Argentina and Australia. Thousands of students flock to Italy every year to attend language and culture courses at universities and privately run schools. The universities of Perugia and Siena are particularly famous.
- **the cuisine and wine** – many of the traditional ingredients of Italian cooking are now used in kitchens and restaurants all over the world. They provide us with good food while at the same time inducting us in the ways of healthy eating. A glass or two of one of Italy's many fine wines to accompany a delicious meal may be a fitting end to this journey through Italy.

We are often told not to dwell on the past. Italy, however, must continue to dwell on and retain so much of her past because, in many respects, it is the passport to her future and to her continuing place in the wider world.

GLOSSARIO	*GLOSSARY*
a favore di	*in favour of*
aiutare	*to help*
alleviare	*to alleviate*
attuare	*to carry out, implement*
la base militare	*military base*
il bersaglio	*target*
la burocrazia	*bureaucracy*
il conflitto	*conflict*
il contratto	*contract*
contribuire	*to contribute*
creare	*to create*
denunciare	*to declare (of income, etc.)*
la denuncia dei redditi	*income tax return*
la disoccupazione	*unemployment*
la divisione	*division*
l'economia	*economy*
le elezioni europee	*European elections*

essere dotato di	*to be endowed with*
l'evasione fiscale	*tax evasion*
fare un sacrificio	*to make a sacrifice*
far fronte a	*to face up to (responsibility)*
la fiducia	*trust*
finanziare	*to finance, fund*
il governo	*government*
l'imposta	*tax*
in seguito a	*following*
influire su	*to influence*
l'inquietudine	*anxiety, unrest*
occupare	*to occupy*
l'organizzazione mafiosa	*Mafia organization*
ottenere	*to obtain*
la posizione strategica	*strategic position*
il problema	*problem*
il profugo	*refugee*
realizzare	*to realize, achieve*
ridurre	*to reduce*
rinnovare	*to renew*
lo scandalo	*scandal*
il servizio sanitario	*the Health Service*
il sistema monetario	*monetary system*
sottolineare	*to underline*
lo squilibrio economico	*economic imbalance*
l'Unione europea	*European Union*

See 'Name that tune', p. 103.

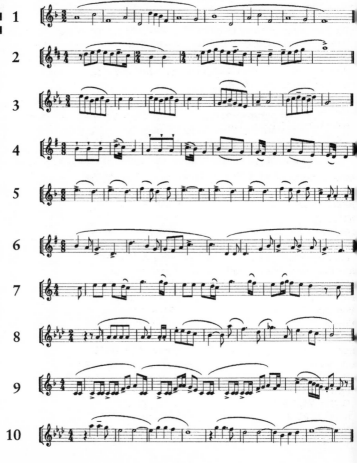